GHOSTS BY LOCH NESS

And Further Tales of the Great Glen and Beyond

GHOSTS BY LOCH NESS

And Further Tales of the Great Glen and Beyond

by

BRIAN DENOON

ILLUSTRATIONS AND COVER DESIGN BY **NIALL MACLENNAN**

ARDVRECK PUBLISHING

Published in **Inverness** in 2011 by

Ardvreck Publishing

13 Lombard Street

Inverness

IV1 1QQ

Copyright © **Brian Denoon**, 2011

ISBN 978-0-9561845-2-8

The right of **Brian Denoon** to be identified as Author of this Work has been asserted by him in accordance with the Copyright, Designs and Patents Act 1988.

A CIP Catalogue record of this book is available from the British Library

Contents

Foreword

Introduction

Chapter 1	Danger Everywhere	1
Chapter 2	Elgol and Leverburgh	9
Chapter 3	A Class Act	17
Chapter 4	Fort Augustus Players	22
Chapter 5	Gun Law	28
Chapter 6	Ghosts on the Auchterawe Road	36
Chapter 7	Inveroich	41
Chapter 8	The Loch Ness Monster	48
Chapter 9	Ghosts by Loch Ness	58
Chapter 10	Old Friend. Cycling Days	65
Chapter 11	Polloch	73
Chapter 12	Sunday Papers. Shinty Hero	78
Chapter 13	A Tale of Two Uncles	84
Chapter 14	The Coming of the Hydro	91
Chapter 15	The Hornby Years	97
Chapter 16	The Golf Course	102
Chapter 17	Victoria Buildings Revisited	110
Chapter 18	University Days	115
Chapter 19	Early Lodgings	121
Chapter 20	The Student Union	125
Chapter 21	Time to Move On	132
Chapter 22	Politics and a Narrow Escape	140

Chapter 23	Aberdeen Trams	146
Chapter 24	College of Education	151
Chapter 25	The Duffel Coat	158
Chapter 26	Norfolk Adventure	166
Chapter 27	Picnic in the Park	172
Chapter 28	High School Folk Group	180
Chapter 29	Comfort Station	190
Chapter 30	The Perfect Round	195
Chapter 31	Nobody's Fault	197
Chapter 32	That's Him, Your Honour	207
Chapter 33	Abriachan	213

FOR SHEILA AND
CATRIONA

FOREWORD

"Ghosts by Loch Ness and Further Tales of the Great Glen and Beyond" is Brian Denoon's second publication. His first book, "Do you say 'Sir' to your Father?" detailing as it did aspects of his upbringing, schooling and student employment in the Great Glen of the 1950s, was very favourably received when it came out in 2009. Brian's unique blend of local knowledge, humourous anecdote and serious social history touched a chord with native Highlanders and incomers alike and made his memoir a "must read" on Lochness-side and far beyond.

The success of his first book should have caught no-one off guard, least of all Brian himself though he confesses to a mild surprise about how well his labours have been received. However, nobody in the parishes to the west of Inverness where the author was brought up and educated was surprised in any way. Many were long familiar with his work which has appeared over the years in the pages of the annual Glenurquhart Bulletin which is published every August to coincide with the Glenurquhart Highland Games.

Brian has of course quite a pedigree both as a writer and a broadcaster. A former school teacher - for many years he was Principal Teacher of English at Charleston Academy, Inverness - he has had a parallel career as a freelance journalist and broadcaster. For a time in the 1980s and 1990s he was a regular contributor to BBC Radio Highland with his series of talks called "The View from Denoon". Beyond that, as well as contributing to newspapers and other more scholarly publications, he also wrote for a number of years on shinty matters for both The Scotsman and Scotland on Sunday.

Here, as the title of his new book suggests, Brian allows his pen to roam more freely. While still having at its core his love of family, shinty and the various communities of the Great Glen, he widens his scope to take in his time at Aberdeen University where, as well as playing shinty, he became involved in somewhat hair-raising student politics. He touches too on his days at Aberdeen College of Education and then his move back to Inverness as a teacher at Inverness High School and his subsequent involvement in the burgeoning folk scene of the Highland Capital. An episode in which he attempted to do his civic duty as a juror in an Inverness Courtroom is also described with humour and sympathy.

Certainly the nature of Brian's subject matter in itself - aided by the sympathetic illustrations of artist Niall Maclennan - makes for an intriguing read. However, what adds a further dimension is the superb quality of his writing. Brian has long nurtured a passion for the English language and here he uses his chosen medium with craft and precision. There have been numerous books written and published in the north about the experience of growing to manhood in a Highland glen: few have been better written.

Fraser MacKenzie

Introduction

With more than a hint of hubris, I ended my first book "Do You Say 'Sir' To Your Father?" by referring to a ghost story that had been told to my parents when they lived in the old schoolhouse in Fort Augustus, at the top of Bunoich Brae. That story was to be the inspiration for my next book. Well, Ardvreck Publications were pleased enough with the reception of my first effort (a second printing had been set in motion and sales of that had been good also) so I was asked to write a sequel.

Memory tells me that I was present on the occasion of the telling of that ghost story, but I really cannot be dogmatic about it from this far-removed viewpoint. Father Philip was the local parish priest in Fort Augustus in those days and I see him as a most sociable and frequent guest in the parental home. We were not of the Roman Catholic persuasion in the schoolhouse, but such was the kind of easy attitude in the village to the Catholic/Protestant divide that the members of the two faiths could commingle without discord, with the only real problem area being that of inter-faith marriage. That was always an occasion for gloomy shaking of the head and admonitory finger-wagging – mainly because of the Roman Catholic church's insistence that all offspring of such a union had to be brought up in the nurture of their faith. Father Philip, with his heavy-framed glasses and round cheerful face atop the black cassock of the Benedictine order of monks always brought a drift of local gossip into our home. Since he visited so many homes of the faithful in the exercise of his duties, he would pick up a vast amount of local gossip. With the help of a glass or two of the schoolhouse sherry, much of this gossip would be passed on. (Sherry, by the way, because my parents' house tended to moderation when it came to alcohol.) I think, actually, I must have been present when he told the tale of the wretched commercial traveller and his terrifying trips along Loch Ness side when he was heading back to Inverness late at night after selling his wares at the Hydro camps up Glenmoriston. I say that because it still stands out so strongly in my memory and I have to say that I used it on quite a few occasions during my teaching days to get the undivided attention of classes. It always went down well.

I said at the conclusion of my last book that the sequel would be entitled "Ghosts By Loch Ness - and More Tales of the Great Glen – And Beyond" and that is what I have called it. I have worded it carefully to ensure that a member of the public who might be tempted to buy it would not be misled into thinking that it was a collection of only ghost stories. In fact, there is just one other episode in this book that could fit that category.

A final point: it was when I was two thirds of the way through writing this collection that I realised that I was running out of specifically Great Glen material, so I decided to extend the education part of my memoirs (the various schools I attended) into my University and Teacher Training College experiences. Those days of higher education in the nineteen fifties seem so strange when compared to today's equivalent experiences. The past indeed is a foreign country. Oh yes, and there is a chapter about childhood experiences in Badenoch – Laggan Bridge, to be precise.

My enthusiasm for the game of Shinty will be clear enough in the light of it appearing occasionally throughout this book, and accounts for the inclusion of the short story "Nobody's Fault" that was published recently in the Shinty Year Book. It sought to explore the problems the Highland sport faces in modern Scotland.

My thanks go to Ardvreck Publications for their continuing faith in me and to my patient wife who had on too many occasions to suffer the intensity of the desperation in my eyes as I passed on to her a print-out of a chapter with the query: "Does it seem all right to you?" Also to Niall MacLennan for his splendid illustrations that bring added life to the pages.

Finally, thanks also to the Shinty Year Book and the Glenurquhart Bulletin for letting me use material of mine, which had already appeared in their pages.

CHAPTER 1
Danger Everywhere

Of the many huge social changes in society over the past half-century, one of the most marked, is the paralysing fear in the breasts of parents of young children about the legion of almost unmentionable threats that lie everywhere, crouching, ready to strike. This has led to a loss of the freedom that the young in my day took completely for granted. It is a cliché used to utter exhaustion that in the past, as children, we were allowed untrammelled freedoms that would be quite inconceivable today. This has to be especially so in the case of country children, of which I was one. The sweep of the wide glen in which Fort Augustus is situated had two rivers that empty into the vast depths of Loch Ness. It has the canal that cuts through the centre of the village with its locks and its still black waters that always brought the chill of fear. It has the hillsides blanketed with dark forests of trees – either the regimented ranks of the Forestry Commission or the more gentle rounded woods at Ardachy towards the west. It has rolling fields and meadows, several of which could be wandered over without fear of a raging farmer intruding. Most of these features were open to exploration by youth and apart from instructions not to be back late for tea, you were really on your own when you had left the house.

According to the mood of the moment or the season, the activity would be chosen. Immediately behind the old schoolhouse, our home at the top of Bunoich Brae, reared the Battery Rock. In those days, it was bristling with impenetrable whin bushes, but we had forced paths through this unfriendly scrub to gain access to the heights from where a magnificent view of the village and the Great Glen to the east and the west spread out before us. I won't pretend that the beauties of nature were uppermost in our minds as we looked out over the village and towards the hills at the other side of the glen, but there was a sense of possession: it was our countryside and it was exciting to plan where we would next explore.

In the immediate hinterland of the summit of the Battery Rock lay a spread of dank and ragged fields that abutted a large wood. This was boggy country and after a spell of rain, it could be treacherous. But the wood beckoned and in it, over the years, we constructed various crude huts that were part of the games our imaginations would conjure up. They played their part and then were just abandoned when we moved off to some other interest. The nucleus of our small gang comprised of my younger brother and myself. Then there was Hector, the son of the Free Church manse and Langley Ludgate who lived in the small house beside the village hall at the very top of Bunoich Brae - and there were various others who joined occasionally and came and went as the spirit moved.

Memories of winter and winter activities are much dominated by the fearsome conditions brought on by the one we endured in 1947. It sort of set the standards by which all others were measured for many years after, as it still holds the record for lowest temperatures over the longest duration since records began. The overwhelming recollection was the length of that winter. It became so settled in that anything other than iron-hard earth, frozen pipes and windows with the permanent rime of frost inside, seemed to belong to another life in another country. Only the fire in the grate in the living room and the one in the stove in the kitchen rendered the house habitable and life liveable. Feet seemed to be permanently cold inside the clumpy tackety boots worn then and the daily routine became one of survival. At one juncture, I remember the pupils in the school being organised by my father to carry Dixie cans in procession down to the loch side where the ice had been broken and where someone filled the cans up with water for us to take back up to the school. As I recollect, it was to the canteen this vital supply was being taken so that the midday meal could be prepared. Oddly enough, with the frost having penetrated the earth to such a depth that all water supplies were locked underground, it must have meant that all the toilets were frozen and out of commission too. That the absence of such a basic amenity to civilised life could have gone unnoticed by me is strange indeed. But that is just as it was. I have not any memory of the nightmare that must have caused. But the upside was that the continuing cold meant that the snow became a permanent feature and the frozen ponds and small lochs were there for our pleasure and excitement. Sledges and their design were uppermost in the list of most desired equipment.   All were home-made and pretty basic. Ours were made by my father and were wooden, though he was prevailed upon to fix on metal runners at one point when it became clear that the performance was much enhanced by this. We didn't have particularly good runs for sledging near our home and had to travel some distance, towing our sledges behind us. The most spectacular, and Cresta Run equivalent, was Glendoe Brae at the other side of the Glen. This is the road that lifts up from the western end of Loch Ness up into the hills of Stratherrick. It is a steep climb; the best part of a mile and the thought of launching oneself on a sledge down that formidable slope with not too many bends in the road was always a mesmerising one. Normally, it could not even be contemplated, since as it was a well-used road, and sledging on it would be totally prohibited. However, during this "perfect storm" winter of '47, the Glendoe road was blocked for many weeks and thus was available for our winter sports. I can see in my memory a brilliant blue sky and a large number of children from the village heaving their variously shaped sledges up the hill. On that day, we were joined by a party of boys from the Abbey school. Normally, the pupils in that boarding school – part of the Benedictine Monastery – were not allowed to mix with us indigenous, but on this occasion the rules seem to have been relaxed. Since they were from a boarding school, not surprisingly, some of them had rather superior-looking sledges. They were custom-built and had upwardly curving-at-the-front runners: some even had steering devices. We contemplated such wonders from the world of privilege with the usual venomous envy. They were a rather exotic addition to our day of adventure with their blood-red blazers and their strange badges. One of the "abbey boys" was tall and gangly and was carrying out some daring stunts – including just standing with legs astride and encouraging his pals to shoot between them. I was beckoned by him to do the same and nervously, lined myself up. I should have noted a sniggering among his blazered pals, but was more concerned with the accuracy of my steering. It would be pretty humiliating to cause injury by scything the gangly one down when he had invited me, one of the common village boys, to take part in their games. I was gliding forward and gaining momentum. The gangly boy was looking over his shoulder, gauging my approach speed and trajectory. What I did not see was the enormous snowball he was holding in front of him at chest height and which he lowered immediately I was sweeping through his legs. I saw the white mass drop in front of me and was completely blinded as I punched through it, careering wildly down the rest of the slope. There were gales of laughter, of course. I had been well and truly caught and there was nothing much I could do about it.

Skates were only things attached to the feet of people in films or in comics, so we were never able to perform arabesques on the frozen ponds or lochs. All we could do was to venture out on to them and slide with the tackets on the soles of our boots giving the required effect. We had become confident that the grey ice we moved over would hold our weight and not open up and draw us into the depths.

One of the obsessions we had then was the construction of huts or hideouts for our games and fantasies. Tree houses were the most labour intensive and one in particular stands out as a source of much invention and energy. One of the huge trees along a drive in the extensive grounds of the Free Church manse had been surveyed by us for some time and it seemed to offer the promise as a possible tree-house site. It had a ring of firm and robust branches that stuck out from the trunk almost horizontally and would be the foundation for a platform of planks that we could nail down. After that, walls could be constructed with other wood discarded from building projects that were taking place at the school where various huts were being built to accommodate the additional subjects that were being introduced in the years after the end of the war. The vast amounts of energy we expended in hauling these pieces of wood into place and nailing them down – all of it being lifted up by ropes – never seemed to bother us. It was the prospect of having a covered space, up in the branches of a huge tree, equipped with seating and any other amenities we could devise, that drove us on. We were quite some height from the ground during all this frenetic effort and there was always the danger of crashing earth-wards. It never happened though. It, like all the others, had its day of fascination before the brittle nature of our commitment to such things in those days found some other project to take up our energies.

By way of stark contrast to the tree houses, we would turn on occasion to the troglodyte instinct that lay within us. Hideouts that were underground. One that took up enormous amounts of energy was constructed down just below one of the compact school playgrounds in what was actually a small orchard full of apple trees. In a space in the centre, we began to dig until we had a quite substantial hole excavated. A raised up mound of earth and discarded bricks was put around it so that it could support a roof, which in turn was covered with earth and divots. The idea was to conceal the existence of our underground hut/hideout from the casual passer-by. It had its access tunnel and, like all such constructions, shelves, seats and other items were fitted in. Being underground, it was pretty dank and uncomfortable. To attempt to make it more homely and comfortable, a small paraffin stove was fitted in with a chimney to take away the fumes. It was an utterly stupid and deadly dangerous escapade and it was only by good fortune that the fumes from that stove didn't suffocate us. Needless to say, this experiment was a brief one and not repeated.

Safer by far to stick to existing facilities. I have described the hut at the back of the village hall that served as our armoury in the chapter "Gun Law". Another such amenity came our way in the form of a disused cadet hut. There had been an unsuccessful attempt to set up an army cadet company in the village, which, for some reason or other, did not survive for long. A fully equipped hut for mustering and for basic drilling was erected just below the gate to the school on Bunoich Brae – on the small level stretch of ground just beside the burn. After it had been abandoned, the hut lay empty for some time, and one day we crawled beneath it. This was possible, since it was standing on stumpy raised pillars. Someone found that it was possible to get into the actual hut by pushing up some of the planks of the floor, and this was used to gain us easy access to the hut whenever we wanted. It had been cleared of anything of value or use, but there were two rooms in it that had been employed as offices or stores, and they were just what we wanted. Once again, we were able to live out our fantasies in relative safety, with the only snag being that we had to be sure that we didn't make too much noise as discovery could have had embarrassing or even painful consequences.

The dangers of asphyxiation in an underground hideout or death through falling from a lofty tree-hut were ever-present, but there were others too in our open and unsupervised lives in those days. I have mentioned elsewhere that our household employed a live-in domestic help. Her name was Margaret Cameron and she came from a large and energetic family that lived over a mile to the east of the village at Portclair. It was always a source of wonder that so many could all live under the same roof in what appeared from the outside to be a modestly proportioned standard Scottish house. But they did, and when we walked out to Portclair every Sunday afternoon with Margaret, it was always into a world of adventure. Two of her brothers, Donnie and Roddie were about my age and were both rough and tumble and exceedingly fit. I already knew that they were both skilled shinty players as they were outstanding in the team from the east side of the canal organised by my father. This was called Bunoich. The other team was called Market Hill. The Cameron brothers introduced us to all the mysterious stretches of country that lay down beside Loch Ness beside and beyond their home. Huge woods that comprised acres of hazel nut trees. These were plundered by us as we packed bags of nuts for future consumption by climbing into the heights and shaking the branches to get them tumbling down. When they were easily prised from their husks, we knew that they were ripe for eating as well as being an enticing brown colour. What damage we did to our teeth by pretending to crack the shells nonchalantly to get at the kernels; actually it could be pretty painful on occasions. But at the time, it was all deemed to be worth it.

Then there was the enormous air-rifle that they had. It was quite unlike any other one we had ever seen and was mostly made of heavy gun-metal with minimal wooden stock. To compress the spring that released the air to discharge the pellet was almost beyond our strength, but it was hugely satisfying to do so.

But the greatest challenge of all was the genuinely frightening "going round the rocks" challenge. There was a sort of small, rock-girt bay not far from the house. The object of the "dare" was to go round the small headland and reach the other side, which was out of sight from the starting point. It was easy at first, then the path, if you could call it that, narrowed and narrowed until you were left with the problem of seeking out footholds and grasping whatever projecting bits of rock you could find. This would not have been much of a problem, had it not been that immediately to your right lapped the black waters of the loch. Deep and menacing. Remember, Loch Ness really has no shore for much of its length. The U of the Great Glen means that from the moment the land gives way to the waters of the loch, it plunges immediately into the unforgiving and merciless depths. The Cameron boys were used to this exercise and would disappear round the jagged headland with a cheerful wave and beckon you to follow. The fact that I had never learned to swim meant that the terror of slipping into these sinister waters welled up as I made my cautious way along the first and easy part of the scramble. As the path gave way to the final heart-clutching point where it was only your frantic grip in the rock itself that kept you from dropping off into the waiting darkness, you strained to inch round the final bulge of the headland to get to the blessed release of the other side and safety.

I was once knocked completely unconscious while indulging in another of our occasional obsessions in those days. This was the construction of what we called "hurleys". They were merely wooden platforms with wheels at each corner with maybe a rudimentary seat at the front; a beam protruded from the front which had the front axle attached to it allowing the vehicle to be steered by ropes. What we yearned for then was the acquisition of a set of pram wheels, which would be by far the best for really fast descent of chosen hills. I had managed just this on one occasion and the newly constructed hurley was taken to the back road from the village that joined the main road at Inchnacardoch. It was known as the "Bruich Dhubh". It was ideal for the purpose of hurley rides because it was usually very quiet and virtually unused by regular traffic. I sat on board the new hurley and off it sped. The new wheels did their job and soon I was moving at quite a spectacular speed down the hill towards the small bridge at the bottom.

There was a sudden flash and blackness.

When I slowly came back to consciousness, I was lying on a couch in a strange room with strange faces looking down at me. I was overwhelmed by waves of nausea and an inability to grasp hold of even the remotest idea of who or where I was or what had happened. It was all quite simple actually. I had thought I was going at breakneck speed down the Bruich Dhubh, but to the overtaking cyclist I was just a nuisance in his way. As he swept past me, the handlebar of his bicycle struck the back of my head violently and I was hurled into unconsciousness. There was panic all round. My companions were alarmed at my apparently lifeless body lying on the road and the cyclist sought help in a nearby house. It was in there that I was carried and deposited on a couch while the doctor was called. He pronounced that I was suffering from concussion and I was transported back to the schoolhouse by my alarmed parents. I have no doubt about the fact I would have been delivered earnest homilies about the dangers of careering down public roads on home-made hurleys, just as I have no doubt that I would have paid not the slightest heed.

Yes indeed, it was more frontier country in those days as far as risk assessment was concerned.

CHAPTER 2
Elgol and Leverburgh

Tales of my parents' early married lives in Elgol came to me in the random way that information seeps down through the generations, but they were given real substance by the recent discovery of tapes I thought I had lost some years ago. I had tested out a miniature tape recorder a few times when my parents were visiting us around a couple of years before my father died in 1990 and their, now long-silenced, voices when played back sound so startlingly clear even through the tiny speakers. They bring on a futile yearning that I should have done this more often. I can only be grateful that I had done it at all on those random occasions.

However, it was really through photography that Skye and Elgol first made their impact on me. Probably in the middle to late forties when I first began to look through the family photograph albums. I was simply mesmerised by pictures that came from an utterly alien world. It wasn't just the starkly different scenery; it was the very appearance of my parents and the people posing with them in these – yes – sepia-tinted products of the early Kodak age. As mentioned elsewhere, my father was Robert Andrew Denoon and my mother was Robina (née MacPhee). She had always disliked her first name and insisted on "Robin" instead.

By the time I was looking at them in this particular snapshot, my father's loss of hair from the front had given him his unwelcome high forehead. My mother's hair too had turned grey with the bringing up of a family of three born fairly close together. And there had been a war in the interim.

So different from these much earlier images.

But there was another deep and strange quality about some of these small square curling prints, apart from that odd tangle of black wavy hair that sometimes fell over my father's forehead and the sight of my mother's cloche hat and shiny stockings.

It was one photograph in particular (I have searched and searched for it in my parents' chaotic cataloguing system to no avail) that got to the essence of the sense of looking far back into a distant mythical land. It showed my father, leaning casually – draped almost – over a rock, pipe in mouth and wearing breeches with long, laced-up boots. Dramatic enough, but it was the background that really set the senses reeling. It was the awesome, jagged outline on the Black Cuillin as seen from close to the shore-line at Elgol. And it was here, in Elgol school, that my father was headmaster from 1929 till 1935, after which he left to return to the mainland and the tiny community of Abriachan, high in the hills above Loch Ness. The uneasy sense I experienced when looking at these images and what emphasised the feeling of distance and unattainability, was that the lives my parents led in these extraordinary surroundings did not include me. I was not born until 1937 – two years after their return to the mainland. There was a sense of, how dare they?

It was the welcome discovery of those tapes that brought all this surging back and it's the memories of my father's days in Elgol as headmaster that dominate their content. He had gone there after a spell of teaching at Tomnacross in Kiltarlity. He and my mother were engaged by then, but their ways had to separate for a spell. In those days, the moment a woman teacher married, she had to give up her post and my mother was desperate to teach. While my father was in Elgol for several years, my mother had gone to Leverburgh in the Island of Harris. This community, re-named in 1920 after Lord Leverhulme, the soap magnate who had many extravagant plans for the village that came to nothing – partly as a result of his misreading of the way of life in the Western Isles and more finally in the fact that he died in 1924.

While my father had a few scraps of Gaelic passed on from his mother, my mother had absolutely none. Again a sad comment on the policies regarding that language in those days. However, she determined to learn as much as she could and armed herself with a Gaelic dictionary and ditto Bible. She lodged with a large family where worship took place each evening, which included psalms and lengthy readings from the Scriptures. These occasions were very heavy going, but she strove to absorb as much as she could. Her most outstanding memory of these days, in what was virtually a foreign land to her, occurred in the local church. She joined the large congregation and all went well enough until one Sunday, after the Gaelic sermon was finished, the minister looked out over his flock – by now beginning to sniff the scent of approaching freedom after the long service – and announced, in English: "As you are aware, we now have in our midst, Miss Robina MacPhee from Tomatin on the mainland. She is the new teacher in our school. For her benefit, I would like now to give an exegesis of my sermon - in English."

And he then did just that. My mother immediately sensed the clenching tension in the church, as the congregation was obliged to settle down in their pews for a further fifteen minutes. One old man, a little in front of her, glared directly at her then bent his head forward to spit on the floor, such was his wrath at this turn of events. It was an excruciatingly embarrassing moment. It was all done as an act of kindness to make a stranger feel at home, but the backlash from a congregation that did not have anywhere lined up in its Sabbath plans, an additional quarter of an hour in the church, was all too apparent. I wish I could tell you that she approached the minister to ask if he might discontinue this generous act of his, but I never got around to asking how it all resolved itself. I do know that she enjoyed her spell of teaching in that part of the world, which was more of a foreign country to someone from the mainland in those days than it would be today. A common factor in my parents' appointments to these posts was their inability to speak Gaelic; yet they were sent to teach in parts of Scotland where Gaelic was much more dominant than it is today. The clear policy behind this is all too obvious to highlight. The corollary was the significant number of Gaelic-speaking teachers who were appointed to posts on the mainland.

My parents married in 1934 in Inverness and they spent a relatively brief spell together in the dramatically situated Elgol schoolhouse joined on to the tiny school. It stands right down by the rocky shore of Loch Scavaig. In the winter storms, spray was hurled at the windows and the whole building would shudder. My childhood was punctuated by scattered references to the people who lived then in Elgol – friends and neighbours – the Lachies, Wee Donalds, Anna Bheag (Anna Robertson) and the dominating presence of the one called "Kate the Rock" (Cait a Bhearaidh). She and her brothers, John and Lachie, lived in a house perched almost directly above the school, near the top of the impossibly steep brae that reared up practically from the schoolhouse back door. In my child's imagination these figures were vague in form and in features, but one quality they all possessed: they were several times larger than life. They were giants and moved easily through that impossible landscape. They were also kind and warm: no dismissive comment on any of them can I ever recollect having heard. The result of all this was that I was left for many years with a mystery – a conundrum that never was properly explained, and with both parents long dead, never will be. Why was it that they never went back to Elgol to visit the place and see the many friends they had left behind? They did keep up a sort of vague contact over the years: I found some greetings cards from Elgol with 1930s date-stamps on them in the correspondence I looked through after my mother died on Hogmanay in 1994. The reason could have been nothing more remarkable than the sheer difficulty of actually getting there in those days.

But a door of sorts did suddenly open in 1964. My wife and I had been married for three years. Still no family but with a brand-new red Mini parked by the side of the brand-new house we had just built. My parents suggested that the four of us should go for a holiday in Skye, based in Dunvegan. (I had suggested Dunvegan, as a close friend and teaching colleague, Angus MacPhee, spent his holidays there with his parents who ran a guest house.) They would pay for the accommodation and meals while we'd pay the petrol and do all of the driving. What an offer and what a bargain. No hesitation.

We were passing through Broadford when the first event occurred.

"Look. I think that's the house. I'll check and see if anyone's at home."

And my father was ringing the front door bell of a typical, small, whitewashed Skye house right by the roadside, B&B sign prominent. It seemed that within moments both of my parents were being wrapped in embraces and cries of recognition. Two small elderly ladies with fluffs of white hair and wearing the universal garb of the Highland landlady were clearly delighted at this chance meeting and for a spell, the thirty-year gap between now and when they had last seen each other was being bridged. This was just a foretaste of what Elgol had in store.

Apart from my powerful memory of my first glimpse of the mountains opposite the school – one of the rare occasions when an event in life actually lives up to the anticipation – the reaction of Kate the Rock when we appeared at her door was quite overwhelming. Large and also landlady-overalled, she just couldn't seem to absorb the fact of the re-appearance of people to whom she had bade farewell almost a life-time earlier. Kate was even larger in life than the image her name had conjured up in my imagination and the welcome from her and her brother John that drew us into their house for all the tea and home baking that we could put away, was in keeping with the atmosphere that was building up around this visit.

Next it was down to the jetty and on to a small launch that was piloted by another close friend of those days. Again the familiar round of hand-shakes, backslapping and anecdotes. This was Malcolm MacDonald, better known as Calum. His launch was called the grandiose "Highland Monarch". (I was told that three years after this encounter, Calum had the narrowest of escapes when he was caught in a sudden storm on his way back to Elgol. He was on his own and the craft was wrecked, hurling him into the heaving seas. Unbelievably he landed in the small dinghy he had been towing and eventually was washed up on the shore where he was found unconscious by rescuers.)

With a party of whey-faced tourists, we bucketed our way across to the other side of Loch Scavaig in the "Highland Monarch". From the tiny landing place, we scrambled along a rickety gangway until we eventually arrived at the unimaginable starkness of Loch Coruisk: silent and ominous – as brooding and sinister a place as you might find on this earth.

Then it was back to Elgol and into Kate's kitchen/living room for yet more hospitality and more torrents of reminiscing from her and others who had by now arrived.

Since we were being more or less excluded from all this past world that was being re-awakened, my eye fell on a wooden panel with a date carved on it. 1947, as I recollect. Underneath this date were carved the names of some of the Hollywood movie industry's finest of those days who had stayed there during the making of one of the most execrable films ever set in the Highlands. It was called "The Brothers" and starred, among others, Patricia Roc, Finlay Currie, Will Fyfe and many more whose names I cannot now recollect. So sad that their eminent presence there could not have left a better film memorial – even if they had clearly enjoyed themselves while staying at Kate's.

This historic panel has long since gone, I learned since. More about that later.

Incidentally, I went to my Penguin-published dictionary of all films ever made to check out the names of more of the cast, producer etc, and to my amazement, it was not included. It certainly has not been lost since I struggled through it on TV just a few years ago – even more aghast at how appalling it was.

But now, back to those recently re-discovered tapes. One of the outstanding stories they contained was about the recently-appointed Elgol headmaster's almost fatal encounter with a lobster. It also has as its *"uhlar"* or "ground theme" the notion of the naïve East Coaster (essentially, someone from the mainland). The event took place in the very early days, before my father had actually moved into the schoolhouse. He was lodging at the Post Office and one day the father (Sandy Rhuadh) of the local postie (Wee Donald) brought a lobster he had just caught. He instructed my father that he was to lay it on its back in the centre of a peat fire, cook it in its shell, and eat it. What he was not told (or he had not heard it) was the vital information concerning the gruesome fact that lobster had to cooked alive! On to the fire it had gone – dead – and soon was disposed of with the enthusiastic help of a tourist who had been staying at the post Office at that time.

The following morning, when my father was in the classroom, the itching began. It built up in intensity and became more and more agonising until he was forced to flee the room and wrench off his upper garments. Far too vicious to be a sudden (and highly unlikely) infestation of fleas, it was clearly something much more alarming. He saw that the whole of his torso was a mass of red weals and blisters – and all the time there was that clawing, terrifying itch. He ended up rubbing himself violently up against the wall to try to get some relief. After a spell, he was able to shrug himself back into his clothes once more and return to his classroom, but the extraordinary discomfort lasted for several days. Shortly after, the doctor from Broadford came to inspect the school and my father told him about the episode.

"You can thank your lucky stars it came out on your skin, or you were dead!" was the alarming response – along with a sly dig about ignorant "East Coasters" making fools of themselves. And it seems that the elderly tourist at the Post Office had just as narrow an escape. He had been violently sick and had suffered similar disfiguring skin eruptions.

The last tale from Elgol comes from a visit I made there over fifteen years ago and a meeting with Colonel Lachie Robertson, one of that community's most famous sons. He was a pupil of my father's in those far-off days and told me of one of the headmaster's escapades that would sit uneasily (to say the least) on today's educational scene.

My father had taken delivery of a .22 rifle, which he had bought for shooting rabbits and scarts (cormorants). The class had noted it propped up by one of the classroom windows and had been intrigued. In the middle of a lesson, they were amazed to see their teacher head towards the window and, still talking to the class, stare out. Suddenly, up went the window and the rifle was levelled. A shot rang out and then,

"Lachie. Out here. Look out past the first rock there. I've hit a scart. Off you go and fetch it..." and shortly after, Lachie was wading into the cold waters of Loch Scavaig to recover the bird.

On dry land again, he removed his socks and beat them against a rock after which he was permitted to stand by the stove until he and his socks were properly dried out. As I have mentioned elsewhere, that cormorant was sent to a taxidermist on the mainland, and its fierce accusing eye was levelled at all who entered my grandmother's house at Victoria Buildings in Drumnadrochit all the years she lived there, from its place below the hall-stand.

It was Lachie who told me about the fate of the carved panel in Kate the Rock's kitchen. It seems that a niece of hers who eventually lived in the house, with the inappropriate name of "The Blonde" (her hair was raven black!), became somewhat confused as she became older and set about removing most of the wooden panelling in the house to use as firewood. The piece with the carved names of the cast and producers of "The Brothers" met the same undignified fate and is long gone.

And I cannot leave this chapter without recounting yet another co-incidence. In our front room hangs a large painting of Loch Scavaig and the Black Cuillin, which includes the school and schoolhouse. This was done by the husband of my cousin, Joan, Neville Weston, who is well-known in Australia where his works have frequently been exhibited and where his articles in prestigious magazines are still being published. I inherited the picture when my mother died in the early nineties. Our neighbour, who moved into the substantial house at the end of our shared drive, was a guest in our house after the painting had first been hung on the wall. He immediately became excited and told us that the ruined house, just hinted at by the artist beyond the schoolhouse, was one that had belonged to his family. He came from Elgol and told me, among other details, that the captain of the "Highland Monarch" who had greeted my parents so warmly all those years previously, was his own Uncle Calum. The usual clichés about the smallness of our world will have to be taken as read.

CHAPTER 3
A Class Act

Recently, I was back visiting my old home village of Fort Augustus. The oldest cliché of such visits is the one about how places and buildings have shrunk in the intervening years. The Fort Augustus Church of Scotland is just one such building. Viewed from the outside now, it looks really innocuous - shabby, even. Inside (I opened the main door and peered in) it is all modern and bright, but the external stonework does look a bit battered. However, the impressive manse that had always seemed to me long ago as the very essence of grandiose buildings still looks amazingly impressive – still dwarfing the nearby squat building that was its reason for existing in the first place.
I spent a large portion of my early childhood and adolescence within it and recollections are of something more echoing, dark and impressive.
The last time I was inside that church was about nine years ago, as I write these words. I felt decidedly odd sitting there: two pews further back from the one we used to sit in as a family – about fifty years earlier. I was there for the funeral of Rev Hugh Gillies who had been minister in Fort Augustus Church of Scotland from 1939 until he retired in 1980.
It's a curious fact, but you never seem to be able to remember the actual last day of something that played a huge part in your life for a spell – such as regular church-going in the late forties and much of the fifties. I can't see the boundary between the remorseless attendance at that church and the days when that attendance ceased to be. Not a Sunday did our family miss nor did we children miss a single Sunday school. All manner of excuses would be paraded to try to get out of this additional imposition on a day already blighted by us having to sit on hard, desperately uncomfortable seats, listening to drifts of words that meant absolutely nothing to us; listening to the strained, combined efforts of the community to make its praise sound acceptable, musically, to the Lord. Donnie Mackintosh's fine tenor would soar above the rest of us, seeming to compete with Willie Jack the organist for dominance: a friendly jousting. Enormous in her vast, black fur coat, Mrs Scott bulked over her

tiny husband in their seat at the front to the far right. The Nelson family from the Lovat Arms Hotel, (KJB Nelson had been one of the immortal heroes of a Scotland Rugby Grand Slam in 1925), sat in the next row. When they had their enticing daughters home from their boarding school, they would sit directly in front of us. My pre-adolescent lustings for them went, fortunately, totally unnoticed.

All that I have taken from my Sunday school experience is the ability to recite the Books of the Old Testament, in order, from Genesis to the four chapters of truncated Malachi. I can't tell you where most of these books fall in the Old Testament and if you were to stop me half way through, I would have to go right back to the beginning again. I also have to gallop through them at top speed. Slow and careful enunciation has me drift into amnesia. This skill is one of my prized party tricks, though.

The pipes of the organ looked exactly as I remembered them: a dull silver, with dun-coloured bands near the bottoms. The organist always fully pulled the curtain on its light rail after he had taken his place, so that he was completely invisible to the congregation. His repertoire was unchanging and some of the dreamy passages of Dvorak he played still drift through my mind. I didn't know it was Dvorak then, of course.

As I looked around, apart from the seventies alterations that had removed the traditional, raised pulpit and replaced it with a more hands-on trendy lectern and the panel of pale wood covering the rear wall with its gold crucifix picked out with a concealed spotlight – apart from these changes, I could have just been deposited by my personal time-machine back in nineteen forty or fifty-something. The funeral service was moving and eloquent and was followed by the slow progress towards the exit where the deceased's family carried out the now-obligatory shaking of hands with all those who attended. For me, afterwards, there was meeting up with people I had not seen or spoken to for over forty years. Brief but fascinating encounters and after all that, a speedy drive along Loch Ness side back home to Inverness.

It was in that church that occurred, back in those far-off childhood days, two incidents seared in my memory for their sheer nightmarish awfulness: incidents where you are trapped and vast seismic forces of suppressed laughter seethe within you and where you dare not allow even a whimper to be released.

The first of these did not actually involve the Reverend Hugh. It occurred one Sunday when we turned up to find that the service that morning was to be taken by a minister from neighbouring Invermoriston. In those days, the Invermoriston minister was the Reverend Turner. I might mention here that there was slight animus between this man and my father which dated back to Home Guard days – something I was not to learn till many years after and to which I have referred in my previous book. Anyway, the Reverend Turner had his own speciality at which he had obviously worked for many years in the pulpit. It was THE PRAYER. These were back in the days when a minister had almost unimaginable opprobrium heaped on his head if it was seen or even suspected that he actually *read* the prayer. The Reverend Turner went to extreme lengths to display to his congregation that he was NOT reading his prayer. He grasped the sides of the pulpit and – with head directed towards heaven and eyes tight closed – he would enunciate each sentence slowly and in as authoritative a tone as he was able. God would have no option but to take the closest note. The PRAYER also followed a pattern. One of the ingredients was the listing of all that we should be grateful for: things dispensed by God. It would enumerate the riches of the earth; the bravery of our fishermen on the tempestuous seas; the armed forces, then moving on to the example set us by the Royal Family. (These were more innocent days.) On this particular day of horror, I remember clearly that after one of his theatrical pauses, the Reverend Turner said: *"We thank thee, Lord, for this tranquil day of worship."* (pause) *"We thank thee, Lord, for the blessed silence of thy House ….."*

It was at this precise moment that someone in the depths of the congregation let slip a handful of coins. They crashed to the floor and, while some ran away and hopped and skipped into the aisle, others did what coins normally do by rotating in that ever-speeding-up dance of theirs before falling silent and still. The church filled with a stunning sense of suppressed explosive laughter. Such timing to destroy the effect of such a pompous man! So perfect, yet not so much as a tiny change in the breathing tempo of that tormented congregation showed what they really felt.

But for sheer excruciating torture, my main memory has to be far and away the worst. It did not involve the whole congregation this time. But it did involve me as a direct (and possibly sole) witness who had followed the build-up to the incident with increasing unease and who had seen and heard the appalling outcome. The Reverend Gillies was to emerge from it all unscathed and with his polished dignity completely untarnished. But enough of the introductions.

Ian MacLean was the church beadle in those days and carried out his duties before and after the service in quiet and unfussy manner. He would ring the bell for several minutes, tie the rope in the hook by the main door, then walk around the side of the church to the vestry at the back to help the minister with the pre-service preparations. From the place where I always sat, close to the wall on the left-hand side of the pew about two-thirds of the way down to the front, I would watch for Ian passing by the windows on my right. When he had passed the final one, there would be several minutes before the door at the back of the pulpit opened silently outwards, towards the vestry. Then I would see the Reverend Hugh's head fleetingly appear as he climbed the steps from the vestry into the pulpit. He would stand for a moment and glance over his congregation before sitting down for a brief spell to go through the final sorting out of notes and so on. All the while, the organist would be looking intently into his mirror to bring his passage from the New World Symphony timeously to an end.

Now you have to use your imagination here. From my seat – out to the left of the body of the kirk – I could see, just peeping above the high side of the pulpit, the tip of what I had long ago realised was the folding seat that the minister sat down on after entering the pulpit. I had worked out that it was the final task of the beadle, after he had helped the minister up the steps, to pull down the seat before closing the door behind him. It had become one of my own small private rituals, as it were, to follow this sequence of events unfold every Sunday.

One of those Sundays, as we were filing in, we saw that Ian wasn't there. Someone else was about to ring the bell. Sitting in my usual place, I listened to the unusually ragged pealing of the bell then watched for the sight of the replacement beadle's head flitting past the windows to my right. Then the regular pause till the door behind the pulpit opened, noting as usual the minister's head rising into view. He did his usual glance over the gathering and made the usual dipping motions before sitting down. But this time there was something different: something was very, very wrong. I could still clearly see the tip of the folding seat. It had not moved. Nothing could be done. The Reverend Hugh was now committed and was sinking out of sight. A pause, and then I clearly heard a sort of untidy, muffled thud. I was rigid. Had anyone else witnessed or heard this? I glanced at my parents; they were inscrutable and no-one was making his way forward to see if all was well behind the ramparts of the pulpit. There was just silence as the organist had stopped. Then there came the faintest of scuffling sounds and for a tiny second, a hand appeared at the edge of the pulpit. A further agonising pause, and the minister's head rose up, and there he was – looking as he always did. Maybe he was a little bit more flushed than usual, but there wasn't the tiniest tremor in his voice as he began the service,

"*Let us worship God. Let us sing to His praise in Psalm ...*"

The congregation in Fort Augustus Parish Church was witness to a class act that day, though perhaps I was the sole person who had actually seen it.

However the damage done to my nervous system in forcing back the urge to explode in crazed laughter has probably never healed. It probably left permanent scars.

CHAPTER 4

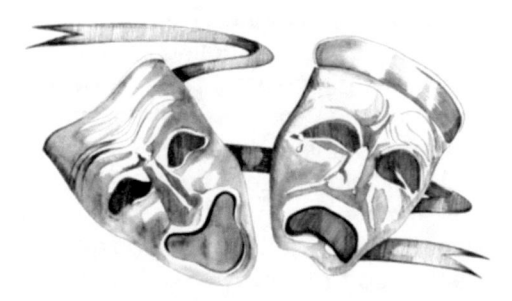

The Fort Augustus Players – Cut Down to Size!

In my first book about the Great Glen, I made passing reference to the amateur dramatic group in my home village of Fort Augustus. It was called the Fort Augustus Players and both of my parents were deeply involved in it for quite a number of years. My mother was an accomplished actress and could portray stern and forbidding characters with unnerving accuracy. Old photographs, taken by a local photographer rather unkindly exaggerate the crude make-up that then was painted on the faces of members of the cast and reveal her as something from the darkest imaginings of the Brothers Grimm. My father never actually took any role in a production, but was the energetic producer of several plays. As in all such amateur dramatic groups everywhere, those who volunteered possessed the basic, essential skills and qualities of self-confidence and, well, no other word for it – exhibitionism. No theatre in the world could exist without such. Among the Fort Augustus Players as I remember them, a few names stand out. Ted Murdoch (one of the dynamic young Hydro engineers) and his astonishingly beautiful wife May. Hamish MacDonald of "Cluanie" with his booming, stentorian voice. Syd Wray of the Forestry Commission. Kathleen MacLaren, who lived just across the road from the old schoolhouse on Bunoich Brae. Ronnie Kirkton, one of the local GPs, Charlie Palmer, teacher of Maths in the Abbey private boys' school – and a collection of others whose names have slipped back into that dark corridor of the memory which becomes ever longer with the advancing years. The only member of that dramatic group I can still contact is Syd Wray and he has been recalling for me, some of the more memorable productions. He remembers one play called "Vitamin X" where he appeared alongside my mother. He also remembers "Entertaining Mr Eccles" where he was on the stage with May Murdoch and Ronnie Kirkton. He told me also that Ted Murdoch took over the role of Stage Manager after my father and Willie MacDonnell had done their stints. When such people came together in a small community it was inevitable that there would be tensions and the Fort Augustus players had theirs. The artistic temperament could be just as combustible in a small community as in the vast production empires of Hollywood. Arguments erupted and flouncings-out occasionally occurred.

Then there was myself. I had a minor role in one play when I was about sixteen years old, the name of which is completely erased from my memory. It might have been a small role, but it impressed on me the fact that acting was no career option for me. I wish I still had in my possession the large excellent photo of me, sitting in profile by a table on the stage and delivering my lines to a female character. Again – who or what it was all about – a total mystery.

Occasionally the Fort Augustus Players would take their art to neighbouring village halls: Invergarry, Invermoriston, Drumnadrochit and I seem to have a dim recollection of Spean Bridge on one occasion. If the truth be told, I have to confess that we had a bit of a conceit of ourselves as might be expected from the largest village, situated in the middle of the Great Glen. Invergarry, to the west, had a village hall that was an extraordinarily rickety and ramshackle relic of a former glory. It was an all-wooden construction that seemed to heave and groan in protest when a typical rumbustious dance was being held in it. A Health and Safety operative today would blanche and have an apoplectic fit if asked to inspect it – especially in those days when almost everybody smoked and dropped their fag ends everywhere. One vivid memory of Invergarry hall is of an event that occurred in 1961 or thereabouts. The famed Scottish troubadours of those days, Robin Hall and Jimmy MacGregor, who were regular performers on the BBC "Tonight" news magazine programme from London and were immensely popular, were doing a tour of Scotland and, in particular, were visiting small Highland venues. I had heard about this and had arranged a lift from Fort Augustus with someone who actually knew one of the duo. We enjoyed the packed and enthusiastically received performance and at the half-time interval, we made our way to the tiny, cramped dressing room behind the stage. There they were – the two stars – who turned out to be totally un-averse to a conversation with fellow folk-music enthusiasts. (I was a member of just such a group in Inverness at the time). It was truly a memorable encounter with a couple of show business figures at the height of their fame and popularity, yet who were totally devoid of pretention or vanity.

But it was the visit of the Fort Augustus Players to deliver a performance in the tiny village hall in Invermoriston, six miles to the east, that our most traumatic experience occurred. The Invermoriston minister, Reverend Peter Fraser, was an earnest and well-meaning figure who strove tirelessly for his parishioners. He was organising a concert for funds for the church or some equally deserving cause and had telephoned my father to ask if the Fort Players would give a performance of their current play for him. This was agreed. I must admit here that there was more than a faint irritation in my father's reaction to the Reverend Peter and some of his works in the community. Quite a number of the pupils in the school at Fort Augustus came from Invermoriston or Glen Moriston and travelled daily there by bus. A small number of them – one family in particular – were profoundly disturbed and acute trouble-makers. On several occasions my father had seen to them being reported to authorities higher up in the chain of disciplinary command in those days and had told his staff that the problem pupil was about to be removed from the school. Much relief all round in the staffroom, but short-lived when it would transpire that the Reverend Peter would plead the miscreant's case so eloquently and energetically that he would appear on the school doorstep again the following week. And he would be totally unrepentant and as troublesome as before. In the minister's defence, it has to be said that he was acting from the very best of motives.

Anyway, my father agreed to the concert appearance. To have done otherwise would have been unthinkable.

The first part of the programme would be the local Invermoriston talent, and then there would be an interval for tea. The whole second half would be then presented by the Fort Augustus

Players, performing – and nothing can drag from the dimmest recesses of my recollection its name – the play in which I had my own small part. My mother was also in the cast. We had props that had been unloaded from the van that had accompanied us and we had our make-up person who made the usual alterations to features as demanded by the script and whatever costumes were required were donned. That was not too complex as the tale was one set in the present day. We felt that we were the equivalent of a small army on manoeuvre and we really meant business. Fort Augustus was about to show the people of Invermoriston what amateur drama was all about. Ours was a team effort by a close-knit and highly drilled company.

The first twinge of unease occurred when we appeared at the entrance to the hall. We had just emerged from our various cars and the van with the props, and approached the doorkeepers who were taking the money.

"Half a crown for adults and half price for children," was the gruff greeting.

"But we're performers. Just arrived from Fort Augustus. You're not going to charge us, are you?"

A blank stare greeted this. Obviously there were no exceptions as far as the stern doorkeeper was concerned. The impasse was only resolved when someone got hold of the Reverend Fraser and told him that the Fort Augustus Players were being refused entrance unless they paid like everyone else. We had had our first encounter with the legendary local character Willack who lived nearby in the local smithy and who doubled up as hall caretaker.

Once safely inside, we watched the local talent as it unfolded in its rustic innocence before us. The tenor who vibrato-ed through a selection of old Scottish airs; the accordionist; the tiny Highland dancers with arms upraised and toes a-pointing; the small boy who played on the spoons and the hesitating recitation from some terrified little girls. The master of ceremonies drew the first half to a close and the applause was thunderous. The community truly appreciated the talent in its midst. The Fort Augustus Players were now in the dressing room, feverishly getting ourselves ready and I was going over my lines again and again with deadly concentration. Then it was performance time.

Places taken: final wishing of good luck and the curtain was swept back. I would lie if I were now to give a description of the actual performance: suffice to say that it must have been to our and our producer's satisfaction. The final lines were declaimed and our tale was told. Back swept the curtains and the hall filled with the gratifying sound of a pleased audience. We had been a success.

As was the custom in those days, the votes of thanks would now follow before the surge to the door and the road home. We emerged into the auditorium to listen to the conclusion to the evening – some of us still with our make-up on our faces. The Reverend Peter was standing up in the middle of the hall and was giving the votes of thanks. I can see him clearly yet, with a small child clinging to him as he was speaking. He thanked each of the local performers by name and paused to allow the applause to flow and then ebb: the singers; the various instrumentalists; the recitation artists; the various small children and the small boy who played the spoons. The last wave of applause rolled over us and faded. We looked at each other. Here it came. We had proportionally been by far the main item on the Invermoriston concert programme.

But the Reverend Peter Fraser was now sitting down. People were gathering up their coats and starting for the door. This was inconceivable.

Then I noticed that someone was tugging at the minister's sleeve. Now he was whispering something into his ear. Thank heavens. This was it. The Reverend Peter stood up. The small limpet child was still clinging to him. He raised his arms.

"Ladies and gentlemen," he called out.

"Ladies and gentlemen. I have just been reminded that I forgot to thank the most important part of the evening's organisation. I am truly sorry. May I thank Willack for his usual excellent door keeping and for looking after the takings in his customary diligent manner."

More cheers from the crowd and the hall swiftly emptied.

Stunned is the only word in the language to even approach what the Fort Augustus Players were feeling at this quite extraordinary gaffe.

Someone must have approached the organisers to point out the blunder, but my memory does not tell me who or if adequate apologies were offered. They surely must have been.

But the scale of our falling to earth had taken our breath away and our drive back west to our home village would have been, along with our wrath, accompanied by dark thoughts about the primitive customs of our Invermoriston close neighbours.

CHAPTER 5
Gun Law
Fifties Style

I suppose that only a few short years after the end of hostilities in World War II, it's not surprising that the youth of my home village of Fort Augustus were pretty much into guns and things that made loud and satisfactory bangs. Indeed for quite a number of years in the late forties and early fifties, this became a bit of an obsession.

Any one of our number who actually possessed a firearm or had access to one was much envied. There were the souvenirs from the recent and even long-ago wars lying around in attics or propped up at front doors or elsewhere. Springing to mind immediately was the revolver that Colin Campbell, who lived in the croft at the other side of the Battery Rock behind the old schoolhouse, had managed to get hold of. It was large, heavy and sinister-black. He would show it to us younger boys and we would crave handling it and feeling its deadly weight in our hands. There was the powerful spring activating the hammer that clicked so sharply and decisively on to the (empty) chamber in the cartridge cylinder. Every time when I would ask Colin if I could have it home for a wee while, the answer was a predictable no. Then, one day, he said that I could, and I remember eagerly going to the door of his house and knocking. Eventually someone came to the door and told me that Colin had left the village and was off to work somewhere far away. So no revolver to show off to my pals.

Another craved-after hand weapon was in Spring Cottage, just up the road from the schoolhouse on Bunoich Brae in Fort Augustus. This was the early home of the local grocery tycoon, Jesse Leslie and his large family. One of his sons was Robert and one day he appeared with a pistol that clearly was a museum piece, but was unmistakeably a revolver with all the thrilling details of wooden handle and dull metal body and barrel. I remember that this one was lent out to me for a brief spell by Robert. He told me that he would leave it under the hedge near his house at a certain time and I could collect it then. And, yes, it was there when I looked for it. I have no idea about the next stage in the proceedings, but I was obliged to hand it back pretty quickly.

During the War, my father had been involved in the Home Guard while in Abriachan and up to the end of hostilities in Fort Augustus. As a result, there was always plenty of the detritus of war lying around the house, from the clips of .303 ammunition in the drawers of the big desk in the front room to the occasional rifle in the cupboard below the stair. Even the poker by our fireplace was a bayonet from the First World War. Over the years it had been plunged into the red depths of the fire so often that it had become misshapen towards the tip of the blade. But the rest of it was quite unambiguous as to its provenance. As I have mentioned elsewhere in my first "Great Glen Tales", he also had a standard issue revolver in its khaki canvas holster, but it was practically never seen by us. The weapon that was legitimately kept in the house and that was not connected with the war, was the pump action .22 BSA that he used for small game when we lived in the hills above Loch Ness in Abriachan. It was occasionally used for more dramatic hunting purposes in those days, as the set of antlers that was fixed on a wall in my grandmother's in Drumnadrochit could attest to. Right in the centre of the skull was a small hole where the .22 bullet had felled the creature by a piece of sheer luck on one occasion in the far Renudin Woods beyond Loch Laide. On all other occasions, it was rabbits that were hunted. (Of course, there was that other dramatic occasion I have referred to elsewhere when the sinister swastika of the Nazi enemy had flitted over his head when he was hunting for rabbits and he had loosed off a futile shot at its retreating black shape.)

Since a real firearm was not possible as far as ownership was concerned, I was stunned when in my early teens my father agreed to buy for me on my birthday a brand-new BSA air rifle. In the early fifties, this was the more or less standard air weapon and was a smart-looking piece of design. It had the .177 bore and could, as well as the lead pellets, also fire the metal darts that all the fairgrounds used for their shooting galleries. In fact, these fairgrounds often used the BSA model that I now possessed. It came with a lengthy list of rules from my father – prominent among which was the absolute embargo on taking it beyond the premises of the schoolhouse. I could use it in the small playground at the back and shoot at tin cans on the wall or inside one of the classroom huts – the woodwork one – shooting at a proper target with the coloured darts. This was all quite amazing as it was a really powerful thing and, if truth be told, not all that suitable for one of my tender and slightly reckless years. (It happens that I still have this airgun in my possession. Lately I have been looking at it speculatively as the latest list of shredded plants in our garden is read to me by an incandescent wife who daily confronts a small, insolent rabbit that sits in the centre of our lawn, nibbling the recently-planted grass. It knows that I am far too squeamish to let loose a lead pellet in its direction now.)

The roof fell in on my happy world one weekend when I had taken a pal back from school in Inverness for the weekend and was brim-full with the primitive delight of the young male when showing off some highly desirable acquisition. And yes, my pal from the big town was mightily impressed with the gleaming wooden stock of my air rifle and the long slender gun-metal-blue barrel with the purposeful sight at the end. That and the satisfying crack when it was discharged really had me puff with adolescent pride. It started with just the merest hint on the Sunday afternoon. "Why don't we take it up the road past the hall and look out for rabbits in the fields there?" slyly hinted my pal. I told him that that was out of the question. The rules were quite implacable and absolute. But face could not be lost, so with the airgun concealed as best as possible, we slipped out past the kitchen window at the back of the house and made our way down to Bunoich Brae. We turned right, up towards the village hall and beyond to the spreading fields where rabbits were regularly to be found. We did not cause any problems for the rabbits, and fairly soon were heading back towards the schoolhouse. It was as we were close to the gates to the Free Church manse that a dark, ominous figure appeared, striding towards us. It was my enraged father who had worked out that our absence together with the absence of the airgun at the front door meant that a strict house rule had been broken. Retribution was about to take place. It was bad enough that I had taken the gun out beyond the house grounds, but that I had done it on the Sabbath. I have mentioned elsewhere that ours was not a strict sabbatarian household: it was more of a continuation of the tradition with which both of my parents had been brought up. It never plumbed the depths of idiocy that could sometimes blight the lives of those living in a true Calvinist culture. It was more a sort of occasional nod in the direction of those strictures - and there was about to be a very definite and decisive nod now. It was more the loss of face in front of my pal from school than the actual verbal onslaught and the confiscation of the gun that caused the greatest bruising to my self-esteem on that long-ago Sunday.

Some of us had organised special hideouts for ourselves in those days and one was an unused small hut that was a lean-to at the back of the village hall just up the road from the schoolhouse. We arranged seats in it and kept various items we used in our various games and activities. And here we kept our small arsenal of weapons. From somewhere had appeared a small bolt-action single-shot .22 rifle. It would have been useful for poachers as it broke into two smaller parts by the turning of a single large screw. It was occasionally fired as it was not too hard to get hold of bullets, but obviously very seldom. Then there was the impressive Webley air pistol. This had come to us from the local doctor, Dr Kirkton. It had belonged to one of his sons who had now become a doctor himself and had outgrown such things. The most impressive was an old Mauser rifle, which we had been told by the one of our number who had found it in his loft that it had seen action in the Boer War. It was not long before I discovered that a .303 bullet would fit into the magazine and into the breech. This was great. We could work the bolt, pull the trigger and eject the cartridge just like the real thing. Why this lunacy? Well, we had been assured that the rifle had been de-activated and the firing pin had been removed. And sure enough, when you slid the bolt out and studied the end of it that pressed up against the base of the cartridge and released the firing pin to do its business, you saw that it did not appear when you released the spring. So, perfectly safe for playing around. How close we were to disaster only became apparent by the merest of chances. I had been playing with the bolt that I had removed from the rifle one day and pulling back the spring that activated the firing pin to watch for the non-appearance of the tip of the pin from the tiny hole in the grey metal. Then it suddenly occurred to me that the bolt, as

I held it in my hand, was not in the actual position that it would be in if it had been thrust home into the breech of the rifle and the protruding handle turned down and locked into place. I tentatively made the necessary adjustment and saw – to my horror – that the tip of the firing pin appeared like a tiny evil tongue, fully able and ready to strike the base of the cartridge and fire the bullet. How close we had come to tragedy. There is no doubt that when playing around with the ancient Mauser, the first act would have been to insert a bullet into the breech, activate the bolt and press the trigger when it was pointing at someone. It can still shock to think of the implications.

These were the days of the Hydro schemes in the Highlands and the vast churnings of the earth that accompanied the building of the various dams and tunnels. They brought to us a sense of living in frontier country and this might have accounted for the highly dangerous activities of some of the younger elements in our community. The level of security at some of the work sites must have been extraordinarily slack, because I knew for an absolute certainty that a certain amount of explosives found their way into very unauthorised hands. I know because I possessed two of those hands. Not even today will I reveal who it was who supplied me with a few sticks of gelignite along with coils of fuse and a pocket full of detonators. Along with these khaki-coloured small packages of high explosive came a total unawareness of just how dangerous they were to the careless handler. We knew that to explode the gelignite you did not apply a flame to it – it would just splutter as it was noisily consumed. It would only explode if it had an explosive set off inside it – and that was where the detonator came into the picture. It was a small silvery tube, open at one end. The fuse was a slim tarry length of rope with a core of gunpowder that fitted into the detonator, which in turn was then pushed into the soft gelignite in its waterproof covering. When the shot was fired, it was just a matter of lighting the fuse and retreating. One day, someone told us that gelignite would become highly unstable if left lying about unattended for too long. It would begin to "sweat" and if that occurred there was the increasingly strong possibility that it might go off if given even the smallest jolt. This was truly scary. I can remember the day when I panicked at being in possession of these sticks of explosive and had decided to get rid of them. I

just went down behind the garage at the foot of the small playground behind the schoolhouse, and hurled the soggy, deadly packages far into the dense whin bushes that clothed the sides of the Battery Rock that rose just behind our home. They disappeared into the prickly undergrowth and vanished forever.
Now, at this point, I have to confess that for just around sixty years, I had believed in the danger of unstable, decaying gelignite. A recent swift check on the internet tells me that this might have been the case with dynamite, that other invention of Alfred Nobel's in 1875, but it did not apply in the case of gelignite. So the fears were unfounded. Phew. That is a relief indeed.
As I have already described in my recent book, the detonators were quite another matter. When they were set off with a short length of fuse to do the business, the effect was dramatic. Early experiments at the back of the garage where there was an old bench that was not required in the woodwork room, showed the violence of the power they contained within their innocuous little grey shells. We stood and watched as the tiny flame spluttered and disappeared down the length of fuse till the thunderclap report told us that we had a really excellent firework for the coming season – much more effective that the wimpish, faint-hearted ones that we could buy in the shops. However, the lump torn out of the bench surface ought to have warned us that this was another whole category of explosive we were dealing with here. I finally parted company with these tiny but dangerous items when I was scared by a neighbour in Innes Street in Inverness where I was lodging at the time during a spell as a pupil in Inverness Academy and had been letting them off around November 5th. He knew by the volume of sound they gave off that I was not using the standard firework bangers. I got off by the skin of the teeth. Then there was the further information gleaned from some source that they were also unstable and likely to go off with even the warmth of the hand. I haven't checked out that one on Google yet.
But the final tale of explosive extravagance will be left to my younger brother who was the one in the family who inherited the practical skills of our father – those gifts which completely passed me by. This is the reason why he became a civil engineer while I became a teacher of English. Anyway, one of

his fascinations around the age of twelve or so was making gunpowder: not the saltpetre, charcoal and sulphur variety but a concoction of his own that contained potassium chlorate among other things. It would go off like an explosive, but left a lot of residue. He designed a gun with a length of tubing for a barrel and bound it to a wooden stock. He drilled a hole in the barrel to insert a stick of cordite from an opened .303 bullet (this was to ignite the "gunpowder") and blocked off the back end of it with a heavy lead plug that was fixed in place by a large nail driven through two holes to hold it in. The charge of powder and the wadding together with the handful of lead pellets were tamped down into place and the target – an old dustbin – was lined up. I was not present at the final act in this experiment, but was off into the village on my bike for something. The parents were not at home either as I recollect. I heard the explosion while pushing my bike up the last stages of the steep Bunoich Brae and saw a billowing surge of smoke erupting from behind the schoolhouse. As I rounded the corner into the playground, I saw my brother stumbling about in some distress and holding his face in his hands. It was pitted with a mass of tiny red punctures as if attacked by a swarm of stinging insects. Between yelps as he pulled splinters of wood from his person, he told me that the gun had gone off, but had not done so as planned. He had held it up and pointed it at the dustbin then he lit the stick of cordite. Then, just before the flame disappeared down the touchhole, he lowered his "gun" and held it under his arm, away from his face. So fortunate a last-second gesture that turned out to be, as when the explosive went off, it did two things: it fired the pellets through the dustbin and left it riddled with jagged holes. It also forced the heavy lead plug at the back of the metal tube barrel and drove it like a heavy calibre bullet clean through the wall of the garage behind him. He would have been stone dead if he had not lowered it at the very last moment. So close.

I really can't remember what tale my brother concocted to cover up what had happened when the shocked parents returned home and saw his ravaged features. What I do remember was that this frightening incident saw the end of such activities. Tranquillity returned.

The poacher's .22 rifle just vanished somewhere; the Webley air pistol is still used by my brother in an adapted form to shoot poison and noxious substances into inaccessible wasps' nests; my father's BSA rifle now hangs on a wall at my brother's house with the firing pin removed and as for the ancient Mauser that had cunningly deceived us into thinking it was harmless, well, my brother recently told me that just before we had abandoned the small hut hideaway at the back of the village hall, he had pushed it into a disused vent that had opened into the hut and covered it over. The hall is still there – I wonder if the Mauser is still in its wall somewhere? And my long-ago airgun gift from a trusting father is still with me. And that rabbit would do well to be a little more careful as it smugly preens itself after consuming another clump of my wife's favourite violas.

CHAPTER 6

Ghosts on the Auchterawe Road

My home village of Fort Augustus had its tales of haunted places such as Ardachy House where the spectre of an old woman was said to move through the corridors at midnight and strike fear into whoever happened to be witness. There were dark corners of the tree-shrouded Forestry roads, which had associations with long-ago tragedies whose memories could conjure up all manner of uneasy images in the mind of the nervous traveller. And of course, there was the greatest mystery of all close to hand – the Loch Ness Monster – whose very existence had been given life by the famous water bailiff, Alex Campbell, who first reported it to the local press in the nineteen thirties.
Like all of the young people in the village in the forties and fifties, I was aware of these stories and was liable to experience the frisson of fear when cycling home from distant places far to the west of the village, along the dark roads. One of my regular chores then was to cycle up to the MacLarens' croft in Auchterawe on a Saturday evening to collect a can of milk for the household.

We knew the MacLarens on several levels. First of all, there was MacLaren's Band. This was a local dance band led by Jock MacLaren himself. He played the fiddle, my mother played the piano and other locals provided the drums and accordion. They played at many local dances and other events and were popular enough. Jock was distinctive in his uncompromising garb: robust tweed and enormous brogues with which he thumped out the rhythm while the music surged and swirled over the eightsome reels and strip the willows. As I have mentioned elsewhere, perhaps their popularity was helped by the fact that they did not charge a fee for their skills. It was just art for its own sake, I suppose.

Then there was the pleasure we had in our occasional visits to the croft. Large spreads of home baking with lemonade for the young guests and the real treat of a run on the huge Fordson tractor with its trailer while Jock was taking feed for cattle at the far ends of the field stretching towards the dark, menacing Forestry trees that hid the River Oich on its way to join Loch Ness.

Then there was another rather more exotic contact. There was a son of the MacLaren family who had been for many years in India in some capacity as a civil servant in the days of Empire. These days were now effectively over and the crofter's son had returned with his wife and family to Scotland. There were huge problems of adapting to life in a war-impoverished land, but the main one was having to live without the small army of Indian servants which had looked after their every need. We were told that the young daughter was unable even to dress herself as that had been done by the Indian "Aya". She was quite helpless. Adaptation to more robust social patterns had to be quick.

It could have been during one of these family visits that the idea was suggested that the schoolhouse could augment its weekly supply of milk by getting some from the croft. In those days, milk did not come to our houses in bottles or cartons, but from the back of the village horse-drawn milkcart at which customers would line up with their milkcans to buy what they required. The milk came from a dairy at the western end of the village beside Lochunagan. So it became my regular task to head off up to MacLaren's croft on a Saturday evening on my bike with an empty milk can hanging from the handlebars.

I enjoyed the hospitality of the croft house and the elderly couple. But in the winter months, the prospect of the run back home became more and more alarming as the time to leave approached. Never did a kitchen seem more warm and safe than when I was anticipating the long twisting road lying between me and the safety of my own home. The roads through the dark forestry plantations were particularly gloomy with the branches of the various pine and spruce trees spread overhead, blotting out what small amount of light might filter through from the night sky. On this particular night, for some reason or other, I was especially uneasy. Maybe it was some stories that we had been telling each other or something I had just been reading, but the result was that the prospect of that mile and a half through the trees on the bike was building up to become a thing of terror. The only thing was to get my head down and to pedal like something possessed. At least I had the comfort of the new piece of equipment that had just been fixed to my bike. Up till now, I had used a battery-powered lamp to pierce the darkness. It was being supplanted by the now latest technology, the Miller Dynamo light. It was powered by a small dynamo that was adjusted to press against the rear wheel and which was turned at speed by simple friction against the tyre. The difference in the light generated was really dramatic. This was effectively the first real test for my new headlight.

The milk can was hung from the handlebars and after the calls of, "Good night: be careful," had faded, I was now looking along the narrow white beam from the dynamo-powered light in front of me. The milk can clattered against the bike and I strove to make certain that nothing was spilled. It was not long before I entered the first tunnel of blackness of overhanging branches and strained to force the pedals round as fast as I was able. Ahead was a brief spell of relief when the road opened out and I would see the lights of the house where Davy Coutts and family lived, some short distance down from the actual road. The comfort of other human presences. Short-lived, as it was then back into the menacing blackness with the trembling, lancing beam of the dynamo all that lay between me and the sheer unimaginable horror of total night.

One of the better parts of the road was a steep brae beside the Forester's office. You could sweep down it and gain the momentum to hurl yourself up the last gentle slope, round a fairly easy corner and then under the huge branches of the old haunted beech tree, to sweep gratefully, at last, on to the open road with its houses and their reassuring lights on either side, till the schoolhouse and home and safety from fears were close at hand.

Now I was rushing down the brae, grasping the swinging milk can to prevent the contents from spilling.

Suddenly, to my horror, I felt a snatching at my flailing gabardine coat, which was flapping behind me. The white beam of light began to flicker and fade. It was as if some dreadful, shapeless thing was swooping through the pitch blackness behind me and was grasping at my coat, tugging at it and trying to drag me from my flying bicycle. I now felt the clutch of sheer terror and all sense of rationality fled. All that mattered was that I get to the foot of the hill and force myself past the final barrier to the world of safety and light that lay beyond that beech tree ahead. The clutching continued and the light flickered over and over again. As if that was not frightening enough, another even more terrifying thing began to happen. Just ahead of me, below the black canopy of the forestry trees, there appeared a flitting, wraith-like shape that undulated and flickered, keeping pace with my desperate headlong hurtling progress. It was just a few yards ahead of me and I was by now in a state of total terror. Then at last the overhanging boughs of the huge beech tree were sweeping overhead. Shortly after, I was looking at the warm friendly windows of the houses and home, blessed home, was beckoning. It was a totally spent human scrap that finally pushed his bike up to the back door and stumbled into the enveloping warmth and safety.

Well, what was it that had caused this apparent brush with the supernatural all those years ago in my early youth? Was it something from Coleridge and his Ancient Mariner? When the traveller on a lonely road dares not look behind because "a frightful fiend doth close behind him tread"?

Nothing like that, I have to tell. The clutching at my coat was the result of it getting caught in the dynamo, which generated the power to activate my light beam. As it got tangled between the small wheel and the tyre, it caused the light to flicker. But what about the pale wraith that seemed to flit below the branches just ahead of me and my staring terrified eyes? This only occurred to me later. It was a wet night and there were puddles on the road. The beam from my light was being reflected up on to these branches and creating that frightening illusion.

Even although boring reason has driven the supernatural away, I still can relive these frightening moments on that dark Auchterawe road and experience a shiver of primitive fear.

CHAPTER 7
The Rise and Fall of Inveroich
A Tale of Not-So-Noble Intentions

My father had played shinty first for Glenurquhart School and then for Edinburgh University until he left there in the late nineteen twenties. For most of my life, he had stared out at me mistily from his sepia team photographs in which he and his team-mates always seemed to manage to look much older than the late teens and early twenties they all would have been when that long-ago shutter would have clicked. He effectively gave up playing after he had left Edinburgh and begun his teaching career: for a short spell in Kiltarlity then to headship of the school in Elgol in Skye; later up to and during the war years in Abriachan with neither of these latter places providing the opportunity of further involvement in the game. It wasn't till he took up the headship of Fort Augustus Junior Secondary in 1944 that he found himself back in shinty country once more. Immediately the war was over, things began to get organised again and the Fort Augustus team was reconstituted and began to compete in the various leagues and cups – it has to be said, not too successfully. Although plenty of excellent players were available, there were always teams like Lovat, from Kiltarlity and the two powerful outfits from Badenoch: Newtonmore and Kingussie, that always seemed to be the regular stumbling blocks to glory for the village.

My father became deeply involved in shinty immediately and in various ways. He had always been a keen DIY man and was particularly good at carpentry and generally working with wood. He made accurate models of tanks for me and my brother which were carved meticulously out of solid blocks of wood and when painted in camouflage colours they looked amazingly authentic. When all the schools in Scotland had their additional facilities for practical subjects built, he made full use of the mass of tools and workbenches that were now freely available to him. And he began to make shinty clubs. This involved searching for suitable timber of appropriate shape – ash, as I recollect. Then, since it was not always easy to find ash saplings with the correct bend at the correct spot, he then began to "steam bend" the wood to obtain the exact shape he required. The process was agonisingly slow and involved special boxes he made that were filled with damp sand. Somehow, this was heated (I honestly haven't a clue how) and the chosen sapling had clamps that gradually bent the wood till the precise shape was achieved. Then the result was pared and polished into the final article. I have to say here that the clubs he made were spectacularly handsome pieces of equipment after the coloured tape had been added for the grips. He made junior versions for my brother and me and we were very proud to own them and to use them.

A good friend of the family then was Willie Jack who had been captain of a winning North Select team before the War. There was a black, silver-mounted caman on display in the entrance hall of his elderly mother's house with which he had been presented. Willie was still a star player in the Fort Augustus team though he had been wounded in action in the recent war. My father made one of his beautiful ash, steam-bent clubs for him and I remember the occasion when he first used it in a match. Within a few short minutes and during the first serious tackle, the brand new club splintered and flew apart. It was not the end of it, as clubs could be spliced in those days of greater austerity and it was soon brought back into service.

My father was also able to put his enthusiasm for the game to practical use by becoming a member of the Fort Augustus Shinty Club committee.

The main problem he identified lay with the neighbouring village to the west – Invergarry. That scattered community had a more formidable team than the Fort and because they were almost next door to us, the animosity between the two was fierce and uncompromising, a syndrome to which the history of our species seems always to bear witness. Actually, the general level of shinty skills in the two teams was pretty much the same – except for a special weapon the Garry had in their locker. The Kennedy brothers. There were four of them and they were extraordinarily skilled players. In fact, it was their presence in the Garry team that gave it its better-than-Fort Augustus success rate. But, like Fort Augustus, they did not have enough overall firepower to bring them top success in the leagues or cup competitions. This had my father and Ronald Guthrie, the local bank manager, start to mull over and eventually to hatch a plot of Machiavellian intent. Quite simply, they decided that if supreme shinty success was ever to come to the middle of the Great Glen, it would require the combined talents of Fort Augustus and Invergarry, linked together in a joint team. Actually, the initial plot was much simpler. Why not try to lure away the Kennedy brothers from their allegiance to Invergarry and get them to join up with the Fort? It was noted that the Kennedys lived at Aberchalder – half way between the two villages. They could just as easily give their support to the Fort and there would be nothing unethical about it. Just their choice.

One evening, the headmaster, the bank manager and three other members of the Fort Augustus committee walked up the road that ran alongside the Caledonian Canal the three or so miles to Aberchalder. They tapped on the door of the Kennedy household. It was answered by one of the brothers, Angie Kennedy. The question was solemnly put to him. "Would you and your brothers consider playing for Fort Augustus instead of Invergarry? We've just walked from the Fort and can confirm that you are, if anything, living nearer to the Fort than the Garry. What about it?"

My father maintained that Angie was tempted at first. However, he then became polite but unbending. The loyalty of him and of the whole family was unshakably for Invergarry. The trump card was that one of the Kennedy parents came from the Garry. "Thanks for calling by, gentlemen, but that's the way it is. Good night." And the door was shut firmly on the proceedings.

The plotters walked back along the canal side to Fort Augustus, mulling over the result of this first move. What next? All were now convinced that an amalgamation of the two bitter rivals was the only answer. And it was going to be realised, one way or another.

I made a radio programme for BBC Radio Highland in January 1986 on the subject, and interviewed some of the main protagonists in this tale.

First of all, Hamish MacDonald, one of the outstanding Fort Augustus players (and, as it happens, a former hockey internationalist for Scotland) thought the amalgamation was an excellent idea. Both teams had good players as well as weaker ones. Put the two teams together and you could have a winning combination. It would also do shinty the power of good.

Hamish agreed, however, that fundamentally it was a Fort Augustus takeover.

"For far too long, the Fort had been the chopping block for clubs like Lovat, Kilmallie or Newtonmore. An amalgam of the Fort and the Garry would hold its own with any team in Scotland."

When asked if there had been any friction between the players from the rival clubs, he said that there was absolutely none. All welded together into a highly effective team. It was on the touchline that the friction occurred. The Invergarry supporters resented the idea from the start. The new team's home pitch would be at Fort Augustus so that the Garry people would have to travel for every fixture and also have to stand among their former rival spectators. Hamish, however felt proud to be part of such a good team, though he mainly felt he was playing for Fort Augustus under another name.

Another pivotal figure interviewed in 1986 was Sandy MacRae. He had been a member of the Invergarry committee that had steered the amalgamation through from that side. He was initially very doubtful about the whole idea. The committee was decidedly not enthusiastic, but was forced to see a logic behind it all. It was felt that for such an important decision, a public meeting ought to be called. First of all, the Invergarry Shinty Committee met at 8pm on August 16th 1948 where they voted unanimously to go for amalgamation. Then the full public meeting took place in the Coronation Hall, where it was given majority approval. One of the secret weapons wheeled into this vital meeting was Father Ninian from the Benedictine Abbey in Fort Augustus who spoke eloquently and enthusiastically for the new team, Inveroich. He pressed the benefits and advantages for both the communities.

I interviewed the three remaining Kennedy brothers on how they felt at seeing their old club disappearing forever. (Archie Kennedy had died in 1978). Donnelly had been very unhappy at first. He had been born in Invergarry but had come around to the idea, whereas Lal, the youngest of the brothers was more optimistic when he saw the quality of the team he was now a part of. When he was asked if he felt that the Garry folks had been conned by the cunning Fort Augustus schemers, he was defensive and said that he had never felt that he was playing for Fort Augustus. He did admit that many of the Garry supporters were deeply unhappy and several simply ceased to support shinty in the district. They felt they had been betrayed by the whole business.

Right from the start, the new team proved to be a formidable outfit. From September 25th 1948, in the MacGillivray League against Fort William to a match against Foyers in December 18th, Inveroich won nine out of eleven games played – one of the defeats being by Newtonmore in the Camanachd Cup at the Eilan.

Angie's best memory was of a game against Lovat at Fort Augustus when they beat the visitors 4 – 0. These were the days when Lovat was one of the top teams in the land. In a game against Inverness – also a really formidable team in those days – the "Inverness Courier" commented favourably on the remarkable skills of this new team to have emerged in the centre of the Great Glen. Inveroich had won that game 5 – 2. Inverness, however, was to get its revenge in the season 1951-52 when they knocked Inveroich out of the Camanachd Cup while on their way to winning that trophy at Old Anniesland in Glasgow against Oban Camanachd.

Hamish MacDonald remembered a game played in a summer's evening against a combined Fort William/Kilmallie team. Inveroich won that one 5 – 0. My own father chose an encounter with Ballachulish when they were at their peak when Inveroich defeated them at Fort Augustus. Sandy MacRae was impressed by their sheer quality. They were an attacking team and drew much praise from the stronghold of shinty in Badenoch after a powerful performance he witnessed against Newtonmore.

So, if they were as good as that, what eventually happened to Inveroich Shinty Club? Well, it folded and disappeared in 1954. Such a brief flaring into energetic life only to be so quickly snuffed out.

One of the reasons seems to have been finance. Another was the Hydro schemes that made such demands on the players who worked for them. It became more and more difficult to get off work on Saturdays to turn up for games.

However, my father in that 1986 interview was withering in some of his comments about Inveroich and its demise. It was a chronic unreliability that had undermined them.

"It was the attitude of some of the players – not all of them, I stress – that was a fatal flaw. They were not interested in playing for the club or the communities, but for themselves. There was simply a lack of team spirit."

He went on, "You expect players in an amateur game to help the organisers. I can't remember players helping to line a pitch before a fixture. I myself lined a complete shinty pitch with some of the team playing shoot-for-goal. It never occurred to any of them to come and offer a hand."

My own memories of that team are mainly of pride in the pleasure it brought to the village to have a team that was able to more than hold its own among the best in the land. Eccentricities on the touchline among the regular spectators stand out too. For some odd reason, the numbingly repetitive cry of a stentorian supporter from the west still echoes in my mind. It was "Face the ball, Kilmallie!" This was hurled at said team throughout the whole of a game. It could drive you insane. Apart from the sheer pointlessness of it all, what else could Kilmallie do anyway? And there was the oddly sinister episode when I had stupidly chosen to annoy a drunk supporter of a visiting team. He had fixed me in his dull, malevolent glare and had begun a lurching run in my direction, accompanied by staccato blistering threats. I was youthful and lithe and not particularly scared and headed to the gate leading on to the road back to the village, across the River Tarff. I thought that I'd swiftly outpace him and then make my way back to the field. Soon I realised that the curses and threats were getting closer and closer. I speeded up, but realised that my pursuer was still closing the gap. I tried to catch the eye of the occasional person I met walking in the opposite direction and get some help, but no one seemed to grasp the seriousness of the situation. I was really panicking now and the matter only resolved itself when the drunk just decided that he had some imperative in his life more urgent than a local urchin who had annoyed him. But it was scary while it lasted.

One last memory of shinty in the days just prior to the creation of Inveroich from Invergarry and Fort Augustus is of the final game between the two teams. It took place at Aberchalder, near Loch Oich. The referee was Willie Batchen from Foyers, who went on to become a famous and much-respected figure in the game. He must have regretted having drawn the short straw that day for this very last game between these angry neighbours. As I recollect, the trouble was mainly on the touchline rather than on the field of play – though it was undoubtedly some incident there that was the actual flashpoint. I can still see the surge of both lots of raging spectators – and not only the male ones either – brushing aside the bemused players and hurling abuse at each other as they gesticulated and threatened. I can see the beleaguered referee blasting his whistle and waving his arms as he tried to restore some order. I looked on in amazement at the contorted features of normally quiet and respectable people from my own home village as they raged at the injustices being visited on their team by malevolent forces – and the focus of most of this communal bile was the unfortunate Willie Batchen. I have not the remotest idea which team won this rather disgraceful ending of the "auld sang" but I suppose it doesn't really matter all that much now.

The final irony though, is that it is Invergarry which has the shinty team nowadays – called Glengarry. Fort Augustus has none. Its shinty players have to travel to the west to get a game with Glengarry, or to the east to play for Glenurquhart.

I suppose you could say it was a just outcome for this tale of long-ago ruthless ambition and imperial arrogance.

As a footnote to all of this, I had a recent contact with a long-ago shinty player from Fort Augustus who, as a young man, turned out for one or two games in the Inveroich colours. Tom Aitchison, who left the Great Glen to live in Sheffield where he joined the police, was able to give me the names of the players who made up that fine team. First, of course, were the Kennedy brothers, Alan Grant from Tomdown, Hamish MacDonald, Ian Grant and his brother Hughie, the three Paterson brothers, Jimmy, Andrew and Jackie, Tommy MacLaren, Donnie and Jimmy Mackintosh and Tommy Cameron.

CHAPTER 8

The Loch Ness Monster
(You Only Get the One Chance)

All of my life, I have lived within sight or within a short distance of Loch Ness. So it is, that wherever I might travel in the world, whenever this fact becomes known, the response is instant and totally predictable.
"Well well. You'll have seen the Monster then?"
(Even as I was typing out these words, you'll note that I have instinctively given it a capital "M".)
Actually, no. I have not seen The Monster. Every fibre and strand of what constitutes my thinking processes denies even the remotest possibility of some saurian hang-over from the Jurassic Age, at this very moment, nuzzling its way through the dark mud at the bottom of the loch searching for food while contemplating a sudden surge to the surface to have a quick look-around and the chance to startle a passing tourist. If it was there, it would obviously be part of a colony of creatures and regular and obvious evidence would be there for all to see on any day of the year.
No, NO. There just isn't any such thing. It's all too ridiculous.
Yet it isn't all that easy. As already mentioned, I was born and brought up in Monster (the capital 'M' will remain in place) country. Its possible existence out there always hovered around in my consciousness while I was young and could have me become truculent, defensive – even shrill - whenever the visiting 'ranks of Tuscany forbore to cheer', or even dared to heap scorn.
You see, there were all those people in my home village of Fort Augustus who said that they had actually seen it. Most

illustrious of all these was Alex Campbell, the water bailiff and local newspaper reporter, who was the very first one to pen the word 'Monster' in an article in the early nineteen thirties. Anyone who ever met Alex felt immediately in the presence of an archetype of absolute Highland gravitas and integrity. He was simply not the kind of man who would ever concoct such a tale. And he said that he had seen it on more than one occasion and gave graphic detail of humps, long neck and reptilian skin, slipping through the oily dark waters. Then what about all those other witnesses – the black-robed monks of the Benedictine Order in the Abbey at Fort Augustus? Several of them had also claimed to have had sightings. During my teaching days, when I was in Inverness High School, I had arranged a visit to the Abbey for a company of Norwegian pupils from Stavanger. Father Gregory was to address them about the history of the building and all were listening attentively. A sudden murmur broke out and then a surge of unrest. The teachers in charge looked to see what was going on in this normally well-behaved group. A few of the pupils spoke to their teachers who then asked Father Gregory if he might pause in his address for a moment. It turned out that most of the party had seen a recent programme on Norwegian TV in which the self-same Father Gregory had been the central figure. And the topic? – a recent much-heralded sighting of the Monster by this tall, stooping priest with his other-worldly air and aura of saintliness. Who could ever have doubted the truth of his account? That was all that these young people wanted to hear about and they were not disappointed. It was the highlight of their visit.

In spite of all that, and the regular flow of tales of sightings during my school years, I was never to be granted that honour or privilege. For several years in the early fifties I travelled twice daily by MacBrayne's bus from Fort Augustus to Glenurquhart School with fellow pupils from my home village and various places in between. The daily journey of around nineteen miles each way meant that the loch was able to be seen intermittently for a fair part of the way – though trees obscured a great deal of it. In all those many journeys, I never saw so much as a twitch on the surface of the loch to hint that the Kraken was awake and moving in the deeps. Nor have I ever since.

Except once. Here is the story. But, first, a little background.

Being a son of the schoolhouse (as already referred to, my father was headmaster of Fort Augustus Junior Secondary School), I had perfect attendance at Glenurquhart School. It was futile for me to try on the sickness stunt to avoid the wrath of the dreaded Chrissie 'Croick' for a forgotten French exercise or some other fearsome retribution, which that school could hurl at the indolent or foolish pupil. (I have to confess that I was both.) All such attempts were seen through by the suspicious parental eye and were useless. One day, though, I did intercept some passing virus and the symptoms were nasty enough to call for a day at least in bed. I would have made the best of it, counting the hours of the passing day and thinking of which grim class I was now missing, and luxuriating in just being at home in my own bed and safely away from it all. This was all to end abruptly when my brother and sister charged into the house that night, straight off the school bus. They were in a state of uncontainable excitement. When they could be calmed down, we were told the startling events of that morning. You've guessed it. You saw it coming. Yes, the whole bus-load of forty or so pupils, the driver and a scattering of other passengers had spent about half an hour watching some "Thing" apparently surging and heaving just below the Loch surface near Urquhart Castle. Sometimes it appeared as if, whatever it was, was actually breaking the surface. In the days that followed, the media of the day made much of it. Several of the pupils were interviewed by the BBC and their accounts also appeared in the press. A surge of excitement in our quiet Highland lives.

And there was I - the pupil with up-till-now perfect attendance throughout my secondary education - missing out on the whole show! You have to admit that as luck goes, it was pretty dire.

I must have heard the programme when it was broadcast, but have no memory of it whatsoever. Just a few weeks before I wrote down these words, I thought I would contact my brother and a friend of my sister's to ask them what they remembered of that long-ago morning on the school run. My brother first. His recollection was clear and it was analytical – and not supportive of the monster legend in any way whatsoever. Here is part of his account – in his own words.

"The school bus, with Sandack (elderly and solemn regular driver in those days) at the wheel proceeding towards Drum,

arrives at Urquhart Castle and stops to pick up Anne Robertson. There ensued a general hullabaloo: "Monster, Monster!" was the cry. Sandack could do little to stop the bus emptying to allow all aboard a better view of what clearly was a disturbance on the surface of the loch. This was in the form of a local disturbance approximately ¾ of a mile from the shore, on a direct line with Dores, i.e. towards the centreline of the loch and moving along this line in a south easterly direction. There was no noticeable object protruding from the surface to create this moving turbulence.

The passengers eventually re-boarded the bus and finished the journey to the school where the tale was told to those in authority. This must have been accepted with some credence, since the ritual thrashings were not administered to the late-comers. Indeed the sighting must have struck some chord with the headmaster Allie MacKell because about three days later, a recording team from the BBC turned up at the school to take eyewitness accounts of the sighting from selected and/or still hysterical pupils. As I recall, all of these were girls. The programme was broadcast a few days later. Briefly, all of the reports were exaggerated, with descriptions which included, for instance: long neck with head and open jaws; varying numbers of humps; erroneous direction and speed of travel; and, most memorable of all, 'the monster displayed a yellow belly, like that of a newt.' (actual words, from a normally sensible friend of my sister and her friend, Theresa, called Bridget.)"

Now my brother's assessment of what had actually happened on that day in the early fifties.

"As you will recall, the most common canal traffic in those days was the small fishing boats from Fraserburgh and Buckie etc, hacking their way back home with their catch from the Irish Sea. Well, on that day, two of these were positioned about one mile in front of the 'hump' with one boat approximately ¼ mile ahead of the other and on a parallel course about ¼ mile to the side: i.e they were not 'line astern'. This is important, and equally so were the prevailing weather conditions viz a light breeze just sufficient to ruffle the surface." To paraphrase the rest of his hypothesis, these wakes crossed each other, and on doing so, caused a disturbance on the loch's surface that could easily be mistaken for something large moving just below the surface.

Now for the recollections of Theresa, my sister's friend, who was also a witness.

"This is a very old memory, but I used to dine out on it when I was teaching. Mind you, the students probably thought I was old enough to have seen Tyrannosaurus Rex in the flesh! What I did see was something moving pretty fast not far out from the shore leaving a sizeable wash behind it. If it was a monster, it was a rather wee one. Someone I mentioned it to suggested a group of otters – which is a nice idea: a wee family of otters out for a jaunt. Of course, we were all out of the bus, agog, but anything that broke the monotony of the bus run was welcome. I don't remember Bridget being interviewed, but we are talking nearly fifty years ago. My father, who was Fort Augustus-born and bred, was always very scathing about the idea of the Monster and even more so about those who got publicity from claims to have seen it. This included more than one monk from the Abbey. But he was a bit anti-clerical."

On several occasions, when I was young, I was chilled by a tale that was doing the rounds then. High above Loch Ness, just beyond Glendoe Lodge, on the south side of the loch, is an eighteen-foot pyramid-shaped monument standing on a rocky promontory. It marks a tragedy that took place on the actual loch, opposite that point. The monument had been erected in 1934, two years after the event. On August 28th, 1932, Winifred Hambro, wife of R. O. Hambro, a director of the influential Hambro's Bank in London, had been drowned. She, her husband and their two children along with their nanny had been enjoying a trip on the loch in a speedboat when it caught fire. All managed to swim to safety, except Mrs Hambro. Although a noted strong swimmer, she disappeared from sight. The distraught husband hired a firm of deep-sea divers to recover the body, but to no avail. Local gossip at the time suggested that it was the fact that Mrs Hambro had been wearing very expensive jewellery that had been the main driving force behind the search, but it is not too difficult to concede that the pain of the bereaved husband would have been the more obvious interpretation. But there was another story about his tragedy that held young audiences in thrall. It went as follows: The divers were lowered into the depths of the loch encased in the cumbersome suits worn in those early days, searching the steep sides of the loch for any caves or indentations which might hold the remains of the drowned woman. Suddenly one of them signalled desperately to be drawn back up to the monitoring craft. When his helmet was removed, the men were shocked to see the diver in a state of rigid terror. He was unable to speak coherently and his hair had turned ghostly white. He was never able to tell what he had seen, but the tellers of this tale made it clear that the Loch Ness Monster was what had terrified the unfortunate diver. No mention of this can be found in the close research done by Fraser MacKenzie of Drumnadrochit in his study of Highland Wayside Monuments, and it clearly is a piece of local fevered imaginings. But it did have an effect on youthful listeners to such tales.

Some of the other more close-to-home sightings I remember could also give one pause for thought. There was, for example, that chapter in a long-forgotten book about the Monster, which was devoted to a mass sighting that took place at my father's school in Fort Augustus. One day, after the morning interval, the pupils rushed in to their classrooms in a state of hysterical excitement. They told their teachers that they had seen the Monster in the Loch, just beyond the mouth of the River Oich. Some time later, a researcher who had heard about this episode arrived at the school and asked my father if he could help. No problem. The pupils were not warned in advance, but on a certain day they were told to write down their recollections of that day. The whole thing was carried out in examination conditions – no conferring – and the results were so impressive that they eventually were given a whole chapter in the eventual book. It was called "The Fort Augustus School Sighting". I have never read that account. A mystery. I have not been able to trace this book.

The moment in my own life when the Monster legend became a myth came about as follows. It was the day when I asked my father what sightings there had been of the creature in the days when he was a pupil in Balnain School up the Glen and later in the secondary school in Drumnadrochit. The epicentre of Monster country. He had been educated there in the early twenties.

Anyway, the conversation went something like this:
"Did *you* ever see the Monster?"

"No."
"Did you know anyone who saw the Monster?"
"No. No-one," he replied.
"No-one? You mean ....?"
"No. We never heard about it."
"You mean that nobody spoke about it – EVER?"
"No. Never mentioned."
Well that really seemed, I suppose, to draw a line under the whole matter.

But the sightings continued. One was by a relative of mine who lived in Inverness and had stopped her car not far from the foot of the Abriachan Brae, about nine miles from Inverness. Something huge and unaccountable by normal standards was surging in the grey waters a few hundred yards from the shore. She had her camera and feverishly struggled to get it set up and focussed before clicking the shutter as often as possible. It was only when she got back to Inverness and checked that she found she had made the most basic mistake possible with a non-reflex camera: she had not removed the lens cap. So no pictures and no fortune from their sale to the world's hungry press.

One of the thought-provoking aspects of this ever-evolving story is revealed when a closer examination is made of the earliest "appearances" of the Monster. I have mentioned earlier that I personally knew Alex Campbell, the originator of the actual name "Monster". He was a familiar figure in our village and, as I have said, was a solemn, dignified and reserved individual. I remember him once appearing at the door of the schoolhouse and asking to speak to my father. I overheard enough of the conversation to make out that he was asking my father's advice on how he should go about writing about his sightings of the Monster over the years. I have no idea as to what my father suggested, but he was certainly encouraging about the idea. As to whether Alex ever addressed this challenge, I have no idea. Certainly I have never heard of anything he might ever have published.

He, it was, who gave currency to the whole legend with his initial use of the term "Monster" to describe something inexplicable in the depths of Loch Ness. It is only when a closer look is taken at the events in the early nineteen thirties and their reporting by

Alex Campbell, to his superiors as a water bailiff and to the "Inverness Courier" newspaper, that slight discrepancies can be found.

On the internet, a study of early Monster sightings by Richard Carter, quotes the first description by Alex Campbell, and it is worth while looking at it again in full.

"At around 09.30 hours on the morning of September 7th 1933, I was watching the loch from the mouth of the River Oich. There was a thick mist and the sun was shining down the loch when I noticed a strange object about 600 yards away from where I stood. It seemed about 30 feet long and what I took to be the head was standing about five feet out of the loch. It seemed to be watching two drifters passing out of the canal into the loch and was turning its head and body very quickly as though agitated. I watched this for a full minute and then it vanished as though it had sunk out of sight."

As Richard Carter observed, this description has appeared in almost every one of the many books about the Loch Ness mystery. However, it is only part of a letter written on the 28th October 1933 to the Ness Fishery Board by Alex Campbell in his capacity as the water bailiff for Loch Ness – a post he held for 47 years.

The rest of this original letter tells a completely different story, however. It goes on: *"Last Friday, I was watching the loch from the same place under the same weather conditions. Shortly, something like I described before came into my line of vision. The same distance as before but the light was improving all the time and what I took to be the monster was nothing more than a few cormorants and what seemed to be the head was a cormorant standing in the water, flapping its wings."*

So, it would seem that this original sighting had proved to be just a mirage and Alex Campbell had recognised it as such. However, in May 1934, Alex Campbell records a sighting in very similar words: *"One morning in May, I was standing near the mouth of the River Oich when a strange object shot out of the water near the Abbey Boat House. I closed my eyes three times to make sure I was not imagining it."*

He went on to describe the head and huge humped body of a strange creature about 400 hundred yards away. He thought the creature could hear the engines of two trawlers making their way out of the canal as it was twisting its head from side to side frantically. As soon as the first trawler came out of the canal mouth, the creature vanished out of sight. He estimated that the body was about thirty feet in length and that the head and neck stood six feet out of the water.

Indeed, Alex Campbell in an early interview about his sightings, explained how easy it was to be deceived by birds and other objects and did not want to have his name mentioned in connection with the Monster. In actual fact, over the years, he appeared in many newspapers and television programmes like Panorama, Arthur C Clarke's "Mysterious World" and Walt Disney's "Man, Monsters and Mysteries". Every book written about the Loch Ness Monster includes the classic sightings of Alex Campbell, the Fort Augustus water bailiff. But the odd fact remains that he did not report his own sightings until after he had reported the sighting of a Mr and Mrs MacKay on March 1933. His father had also been the water bailiff on the loch before him for many years, yet had never reported anything strange in the loch.

None of the foregoing disproves what Alex Campbell claims to have seen, but it does raise several questions.

And my own position? Well, right at the beginning, I placed my cards on the table as a son of the Enlightenment and Rationality, rejecting any notion of the existence of such a creature: it is simply not possible. But, I have to confess, that over the years whenever I find that I am to be taking a drive along the road by the loch, I make sure that I have a camera equipped with suitable telephoto lens, in the car within easy reach. I remember that already in my lifetime I have missed the opportunity of catching a glimpse of the Monster as a result of simple bad luck. I shall make certain that the odds are stacked a little more in my favour should there be a flaw in all my smug rationality. And think of the riches that would accrue to me in the event of my capturing that definitive image.

A good number of years ago, I formulated a theory of my own. During school days, I had been visiting Fort William as part of a shinty team and with a couple of companions, after the game, waited for a late bus in order to go to the cinema. The film was "King Kong". It is difficult to convey the terrifying effect that this film had on me and it provided the basis of many nightmares for many years. It was later, when looking at the famous (and now discredited) "Surgeon's Photograph" of the monster taken in the nineteen thirties, I saw the distinct resemblance it bore to the scene in that film when the crew from the ship, stumbling through the jungle in pursuit of the gigantic Kong who had borne the beauteous damsel away in his vast fist, made a raft so that they could cross a sinister swamp. From the depths, reared a long, glistening neck topped by a head - mouth agape with dagger teeth - that proceeded to pick off the tiny fleeing figures one by one. When that film came out, just around the time of the first reports in the press about the Monster, the world had been gripped by that film which terrified audiences with its up-till-then never-before seen special effects. It does not take too much of a leap of the imagination to suggest that this could have been the origin of the Loch Ness legend.

The two small mysteries that I have yet to solve concerning this matter are, first, what happened to the book that included the chapter about the sighting by the Fort Augustus pupils and the significance of their written descriptions organised by my father, and the other is the non-appearance of any record of the BBC programme with the voices of the Glenurquhart pupils giving their hysterical accounts. Perhaps the book had never got beyond the draft stage. My trawlings through the vast wildernesses of the internet have failed to locate it.

CHAPTER 9
Ghosts by Loch Ness

The chill brush of the fingers of the supernatural has not played much part in my life. I like to see myself as a true son of the Enlightenment where such matters can be attributed merely to the dark churnings of the human imagination. However, there is one series of incidents that occurred over quite a number of years that poses some interesting questions and can stir up that almost delicious thrill that accompanies encounters with the unknown.

Back to Fort Augustus in the nineteen fifties. The local parish priest, based in the Benedictine Abbey, was Father Philip. He was a regular visitor to the schoolhouse and was welcomed by my parents (who were not Roman Catholics) - as were several others of the members of that relatively undemanding Roman Catholic order. Father Philip carried echoes of the "Whisky Priest" of Graham Green fame, mainly in his easy attitude to life and its trials - and the weaknesses of our frail bodies. He enjoyed good conversation and if it was accompanied by a glass or two, then all the better. It was on one of those visits to the schoolhouse that the first episode of the tale of the Loch Ness Side Apparition was related.

These were the days of the Hydro-electric schemes and the huge surging of human activity that engulfed our previously peaceful community. This meant that Father Philip had his priestly duties increased quite considerably by the numbers of his faith who were now living in the workers' camps in Glenmoriston and Glengarry. It meant fairly regular trips to the camps to see them.

It was on one of these occasions, at one of the camps in Glenmoriston, that he was approached by a man who didn't actually work on the hydro scheme there. He was an itinerant salesman who made his living selling clothes and other items from his van to the workers. He seemed very agitated and he told Father Philip that he had been having unsettling experiences on the main lochside road to Inverness, a few miles to the east of Invermoriston. He said that there was a particular spot on the road, at the foot of a long brae, where there was an outcrop of rock and a distinctive black overhang of forestry trees.

The last time he had approached this spot, the lights in his van had suddenly gone out and the engine had faltered and died. For some weeks past, he had had a deep and inexplicable sense of foreboding at this place, but for this to happen was just too much. When he, reluctantly, got out of the van with his torch to see if he could find anything amiss under the bonnet, he shone the beam in an arc round the inky darkness. The black looming trees hissed in the wind and the loch waters lapped close by – all adding to the disquiet that was now gripping him. He told the priest that he had a distinct sensation that he was being watched. He sensed a presence close by. He feverishly fumbled under the bonnet with the battery terminals and the lights returned once more. Back in the cab, the engine fired into life and he sped back along the lochside road home to Inverness.

What would Father Philip suggest he do this evening? He was really nervous about facing it all again. All the priest could do was suggest that he just head back as usual and hope that it was all just coincidental – as it most certainly must be. That was all the advice that Father Philip thought he could give. It really didn't seem all that much a problem anyway. All a flight of the man's over-active imagination.

A week or two went past and, one evening, the parish priest was called down to one of the entrances of the Abbey – the one called the "hospice" (where the casual passer-by could go who might be looking for spiritual sustenance or where the indigent might be given a bowl of soup) – and standing there was the travelling salesman in a highly agitated state. He had had another episode at the exact same spot on the road the previous week. The van had been speeding down the brae and, at the turn at the foot, the lights went out and the engine fell silent. The van coasted to a halt at the precise same spot and the salesman, terrified by now, got out and feverishly looked under the bonnet with his torch. He got the lights to come on again and he looked towards the rear of the vehicle and said that he felt he could just make out a dim figure, with maybe another one behind it, in the faint glow from the rear lights. He didn't wait to find out anything more, but leapt into the cab and sped to the safety of distant Inverness. Father Philip asked about the dim shape or shapes the salesman said he had seen. No real details here,

but just the impression that it was maybe fishermen. It was all so fleeting and he just had to get away as fast as possible. But the immediate problem was how to get back to Inverness this evening? The salesman had decided when he had reached the road junction at the village of Invermoriston that he could not face the dark, tree-shrouded road by the loch. Instead, he turned right, and sped the six miles west to the Abbey at Fort Augustus – maybe even to spend the night there.
Father Philip had an idea.
"I have some business to see to in the town tomorrow. Why not we head off there just now? We'll see what happens and if all goes well, that'll maybe be an end to all of this. I've an address I can stay at in the town so no problem there. Just let me make a phone call."
So off they set. It was quite late now and traffic was light. Eventually the salesman mentioned that there was not long to go now till they had reached the place where it all had been happening. Almost there. The van rounded the corner at the top of the brae and began its sweep down towards the now-sinister corner lying waiting. And, right on cue, the lights flickered and failed, just as the engine cut out and fell silent. In the dim light, the driver struggled to avoid the verge and managed to bring the van to a rattling halt on the gravel on the turn-off, right under the black overhang of the trees. The salesman nervously opened the door and made his way to the front to lift the bonnet. Father Philip, nervous too in spite of the voice of common sense within him urging him that it was all just coincidence. He could only hear the wind in the branches and the noise of the nearby loch. The desperate scrabblings under the bonnet began to have effect, and the sidelights flickered on.
 In the dim, red glow of the rear lights, Father Philip suddenly thought that he could make out a shape just a short distance behind the van. He described it to his listeners in the old schoolhouse that evening, as something that looked like a fisherman – and there might have been another immediately behind it.
He called out, "Who are you? What do you want?"
There was no movement or any sign of response.
His priestly instincts and training now came into play and he directly challenged the dim, unsettling shapes – just as the

engine of the van decided to fire into life once more and the headlights again lanced the darkness ahead. The dim shapes vanished and both of the stricken men now tumbled into the van and hastened to get as much distance between them and that grim spot as they possibly could.

For some time after I had first heard this tale – and, remember, it had all the added authenticity from having been recounted by a man of the cloth – I made inquiries in various places about any accident happening on any of the many fishing boats that used the Caledonian Canal in those days to access the seas to the east and west of mainland Scotland. Had any one of them sunk or had a crewmember or members been lost overboard near that spot between Altsaigh and Invermoriston Bay? No-one I consulted had ever heard of anything untoward that might have had a restless spirit haunting that stretch of the loch's shore.

A number of years after all this, my wife and I, only recently married, and driving my pride and joy in those early sixties days – our tiny grey Mini – were heading back down the lochside after a weekend with my parents at the schoolhouse in Fort Augustus. Father Philip's tale must have figured in the conversation at some point and was in our thoughts as we sped along in our noisy little box. I, like the youthful male of our species, had invested some of my salary as a teacher in Inverness High School in various gadgets for my trendy little Mini, including a couple of totally unnecessary, but very decorative, spotlights on a small chrome gantry at the front. They were activated by a purposeful toggle switch on the rudimentary instrument panel of those early models. As we approached that part of the road where the episode of a dozen years or so earlier had taken place – a few miles on the Invermoriston side of Altsaigh - I mentioned this casually.

"I'll switch on the spots to give us a bit more light at the foot of the brae," I said. "That'll take care of any spooky fishermen."

I flicked the switch for my twin macho beams, but instead we were plunged into dark and blackness enveloped us. I was just able to avoid the verge and miraculously managed to coast to the foot of the brae where we drew up in a state of considerable alarm. As I frantically juggled with the toggle switch and the other light switches I inadvertently managed to turn off the engine. More frantic activity and, to our immense relief, the engine fired up again and the lights leapt into life. I do not need to tell you that there was no investigation as to whether any dim shapes were watching us from the roadside in our desperation and panic.

The next day, I put the car into the garage to have the lights seen to. They told me that there were some faulty connections in my new spotlight set-up that needed some attention. The necessary was seen to and that was an end to that.

For quite a number of years, this was a tale to which we would occasionally give an airing and my wife used it to considerable effect with classes during her teaching days and you might think that would have been the end of our almost-contact with the Loch Ness Ghost.

But you would be wrong.

Another passage of time – more than twenty five years – found me doing free-lance broadcasting with the now-defunct BBC Radio Highland. I did many forms of contribution to the station's output during much of the eighties: talks (the "View From Denoon" thus named by a producer from those days), half-hour feature programmes on various subjects, theatre and book reviews and a long and enjoyable series I did with a then teaching colleague from the High School, Fraser Mackenzie from Drumnadrochit. Fraser had spent many years studying the histories of the many wayside monuments and cairns that are to be found all over the Highlands. Each one was photographed and the tiniest details of its history were recorded in his collection. The idea was that we would head off to one of these monuments: Fraser with his notes and me with my BBC equipment. In those days, I had the bulky reel-to-reel UHER recorder. I would have memorised a basic overview of the monument of the day and when we got there, I would give a description of its appearance and where it was situated in the surrounding countryside. Then my questions would elicit from the expert the story behind it in as interesting and detailed a fashion as we could muster between us.

One of the early ones in this series took us west along the A86 by Loch Ness, past Altsaigh for a couple of miles and to a spot where we could park the car off the main road. I shouldered my UHER as Fraser led the way across the roadside fence, through a field of bracken and into a wood of birch and hazel. We could catch glimpses of Loch Ness, calm and blue, below us through the gaps in the trees. Fraser announced that we were nearly there: the spot where he said a small granite cross had been erected in the early nineteen hundreds to commemorate a drowning tragedy that had occurred in the loch, directly out from this very spot.

It had happened on February the 18th, 1905. A Glasgow businessman, John Hinshelwood and his boatman, Duncan MacDonnell of Livishie, Invermoriston, had been drowned while salmon fishing. Their boat had capsized in a sudden squall. A third member of the party, a boatman called Donald Macdonald, had survived by clinging to the keel of the boat. Hinshelwood had been a guest at Invermoriston Hotel.

It was not till some considerable time after this tale of a long-ago fishing tragedy had been recorded, edited and broadcast on BBC Radio Highland that it struck home with some force that this could have been the missing piece in the strange tale of the Loch Ness Ghost. My inquiries had always centred on a possible fatal accident on a fishing boat, large numbers of which were always making their way in both directions through the Caledonian Canal. The original description by Father Philip when telling the story had simply indicated that the vague shapes seen by the roadside had been "fishermen". Instead of a crewmember of a trawler perhaps it had been the spectres of the ill-fated Hinshelwood and his boatman Duncan Macdonell who were still haunting the loch shore close to where they had died on that February day. But why pick on the hapless travelling salesman, a parish priest – and maybe a youthful couple in a grey Mini - to make their gesture from the other side?

Maybe there have been others who have had their lives interrupted alarmingly while on their innocent way along that stretch of road by the night-time shores of Loch Ness. Or maybe it is just another example of our species yearning for some sign that there might just be something else beyond the world that we experience through our normal senses.

Recent changes to the lay-out of the road at that spot and a widening of it have made it difficult to identify precisely where these events were supposed to have happened, but for all that, I can sense pretty accurately where that van with the travelling salesman and the parish priest had drawn to a nervous halt and they had stared out anxiously into the threatening darkness. And I know that I would not like it if the car I was driving at night were to decide to break down at that spot. Especially if the lights had failed as well.

CHAPTER 10
Old Friend - Cycling Days

Recently, I came across, in my archives, some yellowing sheets of paper dating back to my long-ago teaching days. While enthusing about some of my favourite poets to small groups of senior pupils studying for what in those days was called "Sixth Year Studies", I had been encouraging them to attempt writing poetry themselves. To show that I was prepared to do the same, I set about having a go myself. Most of these efforts have been lost, but I hung on to a few of them, which I thought were not all that bad after all. The following is just such a one, and it neatly introduces the theme of this chapter. I even have the date on which I wrote it. It was on the 30th of March, 1985.

Old Friend

My heavy boots
(Of student job, in fifties holiday)
Crunch along a gravel path
Of memory – and stop.

It's quiet now;
And then I'm on my bike again,
Rushing down some brae familiar,
Aware of every crack of
Each and every spoke
That sagged and strained
With faintly ominous – but unheeded – sounds.

I knew it nut by nut
And bolt by bolt.
Its handlebars askew, a bit.
Its always-rattling mudguard;
Its chain that chose
The wettest day and run most urgent
To whip from sprockets,
And wrap itself in oily twists
Around the hub.

The pedals always jumped
And lurched, and made me wonder, vaguely,
Every day
That human kind
Could ever put its trust in
Something called
A 'cotter pin' ……..

The chrome had left the handlebars
In patches, and
Pitted rust flaked off.
Its brakes, with metal linking rods,
That ought, by all the laws, to work –
But somehow only partly did, and
Mostly seemed just fit
To keep the rims bright and gleaming bands.

From rattling, red reflector
To road that streamed beneath
The front wheel's speeding blur,
I feel that bike of thirty years ago
Still part of me,
With all the surgings and the tensions,
And the drudgeries –
The endless days
Of Highland adolescence.

But as to what became of it -
My slightly ragged, ill-maintained,
Yet faithful – mostly – bike:
When was that day, when
I let it roll into its final lodgement
In the hawthorn hedge
Beside the old, drunk shed …… ?

It's true, I just can't recollect
The way we parted company.

I left that home and moved away

Of course,
But what about the bike?
Did I really simply walk away
And leave it there
To crumple into rust?
Did someone come to buy it? Or
More likely
Lead it off as kindly favour?
Did it ever mould its eccentricities
To someone else's life
And give good service
Like the solid upright citizen
It was?
I'll never know.

My dear old bike:
Your very name – what make you were –
Has gone.
Black and gleaming new
You shone, with thin red stripe:
A birthday present, long ago.
You had the bulky strength
And robust build
That went with long, thin
Stovepipe-funnelled liners.

When did you brush up against
Your iceberg and
Slip from sight?

You carried me so many
Thousand miles.
Each journey had its purpose
That had importance at the time.
But try to add them up,
The lot of them, and calculate
In terms of miles;
Or better still, in tensions
And anticipations, longed-for
Outcomes, yearnings, or just

Simple lusts,
There's nothing left there any more,
Except a few, slow-moving shapes,
Small against a distant, lowering sky.
Yet once
They filled my universe.

It's true, in your case anyway,
They just don't make them like you
Any more!
You'd metal, near enough,
Inside of you
To make a couple of these modern toys
-   or even three!
You were not manufactured –
You were launched!
In front of cheering crowds
With whooping sirens and a spinning
Cloud of workmen's bonnets
Darkening the sky.
The rattling sounds of chain
Drawn taut to hold you,
Turning slowly in the heaving
Iron-grey firth ……..

But, no more nonsense.
Even if I can't remember
Memories exact of journeys made,
You've managed somehow
To rattle back into my life
Today (and why today?)
And I'm, well, pleased to see you
Leaning, quiet, against the old school wall,
Just waiting there,
To speed me down the swooping hill,
I don't care where …………

One of the oldest clichés of life is that once having learned to go a bike, you never forget. Even in your final tottering years, you

can be confident that you could swing a leg over the saddle and maintain, at least, your balance.
Not so.
Many years ago, when in my early teens, I completely "unlearned" the skill of going a bike. It happened this way.
One of the family treats of the Denoons in the old schoolhouse in Fort Augustus was the regular piling into the car and heading west to Spean Bridge, then to almost doubling back and heading towards Badenoch and Strathspey and the small scattered village of Laggan Bridge. There, in the epicentre of this tiny community, was the shop, run by our Uncle Dave and Aunt Annie. Annie was our mother's younger sister and Davie Miller was her grocer husband. I have already devoted a chapter in my previous book about life behind the wheel of the grim behemoth of a van, the mighty Albion, that he used to deliver groceries to his many far-flung customers: these events lay some distance ahead of the episode about to unfold.

Apart from the delights of staying for a spell with a favourite aunt and uncle and our two cousins, Jim and Norman, there was another added pleasure – the fact that our grandparents, our mother's parents, lived quite close by.
About three quarters of a mile, eastwards towards Newtonmore, was an imposing house, Gaskmore Lodge, that stood on its promontory looking westwards along the strath, with its distinctive tower adding authority to its splendid location. In the neat, ivy-clad lodge close by, at the entrance gate, lived my grandparents. My grandmother acted as cook and housekeeper to the owners of the Lodge, the magnificent-sounding Boswell-Browns, while my grandfather was the gardener and handyman. He could not have been more an archetype of the old soldier of the Great War. He was straight-backed and had the bushy walrus moustache (now white) of the kind seen in so many photographs of the men of that era, like "Old Bill" of the famous "Punch" cartoons. In that monstrous madness, he had been a member of the Pioneer Corps, and we learned, long after his death, that one of his duties had been the burial of the mounds of corpses that piled after each insane attack or counter-attack in the churned-up mud of the battlefields. By not the slightest hint or gesture did he ever let slip a glimpse of such horrors to us.

My memory is of his animated voice as he told us stories of Scottish history – the deeds of Bruce and Wallace, being favourites. He was a mesmerising teller of tales. The evidence of his gardening skills was all around in the rolling lawns and well-tended flowerbeds. But his especial pride was a small hill with a scattering of young Scots pine trees growing on it. He had used this to create a feature involving winding paths and additional shrubs, with occasional bench seats installed at effective vantage points providing views of the sweeping strath with its winding river and its tree-clad looming hills.

Gaskmore Lodge had special magic for us. The Boswell-Browns were very hospitable, and the family of the daughter of their much-prized cook was made very welcome. The inside of the house, especially the main front room where we were entertained on those occasions, was mightily impressive. I remember a vast stone fireplace against one wall and pictures and ornaments of exotic appearance. The host and hostess were as typical of their class and nation as you could conceive. He was tall, diffident and blond-haired, while his wife was almost overwhelming in her urge to make us welcome. These occasions were whirlwinds of impressions and the air filled with confident English accents and hospitality. We really delighted in it all. When the tea and other refreshments had been disposed of, it was time to explore the extensive grounds. One day, my brother and I looked into one of the large sheds where the gardening tools were kept and it was there that I found a tricycle standing parked in a far corner. It was wheeled out into the daylight and examined. It was a full-size adult tricycle, with wheels the size of those you would find on a normal bicycle and in a moment I had climbed up and tried to head off on it. To my astonishment, it turned out to be very hard to control. I found that instead of just sitting on the saddle and pressing down on the pedals and heading off in whatever direction you chose, this odd-looking contraption seemed to have a life of its own. It took some time and quite a lot of practice over several days before we were able to set off along the twisting paths of our grandfather's maze on his miniature tree-planted hill.

It just could not get better than this. For all of that holiday, whenever we visited Gaskmore Lodge, it was into the shed and off swirling the manoeuvrable and lively tricycle at breakneck speeds along the narrow twisting paths.

The marvellous holiday came to an end, of course, and we headed back to Fort Augustus in the black Jaguar. As was usual, whenever we got back home from such a holiday, the first thing was the instruction from my mother to head off down to Leslie's shop down by the canal to get various of the necessary provisions. I ran to the shed and wheeled out my bike, steadied it and swung astride it. I promptly fell off, crashing to the ground. Perplexed, I grasped the handlebars again and placed my left foot on the pedal, hopped along once or twice and once more swung my leg across the saddle. Again, immediate crash to earth. I just could not balance it. I had been cycling for many years at this point in my life, and it was quite frightening to find that I had totally lost the ability to balance a bicycle. I can't remember how long it took me to re-learn to go my bike, but it was some considerable time before I regained my former confidence. It was clear soon enough that the lengthy spells whirling about the gardens of Gaskmore Lodge on the tricycle were to blame. I suppose it lies in the quite different skills required to control these machines. A main part of the ability to balance on a two-wheeled vehicle derives from the handlebars and the constant corrections you have to make instinctively to maintain an upright position. On a tricycle, that is not required, hence the initial difficulty with the latter at Gaskmore. The adjustment to this over that long holiday meant that that skill was lost and explains why I pitched headlong on to the school playground in such an alarming manner.

Boswell-Brown himself died some years after these events, and his widow converted the house to a hotel. When I was working at the shop as a student and driving the terrifying old Albion van, I would sometimes walk across to Gaskmore Lodge and the pub there. Mrs Boswell-Brown herself was often behind the bar and an extremely energetic and voluble hostess she made. At one point, fire destroyed much of the original building and its former lustre had gone. Today the name is retained in the Laggan Gaskmore Hotel which now stands on the site and offers its services to the passing visitors to the Highlands.

When I penned the lines of the poem at the head of this chapter all those years ago, the impression might have been given that I have been an enthusiastic cyclist all my days. Well, not really. Effectively I gave it up when I left the old schoolhouse at Fort Augustus and set out into the wider world. At one point I did attempt to take it up again when an advertisement in a newspaper drew my attention to a smart-looking folding bike that proclaimed itself to be ideal for town or city use. Well, I was a total townie by this time, and off went my order form and cheque. Back came the bike and at first it looked just great. However, it had been manufactured somewhere behind the Iron Curtain in a factory where anything remotely like quality control just did not exist. Right from the start, you could peel the chrome off the handlebars like unwrapping a Kit Kat bar. The brakes, when applied, had the actual rubber brake-blocks melt against the wheel rims and leave a black tarry deposit. The tyres both began to wear down before your eyes at the most alarming rate and it was not long before the townie's folding bike was folded up for the last time and hurled into a skip. And that was the end of my cycling career. From then on, I developed the motorists' resentment of cyclists, and began to mutter about the manner in which the rules of the road simply did not apply to them. One way street signs could be ignored just as traffic lights were either at worst totally ignored, or at best, looked on as suggestions that were up for negotiation. I was even heard to rant at the extraordinary dimness of certain members of the tribe who saw that their bikes were never equipped with even the most rudimentary of mud guards. They obviously had worked out the notion that the mudguard-free bicycle was a sign of massive surgings of testosterone, as were the combination of sprayed-on lyca garments and weird helmets. Shudder. All I could do was to bathe in warm satisfaction on seeing, from the interior warmth of my car, the sight of one of them with twin Catherine-wheels of icy cold spray drenching him or her, front and back.

Age has brought a sense of calm, and I no longer seethe with wrath as they weave in and out of the traffic.

CHAPTER 11
Polloch

While writing about the Fort Augustus Players, I had a thought. Good friend, Syd Wray, used to be a member of that group in the years after I had moved on to university and he had taken part in many productions. I remembered that he had once told me he had a number of photographs taken of various productions and I was curious to see them. I had memories of some of the pictures I had seen many years ago, and the recollection of the unkindness of black-and-white film to actors with over-generously applied stage make-up was strong. This was confirmed when I opened the envelope with about eight excellent prints and was transported back a huge swathe of time. My mother appeared in about half of them and it was quite moving to see her again in these strange situations of make-believe. However, it was the sight of Syd himself in the various parts he was playing that also caught my attention. Originally from Glasgow, he had left our village not long after these pictures had been taken. He had been a forester at Fort Augustus for some years and had been, with his wife Moira, a really splendid addition to the village. Their house at Jenkin's Park was a Mecca for myself and my brother and others of our small coterie, in that it was a place of merriment and freedom from the social constraints of the prim fifties. No excesses, of course – just an environment of wit and laughter and music. Syd was an accomplished guitarist and had a truly extraordinary instrument. It was a four-stringed guitar with a cello body. I had just bought a splendid Hofner acoustic guitar and spent many hours of fairly futile effort with it. It was something that I never could quite work out in those days. I was – and I am not indulging in empty boasting here – pretty accomplished at playing the harmonica. I also could get a lively tune out of a button key accordion (though could never use the left hand keys) but when it came to the guitar, I found that I was always locked into a tired mechanical series of chords that were all right for basic accompaniments, but were so far from the flowing swoops and riffs that I yearned to create that I often was ready to give it all up in despair. Syd with his eccentric instrument just strolled through this stuff with casual ease. It was not helped as far as I was concerned by the fact that as a result of an accident some time in the past, he had lost his right thumb.

The first visit to Syd and Moira's new home and place of work in Polloch in Ardnamurchan was in the company of my parents. I drove them there in the family car, which then would have been the rakish, red Riley. We had had our instructions on how to make our way there after leaving the comfortable familiarity of the A82 to the west of Fort William. The real adventure began on the slipway to the ferry at Corran. Something about that stretch of water created the powerful impression of going to a foreign land. The mountains loomed ever more menacingly as we drew closer to the far shore. The distant, white buildings at the approaching jetty took more detailed shape and soon the ramp was crashing down and we held our breath as we waited for the grating of our exhaust dragging over the raised edge of the ramp. We cleared it by enough of a whisker to save us the disaster of a ruptured silencer. On then to the narrow, single-track that stretched far away into the embrace of the dark crouching mountains. This was totally new territory for us, and every detail spoke of strangeness. A small scattering of houses told us we were passing through Strontian. The association of this place with the mysteries of atomic science and the fact that radioactive Strontium 90 was named after this remote corner of the Western Highlands added its own special frisson. We passed the remains of the old lead mines with their associations with the Napoleonic Wars.

We had been well warned that the road was about to undertake a dramatic transformation in its so-far fairly co-operative treatment of the stranger. A remorseless hill lay ahead with a fearsome gradient. Then we were on it. The Riley began to labour as the gears were shifted down lower and lower. Only one left now and visibility was restricted to the immediate foreground of the red pointed bonnet with the knurled cap at the top of the radiator. We seemed to be pointed directly up at the cobalt blue sky. The final double de-clutch into first gear was the last shot in the Riley's locker as we slowly ground our way to the final heave over the summit. We then found ourselves looking down a seemingly endless ribbon of road that swooped and played itself out, looping into distant, dark forestry plantations far below. We knew that somewhere ahead, after we had reached the strath and were driving alongside the loch we could now just make out, we would be starting to look out for the tiny Forestry community of Polloch where a welcome would be awaiting us, and relief from this sometimes alarming and exhausting drive. The countryside became more placid for a spell when we were down on the level, though the darkness of the once-again looming trees reminded us of the sole purpose of this place. Timber: its nurturing and harvesting. A Bailey bridge now, and we were rattling over its wooden planks and then, just ahead, we saw the small – but so welcome – huddle of wooden houses. Now familiar voices were greeting us and the forestry house resonated to the happiness of re-acquaintance.

It was not long before we were able to appreciate fully just how remote Polloch was in those late nineteen-fifties days. Electricity was supplied by a diesel generator. It was turned on only as the evenings darkened, and on weekdays it was timed to switch off at around 11pm. At weekends, it stayed on till midnight. The only time it was on during the day was on a Tuesday afternoon. This was for a meagre two hours, and was to allow the wives to use their irons! Special arrangements had to be made for irons as they used so much power. Tilley and Aladdin lamps were now called into service with their pale mellow light when the generator was not functioning. A large fridge in the kitchen had me puzzled. How could its contents survive the lack of steady power? No problem. It didn't work by electricity. It was gas powered. No, I do not understand at the moment of writing down these memories, but you can check out if you wish. All I can tell you is that it did work. Our exiled friends were highly sociable people and liked to keep up with the news. There was the radio, of course. But this had not been automatic. Several models were tried out and would only work if held at a certain angle while half-way up the stairs. It was the discovery of a "Perdio" radio that eventually solved that problem. As far as newspapers were concerned, they had to be very patient. Their Sunday papers didn't arrive till Wednesday though a daily paper was occasionally brought by the postie from Strontian.

At one point during that first evening, I felt an urge to contact my fiancée who was at home in the manse in Inverbervie with her father who was the minister there in those days. Syd told me that he had no phone in the house, but down the road, a short distance away, was a telephone box. I was handed a torch and off I set. It is only in places like Polloch that you experience real, total blackness at night. I felt it like something palpable and I nervously navigated my way along the beam of light to the familiar red of the phone box. Inside I felt it surreal with the familiar equipment and notices, yet with the sense of being adrift on an ocean of inky blackness. The crude chrome buttons, A and B (which one of these allowed you to make contact with the person you were phoning and let our money clatter into the receptacle – was it Button A or Button B? What distant and now-remote technology.) I can still recall the sense of total isolation I felt while I was speaking to my fiancée across the widest part of mainland Scotland and hearing her voice coming from the minister's study in the sturdy sensible Presbyterian focal point of that small grey east coast town.

Some time after this visit with my parents, my fiancée and I decided that we should make our way to Polloch on our own. It is hard, now, to convey the prevailing social attitudes of the buttoned-up fifties. Even though we had been engaged for some time, there was absolutely no chance whatsoever of straying into forbidden pre-marital activities. Maybe it would have been occasionally possible in metropolitan society, but in the Highlands, it had to remain an unrealisable dream. With just such a dream hovering somewhere around, we set out in the Riley on a pleasant weekend of, what I seem to remember, balmy autumn sunshine. I knew the road by now and there were no surprises. It was exciting and spectacular as expected, though. Again the welcome from our friends was a delight and the anticipated evening of banter and music ensued. We were shown our rooms and it would be quite gratuitous even to hint that faint footfalls in the night suggested we had betrayed the social code of those days, set in grey fifties granite. Memories of crashing streams, velvet darkness and the eerie roaring of the stags are among the most dominant impressions.

Many, many years later, in the late eighties, we drove back to Polloch – travelling by the new road that had been constructed – and were amazed at what we found. Quite simply, it was as if the Polloch of our magical memories, had ceased to exist. Apart from a huddle of wooden Forestry houses there was absolutely nothing we could see that gave us anything to hold on to. The dominant image we had carried with us for the previous thirty or so years, was of dark, looming trees and lowering hills. The place with which we were now confronted had only recently been stripped of all of its mantle of trees. Masses of grey, dead brushwood - the detritus of this great cull – were all that remained. The once-overwhelming scenery had been diminished: hills were smaller and more insignificant and all of that wonderful sense of menace had completely gone. It was just a dull and monochrome little place now. There was only one small spot of colour that linked with those far-off days. The red telephone box where I had stood, enveloped in the Polloch night, was still there. I just had to go into it, for old times' sake. To my utter frustration, the wretched door seemed to have jammed shut. It would not budge. I felt an urge to lift the bulky instrument from its cradle and make a call to our number back home and leave a message. I used my expensive Swiss army knife to try to lever open the door. Unfortunately the clever designers of that instrument had not included a device for forcing a telephone box door, and the appendage I selected snapped. The door remained stubbornly tight shut. It was a curious conclusion to this reliving of memories and one that doesn't even contain a moral or message of any kind I can conjure up. It just happened. And I didn't manage to send that brief message to our answering machine back home in Inverness.

The Wrays eventually left Polloch and returned to (I almost said "the mainland": it had that effect on the stranger) Glenurquhart, where they threw themselves there into local activities, including amateur drama, and left a great impression in that lively community too.

There is little chance that we shall ever see that strange little community in Ardnamurchan again, but the memories of the warmth of hospitality, and the blackness of the nights being torn by the roaring of the stags will always remain.

CHAPTER 12
The Sunday Papers and A Shinty Hero

I have referred to Willie Jack, a close friend of the family, elsewhere in my Great Glen recollections. I had described a ritual that took place in the old schoolhouse in Fort Augustus each Sunday afternoon. That was when I would hurry down Bunoich Brae, across the main road, head under where the old railway bridge had been, and then tap on the front door of the first house on the left. Here it was that Mrs Jack, mother of Willie, lived her widowed life. She was as typical an elderly Highland woman as you could imagine and was a congenial part of the Sunday routine for me. She liked the company of a young person and made certain that I did not scurry away by making sure that there was a cup of tea and a slice of cake ready for me. I would have the schoolhouse copy of the Sunday Express with me and would give it to her in exchange for her Sunday Post. All of us were addicted to the timeless charms and oddities of the Broons and Oor Wullie and this was how we got our fix. This arrangement would have been set up between Willie and my parents so that his mother could have a regular visit on her Sunday afternoon. Again, as I have mentioned elsewhere, I would always pause to look in awe at the black, silver mounted caman that had been presented to Willie before the war as the captain of a victorious North Select shinty team in a match against the South. I had even persuaded her to take it down from its place high on the wall just opposite the front door entrance, on one occasion to let me handle it.

There was always a slight unease in our household regarding Sunday newspapers. Although we did not ever subscribe to the ultra-Calvinist view that such publications were the work of Satan, the fact that we did take them in was not exactly broadcast throughout the neighbourhood.

For some considerable time, it was my task every Sunday – after church had been dutifully attended – to hop on to my bike and head across the village towards the West End Garage, owned by Hughie Grant, to buy the Sunday papers. It is odd, but at this point, I can't remember exactly which ones we actually took in. The only title I recollect with any certainty is the Sunday Express. It would have been a very different thing from its present incarnation, or it would never have been allowed across the threshold. There must have been more, and it is pretty certain that the equivalent of today's sensational "Redtops" would never have been permitted. I suppose it is more than likely that the grimly heavy and unfrivolous "Observer" of those days would have been included.

But there was another reason why the Sunday paper run was jealously guarded by me as mine and mine only. At the old railway station in Fort Augustus, not far from the West End Garage, the MacBrayne's bus which would be heading off east to Inverness on Monday morning had been parked for the night by Sandack, the local driver. This was routine. Amazingly, it was left unlocked and it was just a matter of sliding back the heavy passenger door for a small group of us to find a brief spell of sanctuary from our supervised lives. Packets of cigarettes were fished out and a spell of glorious relative anarchy was relished. I always had to cook up some plausible excuse to explain why it always took at least half an hour longer than it should to get the papers back to the schoolhouse.

But to return to Willie Jack. He had become a close friend of the family, mainly due to shinty. My father was keen that the game, which had been discontinued throughout the land during the war years, should be revived. Willie was a superb player - one of those gifted athletes to whom skills come as naturally as breathing. He had been wounded in the war, but was still able to display his unerring ball control and deftness with the caman. It was not long before the Fort Augustus Shinty Club was up and running again, with my father as one of the moving spirits in the committee. In the twenties, he had been a keen player himself. Willie had that astonishing ability of the natural player by which he really seemed not to require to rush about the field like others: the ball seemed to come to him and he was able to direct it with such an economy of movement and energy that you knew you were looking at a master. If I may be permitted a slight digression here, (and provide a sure give-away that I am a keen supporter of shinty as a game that deserves much more support in the only country where it is played – Scotland!) I have another image in my mind by way of illustration. Some number of years ago, I was at a playing field at Bishopbriggs in Glasgow to watch a shinty match there with my brother. One of the teams had a player from Badenoch in its line-up. He was living in Glasgow at that time, and was turning out for one of the local clubs, and he was another of that truly gifted minority to which Willie Jack had belonged in earlier years. He dominated the centre of the field and in the wet conditions that prevailed that day, he was about the only one who seemed to be free of the splattering of mud that was affecting most of the rest. He played somewhere in the midfield, and sent a steady flow of passes to his forward line with effortless ease. On the adjoining pitch that day, a game of rugby was taking place. The protagonists here were vast and uncouth of physique with bulging thighs and massive heavy necks. Many had bands tied around their heads and due to the fact that the bulk of their activity consisted of heaving against their opponents in grunting scrums from which steam arose in the damp chill air, it wasn't long before the teams were so plastered with mud that they had become virtually indistinguishable. The contrast in terms of sporting spectacle between these two games could not have been starker.

My father was a highly practical man and one of his many skills was working with wood. Camans, or shinty clubs, were mainly available in those days through Macpherson's Sporting Stores in Ingles Street in Inverness. They were well made, but had a reputation for being brittle. So my father set about making clubs himself.

As well as being a top shinty player, Willie was also a fit outdoor person. He was a forester in the Forestry Commission and lived in one of the houses close to the tree nurseries at Auchterawe, to the west of Fort Augustus. He lived, in fact, right beside the Commission offices where the pay envelopes were handed out on Fridays after work. One of the outdoor challenges in those days – as it still is today – was the proximity of the Corriearrick Pass. This defile in the mountains to the south of the village carried the General Wade road that linked up with Badenoch and was built in the early 18th century as part of the pacification of the Highlands after the "Fifteen" Rising and intended for the swift deployment of the Government forces. Ironically, it was used by the Jacobite army in the next rising in 1745, which was much more threatening to the Hanoverian dynasty. Most of this military road was still clearly defined and was popular with hikers of the more robust variety. Willie had suggested to my parents that it would be a good idea one day to walk the Corriearrick from the south through to Fort Augustus. Preparations were made by way of clothing and footgear and the trio set off (and here the exact logistics have vanished from my memory.) I know they went to Laggan Bridge from where my uncle would have driven them to Garva at the south end of the Pass. The whole expedition would have taken two days. Back at the old schoolhouse, I and my two siblings were being looked after by our live-in domestic maid – no real problem for the first night. But as the day during which our parents were to be on their walk across the wild bleak mountains slowly unfolded, anxiety built up till fear for their safety loomed ever larger and more and more tension filled the air. I remember lying in bed, sleepless and terrified, as it got later and later and darkness closed in. Soon all the sounds of the village died away and imagination ran riot. The main sheet anchor in all of this that kept most of the worst fears at bay, was the fact that the guide of the expedition was Willie Jack, whom we had been assured knew the Pass and had walked through it on several previous occasions. We trusted him completely. The massive surge of relief when we heard the footsteps of our parents approaching the back door of the schoolhouse was something that still has resonance at this distant point in time.

His personal life became the subject of some raucous humour on one occasion when the Fort team was playing away from home. There had been a fixture against Boleskine at their pitch down near the shores of Loch Ness at Foyers. I remember that I had gone to the game as a spectator on board the team bus provided by Grant's Garage. When we came to leave after the game, there was no sign of Willie Jack. He had slipped away after changing out of his shinty strip. Eventually, it was decided that we just could not wait for him and the bus began its heavy grind up the steep brae heading for the narrow road back to Fort Augustus. At a point on the road – it was now dark enough to require headlights – a figure appeared from the trees some distance ahead and flagged down the bus. It was Willie, looking somewhat dishevelled. It was all too clear what had been occupying his time and causing him to be late for the bus home. The jokes and ribaldry rang out for most of the journey back home. Indeed, he had been courting someone from Foyers and it was not long before their wedding took place. For many years, he and his wife were close friends of the schoolhouse, until an apocalyptic day saw it all dissipate and crumble. I can remember the day clearly. I was doing something or other in the so-called "back place" – the wooden addition to the old schoolhouse that contained the important Rayburn stove that acted as cooker and source of hot water – when my father burst through the door. He called out my mother's name and it was all too obvious that some crisis had erupted and was going to consume the household.

"What day is it?" he called out desperately. His voice hoarse and almost pleading.

(This was during a school holiday, when such markers in the daily routine can become blurred.)

"It's Friday," called back my mother.

"God," he groaned. "We were supposed to be at the Jacks' for our tea!"

At any time, such a social gaffe would have been unforgivable, but in those far-off days of extreme austerity and rationing, it was about the worst thing you could contemplate. Mrs Jack was, as I recollect, a noted baker and maker of jams and would have spent a vast amount of time in making a sumptuous spread for the head teacher, his wife and their three children. Much time would have been spent on getting it just right. And for them just not to turn up was a real insult. The two households were linked by telephone, but my parents decided not to phone. In those days, all calls went through a local exchange and conversations were far from confidential. They felt that this monstrously embarrassing event was not for broadcasting beyond the immediate protagonists. I remember them, both ashen-faced – heading off up to Auchterawe. Did they walk or take the car? I ask, since my memory seems to suggest that they set off on foot. No matter. The outcome was already set in stone. Willie's wife met them at her front door and made it more than clear that a huge social clanger had been committed by my parents and that a continuing period of frosty relationships would now be set in motion. And that was it. The two households never regained the easy friendship they had enjoyed previously.

My final memory of this man who was a boyhood hero might seem slightly unusual. Among his other attributes, already dealt with, Willie Jack was, for many years, the organist in the Church of Scotland. He was a part of the regular ritual of our lives in those days. His selection of incidental music is still imprinted in my memory. I had not a clue as to what it actually was, when it drifted over my head as I awaited the hour or so of numbing tedium that lay ahead before the freedom that lay beyond the walls could be reclaimed. It was many years later, as I was getting acquainted with various of the classical composers, that a passage of the New World Symphony by Dvorak leaped out at me and drew me back to that small church in the late nineteen forties. Not that it was the sight of Willie at the consol – that was concealed from the eyes of the congregation by a curtain that was drawn tight shut. His only vision beyond his small area was provided by the mirror, which let him know what was happening in the pulpit behind him and allowed the perfect timing for the beginning of the service. When the last note died away, the Reverend Gillies stood up solemnly and looked out over his congregation before initiating the proceedings.

CHAPTER 13
A Tale of Two Uncles

The "Uncles" in the title refer to the MacKell brothers – Alistair and William – who played a considerable role in the lives of our family back in the nineteen fifties and sixties.

Now, those who may have read my last book will already be sighing resignedly. Not again! I have been here before in my lengthy descriptions of the Glen Secondary School under the tutelage of Alistair C MacKell. All who passed through that institution have deep indentations in their very souls from the experience. But I have to confess to feeling that I have been rather negative in my assessments of my former head teacher in past references. I would like to make reparations by stressing that as an educationalist and an inspirer of young minds, his record was outstanding. On a personal level, the quotes from classical literature that can be retrieved from the shadowy recesses of my memory – either spontaneously or when actively sought after – are all there courtesy of his rigorous teaching in the old school.

In any case, it is not that aspect of the MacKell impact on the Denoon family I want to talk about today. You see, the MacKells and my father were cousins. That meant, in the manner of most families, that both Alistair (Ally) and William (Bill) were "uncles" to us as well. Needless to say, it would have been an act of singular folly to have sauntered up to A.C MacKell in full flow in the classroom or school playground and address him as "Uncle Alistair". Apart from the wrath it might have elicited, there was the sheer inappropriateness of such an address in the school environment. Yet there were fairly frequent occasions when our families did meet socially. We might all be invited across to the schoolhouse for afternoon tea if we were staying at Victoria Buildings with my grandmother. (Astonishing to think that five of us – parents, me and my two siblings - could manage to fit into the tiny house at the back of Leslie's Store. But we did.) The visits to the Drum schoolhouse were interesting affairs – though they could be a little surreal. The actual house was dark and oppressive - and surprisingly small. Even the janitor's house at the other end of the central building looked more attractive. My parents were forever commenting on it. They had a similar type nineteenth century standard schoolhouse in Fort Augustus, but it was much more spacious and was set on a hill that commanded a spectacular view out over the village. Drum schoolhouse was shrouded in dark trees. I see a gloomy kitchen, a huge ancient stove and a dark passageway leading to the tiny sitting room where we would have tea and the usual biscuits and scones. Indeed it was always strange on such occasions to be in a room with Ally, the fearsome disciplinarian – surrounded with the everyday things of domesticity – and with him presiding over the bland ritual of afternoon tea. It was incongruous. It didn't seem right. Stern headmasters just didn't do that sort of thing. Then perhaps it was the presence of his wife, Leila, that brought something else quite different to these occasions. One extraordinary thing about both of the MacKell brothers was that each of them married startlingly beautiful women. Leila MacKell was, quite simply, of film star appearance. High cheekbones, wide-spaced slightly tilting eyes gave her a Marlene Dietrich appearance – but without the actress's austere menace. My parents told us that she came originally from Portsoy in the North-East and used, as a young girl, to visit the Glen on holiday at Marchfield. It was there, presumably, that she had met Alistair. She was a quiet and gracious hostess and we liked her. There were two children of the marriage: a daughter, Madeleine, on whom the father doted, and the son, Alistair. He was tall and physically ungainly, but was popular among us in the school – if only because his father made his life barely tolerable at times. Young Alistair was no fool intellectually, but was slow and considered in his responses to the demands of the classroom in those days. This sparked the ire of his father and often we winced at the waves of anger that would sometimes roll over and engulf the unfortunate son. Yet, he seemed to bounce back and was foremost among us to lampoon his father's more outstanding eccentricities of speech and gesture.

The household of Ally MacKell was a thrifty one, and the choice of family car could not have been more apposite. It was a Morris – I think the name was "Countryman" – and had the timber-lined bodywork of its marque. It was very seldom used, as I recollect, and spent most of its relatively inactive days shut away in its small garage across from the back door of the schoolhouse. It was about as dull, functional and sensible a vehicle as you could imagine, and was just quintessentially the appropriate one for such a man. I have only the faintest memories of it ever being backed out and exposed to the rough and tumble of the open road. I do seem to remember that when one day it was sold that no replacement ever appeared.

But it was their choice of cars that really highlighted the difference between these two extraordinary brothers – these "uncles" of our childhood and early adolescent days. While Ally would search out the most economic and least extravagant mode of transport that was available in the dismal fifties, his brother Bill went in the opposite direction. And how!

But before all that, a little about the man himself. Bill MacKell was born in 1904 and in his younger days was outstanding at sports of all kinds – indeed most outdoor activities: a true "Action Man". He became a teacher for a brief spell but found that too tame, so he upped and offed to Nigeria where he eventually became the Federal Adviser in Education to the Government of Nigeria. For this he was awarded the CBE. And it is here that the cars come into the story. His visits back home to Scotland while he was working under African skies were high points of our childhood. To hear from the parents that Uncle Bill and Aunt Peggy were to be visiting us in the Fort Augustus schoolhouse would set the pulses racing. He was a splendid uncle figure: stocky, sandy haired and with a booming, bustling, tweedy cheerful presence.

He keenly identified with the Glen and would insist on the integrity of its inhabitants. "You could leave a five pound note lying on the road and it would be perfectly safe", he would pronounce. He was a keen fisherman and was the founder of the Glenurquhart Angling Club. He was into bee-keeping, but got into occasional scrapes with them as he didn't actually become an expert in that arcane skill. This was amply illustrated when on one occasion he took a hive full of bees to Inverness in the boot of his car. According to a first hand account, there were bees in the car, in the sitting room back home in Inverness and his jacket buzzed for ages. He was also keen on shooting and would spend long sessions practising with Rory, the miller at Mill of Tore. With the miller's .303, they would blaze away at targets 100 yards away.

His wife Peggy was quite astonishingly beautiful in the style of the forties. With her tumbling masses of fair hair and impeccable dress, we were proud to be seen in their company. She was born in Inverness in 1912. Her father had been an engine driver, known as Jock Kyle from his days on the Kyle of Lochalsh line. She obtained certificates in shorthand and typing and worked in a solicitor's office before marrying Bill. I remember them at the Glen Games and on such occasions the small house at the back of Victoria Buildings where my grandmother lived, would be packed with what seemed like standing room only. We always used to wonder what kind of exotic car Bill would have this time. The biggest show-stopper was one year when he appeared with a huge American Ford V-8 saloon. I can't remember the colour, but it had a vast purring engine under a long bonnet - and amazing white-walled tyres. You have to remember that the cars available in the immediate post-War years in Britain were about as exciting in design and appearance as grey slaters scuttling from the light when a log has been turned over. The Ford V-8 stood out among them like the Taj Mahal among peasant huts. It sighed and surged effortlessly on billowy soft springing and to survey the passing world from its luxurious interior was to experience dangerous feelings of social detachment and arrogance. The head tilted back, the eyes narrowed; the nostrils flared a little as the dull peasantry by the roadside stood back and doffed their caps in deference. Well, not quite. But, you get the picture.

On another occasion, the exotic car experience was an initial disappointment. We were at Drumnadrochit visiting my grandmother at Victoria Buildings, looking through the piles of Illustrated London News magazines that were stacked under her radio table by the window. The endless pages of sepia photographs of the First World War dead never ceased to morbidly fascinate. A loud rattle at her front room door and the booming, "Anyone at home, Maggie?" signalled Uncle Bill, Aunt Peggy and Neil, their son, paying a visit. The house filled with loud chatter and the inevitable preparations for the *strupag* while we sped out to the road to see what manner of product of Detroit was parked out there. Instead, we stood and looked in amazement at a black, squat, almost crab-like vehicle with wide-spread front wheels and flattened-looking profile. It was that essential of the early Maigret series on BBC black-and-white television (though we were not to know that then, obviously): a Citroen "*Traction Avant*". Its distinctive radiator with the double inverted "V" cried out for attention and soon we were off for a run through the village and up the Glen. And I was won over to its initially strange appearance by getting to sit in the front seat – where the driver ought to be sitting! The gear lever was an odd-looking stalk that emerged from the dash. All in all, it was yet another triumph for our Uncle Bill in terms of living up to our expectations. The Citroen was yet another head-turner as we swept through the village and headed up the Glen.

Bill MacKell was an ardent Liberal and it that capacity would visit my father in the schoolhouse in Fort Augustus: he (my father) also believed in that traditional Highland political cause. The charismatic John Bannerman (Grand Slam Scottish rugby hero of the late twenties) was Inverness-shire candidate then and Bill and he were regular visitors. My overwhelming memories are of Bannerman's huge, craggy features, of booming voices and yet more tweed. Later, Bill became Russell Johnson's adviser when he became MP for Inverness-shire in the early sixties and he (Bill) actually rose to becoming Vice-Chairman of the Liberals in Scotland.

By this time, I was old enough to have just passed my driving test in the 1939 Jaguar my father then owned. During one of those visits, someone suggested we head off down to Inchnacardoch Hotel, a mile or so to the east of the village, for some reason or other and I was keen to show off my mastery of the arcane skills of double de-clutching – essential for the subjugation of that formidable car. Alas, the day was to turn out an occasion of deep shame for me. We had just swept up the drive to the front entrance and I had casually stepped out and opened the back door of the Jaguar to let Bill get out. I then swept it shut and froze in horror at the hoarse bellow of agony that exploded right behind me and echoed from the dark trees behind the hotel. I turned to see my favourite uncle doubled up with crimson face and contorted features as he clutched one of his hands. I had caught it between the door and the pillar. Luckily it had not broken anything, but I was reduced to a state of terminal, crushing shame and embarrassment. Such a loss of face in front of such people. A deep scar in the psyche for life.

A final memory of the two uncles concerns the home up the Glen that they kept as an occasional holiday or weekend place. Now, we always referred to it as "Strathnacro". Wrongly, as it happened. "Hazelwood" the house was actually called. This house stood up at the top of a rough path that led up from the main road. It was surrounded by trees and the overall impression was dark and brooding. It had been the MacKell family home and the two sons insisted that it remain unchanged from the days when their parents were alive. I even remember a story from my mother that in the early days of her marriage, Leila MacKell, on her first visit to the house, had adjusted or moved an antimacassar on the back of a chair. She was firmly disabused of any notion that anything in that house was ever to be shifted from its traditional place.

I said that the foregoing was the final memory, but another piece of surprising information connected with Hazelwood just came my way. I had contacted my cousin Neil, in Banavie, to check out some final details about his parents. When we were talking about the family house up the glen, he had reminded me that there was no road up to the house and visitors who came by car had to park down at the roadside. That was how the brothers wished it to remain. However, there was one exception to that rule. Alistair at one point in his life bought himself a motor cycle, and it was able to scramble its way up to the house on the stony steep path. The image of Ally MacKell, the huge looming presence of my schooldays, astride a motor bike is one that has come to me rather late in life and one that I find rather difficult to cope with. I can never see him as a biker.

And, almost as an afterthought I have to add, Bill was almost instrumental in my wife and I taking a huge decision early in our teaching lives. In our brand-new house, one of the earliest guests at our dining table were Bill and Peggy. He still had his connections in Africa, and had suggested to us that there were openings for teachers of English in the part of that vast land where he had recently been a prominent and highly influential figure. "Just say the word, and I'll be able to open some doors for you. Just the thing for young folks looking for a bit of adventure. And your salary will be excellent as well. Have a think about it."

Well, we did think about it, but not for too long. The bonds that had us tied to Scotland, and especially the Highlands, were strong and not for casting loose. But it still is an interesting speculation – even at this distance in time.

CHAPTER 14

The coming of the Hydro
The great switch on

As I set about recounting the coming of mains electricity in the late forties to a large village like Fort Augustus and the vast excitement of it all, I am aware of the absurdity of such a scenario to generations behind me. To them, the presence of electric power within the home and everywhere around them is as unremarkable as the water that comes from the taps when they are turned on. It's just a simple mundane part of everyday life.
Yet, the first sentient years of my life, in the village of Abriachan in the hills above Loch Ness and later in Fort Augustus, were lived in houses that had us huddle in one of two main rooms downstairs in the winter time, with the heat radiating from a fire that required constant tending, and light coming from one of three different sources: the silent Aladdin lamp, the

straightforward paraffin lamp with its wick and the drama of the hissing Tilley pressure lamp. Reading was only possible within the pool of light surrounding one of these sources and to move to another part of the house, along dark flickering corridors, required you to carry a lamp of one or other of the sorts already mentioned. It was not an especial hardship at the time; it was just that you really didn't know any alternative. Well, you did: you saw films in the local hall and people switching on lights and various implements, but these were in places exotic and far away. Yet, in Fort Augustus, it was not as clear-cut as that. One half of the village actually had a supply of electrical power – the side on the western side of the canal that ran through the village. It was power supplied by the Benedictine monastery. It was direct current and it had its severe limitations. It was at the whim of the weather for a start. The actual main generator was a mile or so from the village in a small anonymous stone building at the western end of Loch Ness. You headed out along the road towards Glendoe Brae, then you turned sharp right along a narrow track, all the while aware of a stream of swift water skimming along by your left. As you approached the small featureless building, you also noticed a humming sound that became increasingly louder until you realised that it came from inside that building. This, in fact, housed the generator that was powered by a fast flow of water that rushed down a concrete-walled channel that had been built by the monks to tap a source from somewhere in the distant hills. This was the power source that kept the lights in the huge monastery going, and what surplus there was went to the lucky villagers on the same side of the canal as the Abbey. It was simply not possible to take the power cables across the canal to the darkened east side where we lived. Since this power depended on the flow of the water, it is obvious that when there was severe frost or ditto drought, the generator might cease to spin and the lights would flicker and die. But the resourceful community of monks had this covered as well, and on these occasions, the thump of a huge diesel engine would announce that rescue had arrived. We on the east side of the canal would look at the light switches on the walls of the houses of our friends with deep and corrosive envy so when it became clear that the main power from the post-war Hydro schemes was heading our way, the craving became more and more intense. We longed to see our own houses equipped for this magical addition to our lives. Actually, apart from the fickleness of the weather being a problem with the Abbey electricity, it also limited the householders to light only. As far as I recollect, they could not have electrical machinery plugged in: the system could not support that.

The Abbey arranged film shows in a small wooden hall inside the walls of the original Hanoverian fort. These took place, as I recollect, on a Monday evening – though I could be wrong on this. It does seem an odd time. The advantage for the audience was that there was not the pounding threnody of the engine in the background to power the projector. The smug Abbey had its own power. On our side of the canal, in the village hall at the top of Bunoich Brae, when we attended the film shows put on there by the Highlands and Islands Film Guild, this irritating but essential accompaniment filled the air and dominated the proceedings. The engine in the back of the small navy-blue van that brought the cinema to our village was inclined to be fickle on occasions and would sometimes falter during the more tense moments of some drama and flicker and growl into silence and darkness. This was the signal for the unfortunate man in charge to flee the hall and with torch and spanner, try to coax the wretched engine back into life once more. With a hall full of frustrated cinema-goers simmering close behind him, his job on those occasions was pretty unenviable. But he was a skilled operator and I only remember one occasion when the breakdown defeated him and he was obliged to refund our money. All of this, of course, disappeared into the dim vaults of history when the mains electricity arrived.

As far as our family was concerned, I was the main messenger in the old schoolhouse in bringing the latest progress of the power cables as they marched towards our village. The power was from the general area of Beauly originally and came over the hills, dipping down into the Great Glen some eight miles to the west of Urquhart Castle. The cables then followed the main road alongside the loch till Invermoriston and then on the final six miles to Fort Augustus. I was then attending the Academy in Inverness and came home each weekend in MacBrayne's bus, buoyed up by two surging excitements. First, just getting back home to parents and siblings and away briefly from the school I so disliked, and, second, looking out for the electricity poles and how far they had reached along the lochside. As soon as I got in to the house, I would tell the household that they had now reached beyond Altsaigh. Then we'd calculate how far they had progressed since the previous weekend and guess when they'd actually arrive at Fort Augustus. Long before the cables actually reached the village, we had been virtually living with a cheerful team of electricians who wired the whole of the schoolhouse as well as the school. Bulb sockets hung from ceilings and power points were fitted to skirting boards. An electric cooker appeared in the "back place" - the wooden appendage to the traditional stone schoolhouse, and an electric iron as well.

For some reason, the new electric kettle stands out for me as the symbol of this transforming miracle in our lives in those days. It was of the most conventional kettle design: it crystallised all of the essence of just being a kettle in its uncompromising Victorian design. It was made of burnished copper and if it were not for the four small "feet" screwed to the base, it could happily been placed in the centre of the red, glowing coals of a kitchen fireplace. So, our house was all equipped to join the twentieth century quite some time before the Great Switch-On Day arrived. During my fantasies, as the bus trundled west along the loch side, I used to imagine some kind of ceremonial occasion. But the reality was totally devoid of drama. For some time, I had not been delivering my reports since the dark poles had long arrived bearing their triangular branch supports tipped by the large, brown earthenware insulators for carrying the sagging electricity cables. We just had to wait. Then, one Saturday, when I was just leaving the kitchen to get my bike to head off somewhere and was talking to my mother, one of the regular electricians appeared. We hadn't even noticed him: he was such a familiar presence in the house. Just as he was heading for the door to leave, I asked him how long till the power came on.

"It's on now," he said.

"Eh?"

I couldn't believe it!

"Look," and he flicked a nearby switch to light up the bulb above the kitchen table. And in that nanosecond, our lives were transformed for ever. I sped round the house pressing switches and delighting in the magic response. Never again the faint light from the candle or paraffin lamp as you moved from room to room. Everywhere was now bathed in uniform crisp brilliance.

My mother now filled the amazing copper kettle and switched it on. We both sat and watched and listened to the stirrings inside its burnished carapace, then saw the steam bursting from the lid and the spout. An unforgettable moment indeed. Though all the rest of the story would have been the usual anticlimax that our restless species is doomed to experience when a much longed-for event actually manifests itself.

After the arrival of the electricity, the next big event was the coming of television not all that many years after in the mid-fifties. I was now a student in Aberdeen University and pretty well used to TV in my lodgings and in the Students' Union. It was thrilling to think of this wonder being available in my home village back in the Highlands. The early signals did not really benefit the village of Fort Augustus, so local engineers and energetic people looked for the best location on the Glendoe hillside to set up an aerial that would serve the whole community. Here again, it was the anticipation and the mounting excitement that lingers on. I remember coming home from Aberdeen for a weekend, and seeing a small, grey metal television test set, sitting on a table in the front room. It was a temporary expedient from MacDonald's general store in the village to tide us over till the main mahogany-encased super set was delivered. It was Sergeant Bilko on screen on that first occasion in the old schoolhouse. I still have a special place for him in my affections.

The wait for the posh set was agonising, but eventually, when I was at home not long after during a holiday, the van from MacDonald's arrived and the installation took place. The television was encased in polished and grained wood: a really handsome piece of furniture. And to keep up this illusion that it was nothing so common and unsophisticated as a device to bring entertainment into the house, it had a jointed pair of sliding doors that could be drawn across the screen when viewing was over for the evening. On its handsomely-turned wooden legs, it could then just look like any other piece of smart furniture designed for a well-set-up respectable sitting room in a Highland schoolhouse. It had the advantage of a larger screen and a better picture than the temporary one we had been using up till then and it is hard from this distance to relive the sense of sheer excitement when anticipating an evening sitting in the front room watching the then single channel that was available to us. It was a year or two later that, when looking at the little panel on the top that had a flip-up cover, I saw several positions that the main switch could be clicked over to engage. One of them brought the amazing sound of a local news bulletin being delivered in an accent that was decidedly from our part of the world. It was coming, I discovered much later, from a small studio on the Black Isle at the foot of the main television mast. I always made a point of tuning into it and became quite intrigued by it. Our sense of being humble peripheral figures on the edge of society in those days made it almost inconceivable that a news bulletin could come over the airwaves in an accent close to our own.

Many years later when I was talking to a teaching colleague in the High School in Inverness and describing this, he told me that he had been the man at the microphone! He had answered an advertisement while he was a student and had cycled once a week up to the small studio to do his turn at newsreading during a summer holiday. My last memory of that splendid old television set was witnessing the amazing sight of the astronauts on the moon's surface as Armstrong voiced his thoughts across the void to the tiny pale disk hanging in the blackness above him.

CHAPTER 15
The Hornby Years

It took a programme on BBC to set me off exploring this particular stratum of memory. It was the sight of another faux-naïf inquirer of the experts on "Antiques Roadshow" who was presenting his collection of Dinky Toys, all in their original boxes and with paint unscratched, to be told that they were well nigh priceless on today's markets.

A first and obvious observation: what on earth sort of child would accept as a gift, or would save up and purchase, a hugely desirable item like a Dinky Toy and instead of parading it in front of his pals, and playing with it, would consign it to its box with its wrapping and shut it away in a drawer or cupboard, not to be displayed till some remote future date. These marvellous models were made to be played with and to fill our imagined landscapes in sandpits or on table-tops with cars, buses and lorries that were so satisfactorily real-looking. Soon they would become scuffed and worn and part of the childhood world. Then they would slip from sight in the natural way with all such things.

Actually, it was the name "Hornby" that was the weaver of the greatest fantasies and yearnings for us in those days. This was the firm that originally manufactured the Dinky Toy range. But mainly, it was the magnificent model railway systems that were created in the Hornby factories and held the greatest allure. Alas, they were far beyond realisation for me as they were simply too expensive. They could only be gazed at in shop windows or toy departments in places like Edinburgh, but never actually handled. Luckily, however, the craving could occasionally be assuaged. The head forester, Mr Drummond, who lived in palatial grandeur in his large house near the end of the Auchterawe road to the west of the village, had three children with whom we would occasionally play. The son of the house possessed an almost-impossible-to-imagine, magnificent Hornby train set. It was spread in a large lay-out in a room set aside for it. There were stations with platforms and sidings, signal boxes, tunnels, signal gantries, and points systems. The main rolling stock consisted of one amazing locomotive with the full complement of driving wheels, bogie wheels and coupling rods. There was the tender and there were carriages with real transparent windows – indeed, the whole set-up was a total dream for anyone who had been gripped by the special attraction of railways that seems to affect the majority of young males.

Some time before I had made contact with this model railway nirvana at the head forester's house, I had been seduced by a train set that appeared in the window of a small shop in the centre of the village near the canal bridge. On the lid was an illustration to fire the imagination. It depicted a locomotive powering its way out of a vast station with a lengthy train being hauled behind it. Smoke and steam in billowing clouds spoke of noise and energy and completed the seductive image. It looked superb. I just had to have this train set and the saving up of funds began. I had to beg frantically for help from the parents as it was beyond my own feeble resources, and reluctantly they relented. On the day I had accumulated enough, I sped to the shop to achieve fulfilment. It was still in the window. Relief. When I got home and opened the lid of the box, I can still feel the vast disappointment that swept over me as I looked down at the meagre contents. The locomotive and the two miserable carriages were cheap and tinny looking and had only the most superficial resemblance to the real thing. The minimalist set of rails when assembled made up a meagre circle and I don't think I really ever spent any time with it worth mentioning. A dismal disappointment and wrecker of dreams. I suppose I could say that it was an early lesson on the duplicity of the advertising industry. I was on the rebound from this episode when the Drummonds moved into the Head Forester's house and the gates of model railway paradise were opened to me. There was never to be anything like the Drummond model railway ever installed in the old schoolhouse, but there were to be other interests and compensations.

The other wondrous creation of the Hornby designers was the Meccano system. These sets of differently shaped metal components with the holes drilled in them were the materials with which the most remarkable working models of industrial cranes, vehicles and so on could be made. The main model that adorned the advertisements for the Meccano system was a gigantic crane like the one that dominates the skyline of Glasgow and the Clyde. Such a creation was far beyond the scope of the basic Meccano sets, of course. You could follow the instructions that came with every set, or you could launch out on your own and let your own imagination take over. What made this system so especially desirable was that when you had exhausted all the creativity that came with the set you actually had, you could move on to the next level. If you owned Meccano set number four, you could buy number 4A, which had all the additional components required to give you set number 5. The higher the number, the more components you possessed and the more gadgets accrued. There were sets of gears and pulleys that could be driven by motors. There was the basic clockwork motor, but far and away the most brilliant power source was the steam engine. This was a rather expensive extra. It was fuelled by methylated spirit and when the water in the boiler was thrumming away, the pistons got to work and whatever contraption you had constructed, leaped into action and became alive. I can't recollect what number of set I eventually managed to build up to, but it was pretty near the final one. There were spanners supplied and the small boxes of nuts and bolts had to be carefully looked after as they were forever getting lost. Without these, the nuts and bolts, that is, the whole system broke down. It was a pretty large and complex collection of red and green components of all shapes and sizes that eventually came into my possession, and it provided huge enjoyment.

I mentioned at the beginning of this chapter that it was the sight of Dinky toys on 'Antiques Roadshow' that had set the memory turning. It also called up another episode of a very odd nature that occurred at Lenie, overlooking Loch Ness at the place where the unfortunate John Cobb was to lose his life so publicly a few years later when he was attempting to gain the world water speed record. I had been into Inverness with my father, by bus, and at some point had managed to prevail upon his better instincts to buy me a rather more expensive than usual item from the Dinky Toy range. It seems strange to recall the actual model I had been yearning for, but I can see it yet in all its ochre and red livery. It was a dust cart. I think that it was because it had a tipper and the covers on the back slid open that I was attracted to it. It had a tiny handle that operated the tipping mechanism and that made up for the distinctly unromantic nature of the actual model itself. No matter, I was sitting beside my father in the MacBrayne's bus as it trundled its solemn way with 'Sandack' Macdonald at the controls. As we were passing the viewpoint at Lenie, there was a burst of animated talk from the front of the bus. My father and I looked up and saw that there was a hold-up of some kind of the traffic – both ways. As we got closer, it became apparent that something serious was happening. A car was slewed off the road, and its front wheels and bonnet were suspended over the dizzy drop to the waters of the loch far below. Only the taut wires of the fence at the roadside were holding it from tumbling to destruction. A knot of people was staring down and also out to the loch. Sandack had heaved on the handbrake by now as it was clear that no-one was to be moving on that road for some time. It was totally blocked. Gradually the story emerged. The perilously suspended car had been carrying a dangerous patient from one institution to another, under supervision. The supervision could not have been all that secure, as the patient had apparently and without warning, grabbed the steering wheel and lunged the car towards the fence. When it failed to break through, he then flung open the door and shook off all attempts to restrain him, while he plunged and rolled down the steep grassy slope to the water's edge far below. By the time we arrived in Sandack's bus, the crazed individual had struck out from the shore and was swimming desperately in the chill waters of the loch. Someone must have telephoned from a nearby house or driven back to the Police Station at Drumnadrochit and raised the alarm. As we watched, mesmerised, from our vantage point, we saw a motorboat appear round the headland from the direction of Urquhart Castle. It contained several people, one of whom appeared to be the Drum policeman. What followed was a crazed pantomime in which the fugitive, who was an amazing swimmer, continued to elude his desperate pursuers. They would position the boat close to him and one or two would reach overboard to try to grab him, while he would just as swiftly dive out of sight and bob up at the other side of the more and more unstable looking craft. Eventually, they managed to manhandle him into the boat and it sped as fast as it could round the headland and out of sight. By now there was a considerable number of vehicles completely blocking the road and it took some time to get them all moving again.

I never could look at my Dinky dustcart after that without thinking of the frantic, tiny figure swimming out into Loch Ness and defying his pursuers for well over an hour as he threshed his way through the chill waters. It was some remarkable performance he put on for the cluster of spectators staring from the road high above Loch Ness that long ago evening and it is odd that we never really found out any real background details to this event. Who this desperate man was or whatever eventually did happen to him I never discovered.

CHAPTER 16

The Golf Course, the Tennis Court and The Fashion Model

Two features of life in the village of Fort Augustus that had fallen into disuse during the years of the Second World War, were the tennis court and the golf course.
In the fifties, committees of various local people got organised and set about bringing these facilities back to life.
My father became involved in the revival of the nine-hole golf course out at the western end of the village, alongside the canal. The years of inactivity and neglect had seen it revert to its wild natural state so that it looked nothing more than a stretch of featureless moorland with a small rickety wooden hut that had been the clubhouse in happier times. The course itself was covered with dense, springy heather and the original fairways were just discernable although the greens had all but vanished. Teams of local volunteers were organised to clear the fairways and to bring the whole thing back to life. The owner of the local hotel, the Lovat Arms, J B Nelson (one of Scottish Rugby's Grand Slam heroes of 1929) was one of the other prime movers in this enterprise. He was owner of a large Ford V8 shooting brake, with the distinctive wooden bodywork of that extinct style of vehicle and had lent it to help with the movement of various materials. One of these tasks was the shifting of large boulders that had somehow accumulated and become an obstruction. They had presumably been dumped by some farmer or landowner and when I was doing a stint at one point in the operation, I was asked to shift some of these boulders with the large, powerful Ford. It sagged and rolled on its suspension with the weight, but I got my rush being in control of such a machine, even in such non-dramatic conditions.

It was a pretty impressive sight when the original course emerged from the ruins of several years of total neglect. From the medium length first fairway with its tee immediately in front of the small restored club-house, heading out to the west, then doubling back, then crossing over eventually towards the canal where its longest fairway and biggest challenge lay, soon after to face the shorter tests of skills; gradually working your way via the deadly dog-leg and back to the clubhouse once more. The setting of the course was spectacular and it provided a superb couple of hours or more of golfing activity. But, as is so often the case in life, there is a worm embedded in the bud. In my case, it was that however enthusiastic you may be about a sport, if you have not been gifted with that essential, almost magical, co-ordination of hand and eye, no matter how often you address a golf ball perched up on its tee, and sweep the head of the driver in a perfect arc to smite it in that spirit lifting trajectory you had planned for it, it might only do that for you on just a sufficient number of occasions to tempt you back to try again and again – on into infinity or till decrepitude has the sinews wither. Being a shinty player, I felt I had a distinct advantage in the business of hitting a ball with a club. The only thing was the smaller striking surface of the golf club and the considerably smaller ball. But to counter that, there was the fact that the golf ball for its initial strike was perched on the top of a little plastic or wooden peg. So, I have to report that the very first time I hit a golf ball, it eased its way, ever-climbing, into what I thought was the distant stratosphere. This game was a daudle: it was almost a disappointment. Not a real challenge. It did not take long to work out that it was a game that contained all the warped interpretations of all the physical laws in the universe, and that these laws would all – singly or in conjunction with others - work against you if you did not possess that mystic quality or power that the tiny percentage of the human race who had conquered golf could call upon. The weird quirkiness of the game can be illustrated by my own father, with whom I had played many rounds when in my student days. I have referred elsewhere to his own shinty history in Edinburgh University in the nineteen twenties. Well, he was one of that odd band of players of shinty who are right handed, yet find it easier to hold the club and play the ball as if you were left-handed. This is such a marked feature of shinty that studies of this phenomenon have been made in places like Kingussie and Newtonmore where many of the right handed members of local golf clubs actually play with left handed clubs. Weird, I know, but one day when my father was trying to address a ball that had nestled up against a fence post and was virtually impossible to play, he muttered the observation that if he had a left handed club, he could have hit it without any bother. He went ahead with that idea and bought a left handed wood and ditto mid-iron that nestled in his golf bag with the conventional clubs. It certainly raised eyebrows when he would approach a ball in an awkward lie and announce casually that he'd try his left-handed club. Certainly with partners who were strangers.

The revived golf course in Fort Augustus became a great success and is still there, though it is many decades since I trampled the heather in some of its more remote reaches with seething futile rage burning in me. I will now leave Fort Augustus Golf course with a final image. It was the sight of Hamish MacDonald, local ace shinty player, practising pitching shots on the ninth green when it was a quiet day on the course. He had dropped a couple of dozen balls at his feet and was drifting them, one after the other, on to the green. All of them hit the actual green and a few of them actually trickled their way into the hole. It was his comportment that really was the main source of amazement. Instead of shouting hoarsely in crude triumph at the sight of the disappearing ball, he just tapped another one into place and proceeded to loft it in the same direction, with apparently the same expectation. That was one of the sights that told me I would never be a golfer. At that point in time, I could have counted on one hand the number of times I had actually managed to land on that abomination of a green.

I cannot remember if the revival of the tennis court came before the golf course, but I do know that I did not play any part in its regeneration. There was no actual clubhouse nor did there appear to be any organised club activity in its early days. I just found myself heading down to the tennis court to play a game or two with various of my local pals and that was it.

These were the days before the TV coverage of tennis that we take for granted now and I don't really know how I picked up the rules and the finer points of scoring. I just turned up at the tennis court beside the old abandoned railway bridge close to Bruce's Buildings. The tall fence of appropriate netting kept the balls from bounding into neighbouring gardens. We just opened the gate without reference to anyone and got on with it. The court itself had a dark, dusty surface and had the permanent markings in place. The net had to be raised into place and the precise height measured with a tennis racquet. Like golf, this game had its moments of exultation as when a service powered its way low over the net and left an opponent floundering. But it too had its longueurs when the ball stubbornly refused to remain within its designated boundaries. The familiar experience of high achievement followed by dull spells of mediocrity.

A story of the tennis court's pre-war days came to us from Peter MacDonald from Portclair. He was known in the village simply as Peter Portclair. He was a skilled raconteur and kept us much amused during days on the hills working for the Forestry Commission. He was also a performer at local concerts where his fine singing voice was a popular feature. His singing abilities also saw him as precentor in the local Free Church. This was always a source of amusement to us, as Peter's stories out on the hills during the bracken-cutting or in the nurseries at the weeding would hardly have been approved by the congregation. Let us just say that they were robust in subject and in delivery.

He told us of an occasion when he and a small Yorkshireman called Charlie Hill, who lived in Auchterawe to the west of the village and also worked in the Forestry, had been having a game of tennis. The game had not been going very well for Charlie, and after one particularly futile flurry, it was his turn to serve. Peter called out, "Balls to you, Charlie!" and threw them over the net towards him.

A pause here to set the scene with specific reference to the natural demotic of the county of York. People from there have a distinctive accent and way of pronouncing certain words. This is essential in getting the best out of this tale. In Yorkshire, the natives pronounce the word "duck" as "dook" and "luck" as "look". And then there is the problem with the often overused, forbidden, Anglo-Saxon monosyllabic swear word that still sits uncomfortably on the page.

To resume: Peter had just thrown the balls over the net to Charlie, calling out, "Balls to you, Charlie!" The small choleric

Yorkshireman hurled down his racquet and roared back, "Balls to thee and f*** thee! I told thee I couldn't play ****ing tennis!" I leave you (if you so desire) to fill in the asterisks with the appropriate sounds as they exploded into the quiet air of a summer day in long ago Fort Augustus.

But it was tennis and that little grey court by the canal that was to bring a brief other-worldly summer experience that really set the youthful emotions pounding.

My sister's closest (and attractive) friend Theresa lived in Bruce's Buildings. She had a cousin from the south of England who occasionally came to stay during the summer. What I had heard of her up till that point was exotic enough. Her name was Trixie Henegan and it was whispered that she was a fashion model in distant London. When I came home for the university summer break early on in my student days, I was told that she had arrived for her holiday in the village. Early glimpses I got of her confirmed that she was something quite alien to our small Highland community. Quite simply, she was stunning of appearance. She was a petite version of the modelling ideal of the Fifties fashion scene – in fact it was only this that had prevented her from being one of the elegant procession of haughty beauties who ruled the catwalk in those days. If you are old enough, just visualise Barbara Goalen who dominated that scene. But Trixie was not quite tall enough to become one of that privileged band. Instead her modelling was mainly for fashion catalogues – but it was modelling and it was her startling good looks that ensured her some success.

While in Fort Augustus, Trixie liked to play a game of tennis and would join us occasionally. This developed to my advantage when I was staying at home for a while early in the holidays while still casting around for a job. The beauteous one took to coming up to the schoolhouse to call on me to join her at the tennis court. My brother and I used to sleep in a small wooden shed at the bottom of the front lawn of the schoolhouse during the summer months. We just called it "The Cabin". One of these summer mornings, I was wakened by a loud tapping on the window, right by my head in the top bunk. Framed in that window were the ravishing features of the fair Trixie. And she was calling MY name. That walk down through the village, with my tennis racquet gripped sweatily and Trixie in her brief shorts by my side was quite the most terrifying experience of my life up till that moment. Quite simply, she was just too damned attractive. I was well out of my league. Heads were turning and the male drivers of passing vehicles were gawping. First at Trixie and then at the be-spectacled and unprepossessing companion by her side. I felt their querulousness and disbelief. But when we made it eventually up the canal side to the tennis court, the smack of the tennis balls and my desperate efforts to show off to her soon took over. They were indeed mesmerising occasions but that is all that they could be. Nothing could come of this liaison beyond the companionship of the blaize and the baseline and Trixie continued to flit in and out of my life briefly for a marvellous few tingling weeks of that summer.

That summer, she had been working for a spell as a receptionist in the Lewiston Arms Hotel near Drumnadrochit. Then she went to do similar work in Fort William. Her love of the Highlands had drawn her temporarily from her life in London and this, alas, was to be her undoing. While in Fort William, she met with and had been captivated by the handsome son of a wealthy sheep farmer and soon marriage was on the horizon. The signs however were not propitious. A visit he had made to meet Trixie's parents in the south had been a disaster and they were deeply unhappy about the whole affair. But in such matters, little can be done to dissuade and the wedding was set to take place in the Abbey at Fort Augustus in November 1958. A large number of guests were invited and the local hotel laid on a sumptuous reception. It was a significant event on the social calendar – the wedding of a beautiful London model and a handsome young Highlander. The result was considerable press interest and the arrival of a large number of reporters and photographers.

My parents were guests, but I was in Aberdeen for the first term of my third year at university there. I remember opening a newspaper to see the stark, smudged headlines shrilling something like, "Fashion Model Left At Altar as Groom Flees". The story was everywhere and it attracted further hordes of reporters to the village to feed on this rich source of copy. They were desperate for background details. Quite a large number had been present for the actual wedding and were frustrated not to be able to get photographs of the distraught Trixie and her parents. Quite simply, the village closed ranks to protect the family from unwanted publicity.

The church had been brim-full of guests and Father Philip, the parish priest was presiding. Trixie and her bridesmaids had arrived, but of the groom and the best man, not a sign. When he did eventually arrive at the church, he approached Father Philip and announced that he was 'not feeling well'. Then he abruptly left. He and his best man were last seen driving at hectic speed out by the west end of the village, heading back to Fort William. The stunned gathering was invited to the Lovat Arms Hotel but the atmosphere was one of total disbelief and embarrassment – and pity and sadness for the deserted bride in her finery. Later she was smuggled out of the hotel in a van belonging to the local grocer, Leslie, to avoid the encircling pack of reporters. Later she was secreted to Dalcross for a flight back south to her home.

It was now that the remarkable response of the people of Fort Augustus came to the fore. The community had very much taken to Trixie and were outraged at what her loutish fiancé had subjected her to. As a result, the reporters from the various newspapers all over the country found it impossible to get quotes or any assistance in filling out their stories. One event really encapsulates this. Trixie's father and uncle were walking down the canal-side, when a reporter with a flash camera jumped out and took a picture. Before he could utter a word, both of the men rushed at him. Trixie's father grabbed the camera and hurled it into the canal. Naturally furious, the reporter headed for the local police station to make his angry complaint. The response from Sergeant Irvine was along the lines of: "If I hear you have been troubling this family again, you'll be lucky you don't follow your camera into the canal."

Trixie never lost her love of the Highlands and eventually became a teacher. At her recent funeral, that love was indicated by the picture of Fort Augustus Abbey on her funeral order of service.

A final footnote to this story: the fleeing bridegroom, in later years, became a regular competitor in the popular TV programme, "One Man and his Dog". I knew about his history when the series was on air. When he was on screen, performing with such skill on the hillsides with his sheepdogs, I could not but feel a chill when looking at this man, remembering his unspeakable behaviour all those years before.

CHAPTER 17
Return to Victoria Buildings

I have visited Victoria Buildings once before in the pages of my last book, remembering the remarkable grandmother of mine who lived there till the early seventies in the small house tucked away behind the proud commercial statement of Leslie's Shop ("Leslie's Stop: The Spot To Shop" as the bold declaration on the front of the building called out to passers-by). In the early fifties, I spent an academic year in a school in Inverness when, instead of looking for lodgings in the town or staying in a hostel, I stayed with my grandmother instead – travelling in to the school every morning and returning to Drum in the evening in one of the multi-coloured Bedford buses of MacBrayne's fleet. If it hadn't been for the scholastic side of that year of my youth, I think it could have been summed up as one of my most enjoyable and happy of all.

And the reasons for that? Well, Drumnadrochit and the small house behind the shop were extensions of my home – which was then in Fort Augustus in the schoolhouse there. It was far enough away from the strictures of home and parents to allow a modicum of freedom. Although my grandmother had as strong a code of Calvinist ethics as the next Free Church adherent, she also possessed that fatal weakness of all grandparents: a tendency to benign indulgence when dealing with her grandson. I would exploit that rather ruthlessly on occasions, I fear.

When the evening bus had passed the foot of Abriachan brae, it heralded a sense of homecoming as each landmark along the road was noted till we were passing by the long line of the mighty trees past Drumbuie. She always had a substantial meal waiting and she was a great cook. The only blight on the evening that stretched ahead was, of course, the homework. The school in Inverness was a pale inadequate compared with the Glen school in those days when it came to that accursed imposition. Glen pupils groaned under the weight of the tasks heaped upon them by most of the secondary staff there. My burden from Inverness was bad enough, but was tolerable. But I was inclined to do as little as possible because of the many temptations that Drum spread out for me just beyond the narrow little lane that led out on to the road where you looked down over the bridge towards the village.

First of all, there were the local lads. I had met most of them already in Drum school, but some of them had left school and were now revelling in the heady freedoms the world now offered them. I will avoid the temptation to name names, but you know who you are, gentlemen.

Two in particular do stand out, though, as companions of those summer and autumn evenings when I should have been engaging my intellect with the complexities of Higher French or Chemistry. One of them was an apprentice mechanic in an Inverness garage and now owned his own elderly car that he kept in good repair and in which we swept round the three villages regularly to look out for whatever action might be available. The engine had a particular highly distinctive knocking sound. It broadcast its arrival long before it had breasted the small rise in the road below the stately house of Miss Burgess on its way down the Glen from Polmaily to pick us up for our evening spin. The fifties were relatively restrained and douce indeed, but just the thrill of the transport itself and its potential with the local talent had to be excitement enough. Most of the time.

The other memorable figure in those days was the manager of the local branch of Leslie's grocery shop in Victoria Buildings. That shop was part of the Leslie chain that had outlets in every community in the Great Glen – and one in Tain as well. There was also the excellent Mitchell and Craig's delicatessen in Inverness and a wholesale warehouse in the warren of tiny streets that used to be where the modern developments in Falcon Square are now. The dapper *capo di tutti capi* of this organisation was Jesse Leslie himself who lived in Fort Augustus and ran things from there. If truth be told, we from Fort Augustus were a little bit proud of being from the HQ of this impressive grocery empire. Anyway, at the time in question, the manager of the Drum branch was Gordon Leslie. He was one of Jesse Leslie's four sons and was a popular and laid-back character. He had lazy sort of good looks and his wife was extremely attractive. We were quite a bit younger than he was, of course, and were rather flattered that he would take any interest in us. He had another quality too – the aura of intrigue of a man who had travelled far and had been involved in and survived dangerous places and times. Britain is a bellicose nation, as all the evidence of history tells us, and shortly after the vast upheavals of World War II, some of its armed forces were deployed in the cauldron of Palestine at the time of the formation of the state of Israel. One of the branches of the British forces then was the Palestine Police, and Gordon had volunteered to serve in that instead of one of the more conventional options of National Service. He was in the Palestine Police in the last years of that force's existence (it was actually disbanded in 1947) and witnessed some of the most violent incidents and atrocities that occurred in that, today, still tortured and agonised land. The ruthlessness of both sides – that of the Police on the one hand and the Stern Gang and other Jewish groups was sometimes hinted at darkly by Gordon when he would speak of those days. Sparingly, as it happened.

But Gordon also had an extraordinary car. Now, I have had a few problems with this part of my narrative: exactly what make of car it was as opposed to what memory told me it was. I had been about to say that it was a huge MG saloon with a very long bonnet and vast staring chrome headlights. It was at this point I hesitated. You see, the MG marque is associated with the small, traditional sports car – the MG Midget. My father had one before the War. I had been checking up various details with Gordon's brother Robert who now lives outside Inverness. When I mentioned that Gordon owned a huge MG saloon car, doubts were apparent – though Robert did agree that it was some car! Nothing for it but the infinity of Google and in a trice, I was looking at a website that lovingly traced the history of the MG car from inception to its recent ignominious and inglorious end. And there it was! In 1939. A saloon model was produced in very limited numbers (fewer than 400 actually) that had a big 6-cylinder engine with a 2.6 litre capacity. Gordon's car, without a doubt.

I had just recently passed my driving test in my father's equally out-of-the-ordinary car – his 1939 SS Jaguar. So when Gordon one day offered us lads the chance to go off into Inverness to go to the pictures in his monster MG, excitement went off the scale. I can't remember who did most of the driving, but I did persuade the senior member of our group that I should have a shot. The black Jaguar (BCX 909) was a fearsome thing to drive as many cars in those days were, so I felt totally confident that Gordon's MG would be no bother. Memory of my brief contribution to the evening's drive was of staring fixedly through the narrow windscreen, along the etiolated bonnet and trying to concentrate on the timing of the double de-clutching - essential to moving through the primitive gearbox without making the night hideous with the scream of tortured metal.

Cars? Drivers today? Hah. They don't know they're born.

Two more memories of Victoria Buildings from the fifties.

One of the lads who was an occasional member of our easy-going Drum group in the evenings was called Colin. He worked in the bank and was a bit older than the rest of us. Good looking, easy going and good fun. I lost touch with him completely after the Drum year came to an end. Many decades later when coming to the end of my teaching days, I would occasionally mention to my wife that I had seen a man in the town who reminded me of Colin from the bank in Drum in the fifties. And that was as far as it went for many years. In fact, a ridiculous length of time elapsed before – and not all that long ago – I actually stopped this person in the street. I steeled myself and asked directly. It was his distinctive gait that really had me convinced. A sort of hurrying, forward-leaning style.

"I know this might sound rather silly, but did you work in the Bank of Scotland in Drumnadrochit in the fifties?"

"No," came the reply. "But my brother Colin did."

Amazingly, I was speaking to Duncan, Colin from Drum's identical twin brother! How's that for co-incidence? Needless to say, we greet each other whenever we meet nowadays.

And the last of the memories of Victoria Buildings from those days concerns my grandmother directly. As I have mentioned elsewhere, she was devoutly religious and a regular church-goer. On the few occasions I stayed over the weekend in Drum, there was no escaping the vast Victorian gloom of the original Free Church at Milton. A wrathful God was regularly borne witness to there from the high pulpit, under the dark beams. A good friend and regular visitor to the small house at the back of Victoria Buildings was Peggy MacPherson, a teacher in the Primary department of the Glen school. Peggy was as zealous a church-attender as you would find in any congregation in the land, and I can still see her sitting in front of the fireplace as the ritual of the *strupag* was getting under way and announcing to my grandmother,

"I'm just back from the communion in Beauly, Maggie. The sermon was beautiful." And then would follow a lengthy synopsis of the theme of the sermon, to my grandmother's solemnly nodding approval and deep appreciation. I was a stupefyingly bored witness to those occasions.

A part of the bedtime ritual of every evening that I stayed there that year, after the cup of tea or cocoa, was the reading of a "portion" from the Bible. This became my duty. The very old and limp-covered (a sort of velvet material) Bible was handed to me and I had to read three excerpts. One was from the Old Testament, one from the New and it was all rounded off with a psalm or paraphrase.

I would put all my efforts into getting the tone just right as I knew it was a matter of vast importance to her. I think, however, she would have been saddened in her unquestioning faith had she known that I was just doing no more than any other performer as I intoned these verses. It was all an act on my part. But a good one, I think.

CHAPTER 18
A Fifties Educational Experience
University Days: Aberdeen

Intimations of the fact that I was not going to avoid a university education came rather early in my development. My mother, in particular, was hugely proud of her own education in Edinburgh University in the nineteen twenties (where she met my father) and this coloured much of my upbringing in my school days. The topic was forever coming up when matters educational arose in the round-the-table conversations that took place in our house as a matter of course in the late forties and the fifties. This was pretty frequent, since both of my parents were teachers. My father's first teaching post had been in Kiltarlity in Inverness-shire. Then he became head teacher in the spectacularly-situated primary school in Elgol, built right down by the shore of Loch Scavaig in Skye with the operatic drama of the Black Cuillin rearing out of the sea opposite. From there, he returned to the mainland in 1935, to the small community of Abriachan, overlooking Loch Ness. His last move in 1944 – and the post he held until he retired in 1971 – was to Fort Augustus, at the western end of Loch Ness. My mother's early teaching experience was circumscribed by the absurd rules of those days that prevented married women from taking up teaching posts. She had begun in Leverburgh in the Outer Hebrides, but after she had got married in 1934 that was the end of that until after the Second World War, when she was able to take up the job again in the primary department of Fort Augustus Junior Secondary School. This job she held until 1971, when my father retired.

When I was a pupil in Glenurquhart Secondary School in the early fifties, it was not uncommon for us to be friends with some of the senior pupils. A few of those went on ahead to university – in particular, one of the extremely bright lads, Calum MacLeod, the brother of one of our teachers, John MacLeod of the English department. John MacLeod was somewhat of a hero to many of us, as we had learned that he had been in the Royal Navy during the recent war. After Calum had left the Glen school, he kept in touch with us by letter and I can remember the sheer amazement at the pictures he painted of student life in Aberdeen in those days. It was such a universe away from our own strictly disciplined lives. One notorious incident of the early fifties (1952 I think) he described was the violent attack by the police on the students who had congregated at the Kirkgate Bar on Upperkirkgate for the traditional drinks after the installation of the newly-elected Rector of that year, the then highly-popular comedian, Jimmy Edwards. For some reason, there had been a deep hostility directed at the student body from the police force then, and this event proved to be an excuse for some heavy-handed treatment. A minor incident when a police cap was tossed around and snowballs thrown brought a full, baton charge, which resulted in a considerable number of injuries and arrests. It was a source of much recrimination and controversy at the time, and I remember thinking that I couldn't wait to get in among that sort of action.

When I eventually managed to accumulate the requisite number of Highers and Lowers and got acceptance to Aberdeen University, it wasn't before the narrow escape I had of being press-ganged into the army. In those days, every able-bodied youth of eighteen was liable to be called up to do his National Service in the army or one of the other services. Because there had been a delay in my acceptance for Aberdeen University, by law I now had to report to the Northern Meeting Rooms in Inverness where the selection was to take place. There, along with a large bemused number of others of the same age, I was subjected to the indignities of the physical examinations by a series of men in white coats. I remember the room into which we were herded on one occasion for what was termed the "Intelligence Test". We sat at standard desks, like a classroom, and the papers were handed out. On the command of a uniformed sergeant who was in charge, we turned over our question papers and silently set to our task. I remember the first question to this day. It was "How many inches are there in a foot?" and the rest of the test was of a similar challenge. When I had handed it in and had it checked, I didn't know how to react to the brusque assessment from across the other side of the sergeant's desk: "Another bloody professor. There's a lot of your kind in today." We were asked if we had any preference as to which branch of the army we would prefer. I remember saying that Transport would be my choice. I suppose I saw myself driving some vast military mountain of machinery. Who knows: maybe a tank? I was keen on this sort of activity in those days because there were jobs available around my home village where you could drive commercial vehicles. I suppose I was too humble even to hint that I might like to be considered as officer material. It certainly never crossed my mind. After the medical and general test, I was told that I was suitable material for the defence of the realm and that I would be hearing presently as to where I was next to report. I still possess my "Certificate of Registration" with its stern warnings about what I must do and not do.

On Her Majesty's Service
READ THIS CAREFULLY

Care should be taken not to lose this Certificate but in the event of loss, application for a duplicate should be made to the nearest office on the Ministry of Labour and National Service.
You should not voluntarily give up your employment because you have been registered for military service.
This Certificate must be produced on request by a constable in uniform.
A person who uses or lends this Certificate or allows it to be used by any other person with intent to deceive renders himself liable to heavy penalties.
My registration number is IMM 15388 and my full signature is there in innocent-looking cursive script. My name, laboriously penned a whole life-time ago. A strange window on to a distant land.
There was nothing to suggest other than that I would be spending the next couple of years in uniform going through all the indignities that we already knew lay in wait for us in those days. I can't say that I was actually afraid, but I would have preferred not to go at all. Any contemporaries who had donned the uniform testified to the grimness of the initial training followed by the tedium of much of life afterwards. That is, unless you were lucky enough to get an overseas posting where there was nothing particularly dangerous happening. Always remember that in places like Malaysia and Cyprus in the fifties, there were

trouble spots where life for the forces could be far from pleasant. Friends of mine from school, like Duncan MacLeod, the son of the Drumnadrochit policeman, actually were involved at the sharp end in the disastrous Suez debacle. In the curious way of our species, I could feel the sense of disappointment of not having been among those who could recount their tales when home on leave, but it existed alongside the selfish feeling that that sort of life might not be the best one for me. However, all this disappeared completely as a possible immediate future when I got a letter telling me that I had been accepted by Aberdeen University's Arts faculty and would start there in October 1956.

I think I was aware then that being a student in those days was to be part of a small and very privileged group in society. Only a tiny percentage of school leavers actually went on to that level of education. In the fifties, there were around 1,900 students in Aberdeen University compared with the 13-14,000 there today. In short, we felt rather pleased with ourselves. To be a student was a source of pride so that anything that would tell that to the world was an important item in one's accoutrements. My dearest wish in my early days there was to come home to Fort Augustus for a weekend wearing the full student regalia. There would be the dark blazer with its silver buttons and the sunburst badge on the breast pocket. Of all the Scottish universities, Aberdeen's crest was by far the most flamboyant. Next was the duffel coat with its wooden toggles and twine loops for fastening it: the hood, so useful when the piercing winds from the North Sea knifed their way through the granite city streets. Then there was the silk tie with the beautifully stitched, tiny badges in their regimented rows (so desperately expensive an item) from Esslemont and Macintosh, (*"Appointed Robe makers to the University"*). Or maybe it would all have been supplied by that other establishment on Bridge Street whose motto was *"The prudent student, like most gents with sense, makes a practice of going to Patrick McGee."* This latter was agent for all the university regalia, even to the Air Training Corps. Note that no reference is made here to women students. O tempora, O mores. Actually, it wasn't till my second year, because of the cost of these things, that I actually managed to get my hands on a blazer and badge but the duffel coat and scarf were within financial reach almost right away. But here, another slight irritation. For some odd reason, the Arts faculty scarf was the only one that didn't have the long, contrasting-colour longitudinal stripes that all the other faculties had. Instead we had an enormous blue square of material, cut by diagonal yellow stripes and with regimented rows of university crests. It had to be folded in a special way in order actually to be used as a scarf. If opened out fully, it could almost have been used as a bedspread. It was the year after I left, when I had completed my year in the Teachers' Training College, that the Arts faculty finally managed to get around to having a proper undergraduate scarf. It had the proper length and breadth and had stripes of green, white and dark blue. Too late for me though.

It is well-nigh impossible to convey the mixture of fear, anticipation and wonder that accompanied the first step I took into university life. It seemed to me to be something vast: toweringly and intimidatingly beyond my puny capabilities. Let me try to explain. My progress to that level of education was not without its problems. I will not in any way say a word against my parents who were highly ambitious regarding my education – I was the oldest in a family of three – but I would suggest that the sheer driving force of my mother had the opposite effect that she hoped on my approach to matters educational. The tales of university life and the difficulty of the academic side and the necessity of constant application as a student in order to graduate were force fed over many years, so that I found myself in a mind set that said that, quite simply, I was quite inadequate to the task. Now, I know that this sounds like passing the buck for my own failings, but not so. My struggles with my final Highers in order to gain entrance were as much the result of my own laziness and silliness, but the sense of the whole thing being totally beyond me was always there and it played its part. It all sorted itself out in the end, of course, but there were a few years of mental torment before that happy eventuality. I remember that when we were children, we had been taken to Aberdeen for a holiday when we stayed in a small hotel in the outskirts of the city, on a tram-route. Apart from the intoxicating sound of the trams as they hummed and ground their way to their mysterious destinations until well into dusk, I can remember vividly the darkness and vastness of Marischal College with its dizzying views from the main tower. Aberdeen was a real city and very unlike Edinburgh in appearance, which we knew better up till then. It had been described to us as the "Silver City" before we went there, but to us it looked more drab and grey than silver. It did possess, though, that major essential feature of city life then: the green and cream liveried trams that moved in their stately processions along Union Street and the other streets. The city that awaited me in October 1956 was essentially what I remembered from that family holiday.

CHAPTER 19
Early Lodgings

I just have no memory as to whether I had gone through to Aberdeen beforehand to check out my first lodgings. Clearly I must have. But it is my first arrival as a student in the vast echoing station in the city that I remember as overwhelming. The train was packed with many students from the Highlands and from Inverness and immediate hinterland. As we stopped at the many stations on the journey east, we picked up more and more and the accents became more strange. The sense of travelling into a foreign land was strong. I had no one I knew with me that day and at first felt somewhat isolated. Most of the rest seemed to be in groups. Their behaviour was as boisterous as that of any young people who were leaving their homes and schools and the normal restrictions they had lived with up till then. However, I did soon fall in with a tall, very Inverness lad, Roddy Whyte, with whom an instant rapport was struck. He told me that he had come from Inverness High School – one of the two large secondary schools in the town in those days. Inverness Academy was the academic establishment and the High School catered for the non-academic. It had until recently actually been called the Technical High School. Roddy told me that he had been the very first pupil from that school to have qualified to go to university. Such were the sharp divisions in education in those days.

The actual first arrival in Aberdeen in the "student train" is fixed indelibly in my memory. The train from the west used to stop at Kittiebrewster to let off passengers and a few of our number disembarked there. The rest of the journey was fairly brief and we passed the seemingly endless ranks of austere city housing before the spreading out of the railway lines told us that a large station was a short distance ahead. To the right, beautiful city gardens reminded me of Princes Street Gardens in Edinburgh even although Union Terrace Gardens were much more modest in scale. The station, when it engulfed us, was standard Victorian gothic in cast-iron filigree and glass with – in those long pre-Beeching days – a myriad of small platforms to take local trains along the long-ripped-up lines to the many communities in the hinterland. It all seemed vast and echoing and overwhelming. A true city railway station. As we were pulling up at our platform, I noticed a mass of other students beyond the ticket barrier, all staring and with some waving in our direction. These were the ones who had arrived earlier and were waiting to greet friends on our train. I was glad that I had teamed up with Roddy Whyte or I would have felt extremely alone.

My first lodgings were on Ashley Road. This is a residential street that branches off Great Western Road, opposite St Swithin's Street. (An elegant distant relative of our family, from my father's side, who had connections with Shewgly House in Glenurquhart, lived on St Swithin Street. Later I was occasionally to visit her and wonder at the pictorial evidence of her days of life in India when her family had scores of servants to look after every tiny aspect of life in those insanely pampered days of imperial privilege. She was known to us as "Aunt Elena". She was kindness itself, but could not help but carry an air of hauteur about her.) I stayed at an address roughly half way along Ashley Road on the left hand side. No idea now of what the number was – or who my landlady was - but it was not a happy introduction to the student life. The main problem for me in my first year was a simple one of lack of cash. Because both of my parents were teachers in full time employment, I didn't qualify for a student grant. I was therefore totally at the mercy of what my parents deemed adequate to keep me alive during term and living far from home and its taken-for-granted comforts and certainties. It was a huge shock to my system. At this stage, and with my parents long-gone, it would be inappropriate to point the finger of blame, but suffice to say that their mind-set and sense of fiscal values really belonged to their own student days of well over thirty years earlier. My pocket money for the first spell was ten shillings a week. With the cost of incidentals admittedly being unrecognisable in today's world, that sum might just get one by in cups of coffee and sandwiches and even tram and bus fares, but since my Ashley Road digs only provided breakfast and the evening meal, I had to be able to buy lunch for myself every day of the week. And all of that from the ten-shilling note I got in an envelope from home each week. It didn't take long for despair to set in. The sheer awfulness of being in the Students' Union around lunch time with the aromas from the various snack bars and restaurants in the building being wafting about – and when I had not a single coin of the realm on my person - soon found me regretting ever having made it to this level of educational achievement. It actually became so bad during the latter stages of that dismal first term that on some days I made my way back to Ashley Road in the early afternoon and crept up to my room so that I could sleep off the pangs of hunger till tea time. And even that yearned-for hour, when it did arrive, failed to live up to expectations. The catering in these early lodgings was pretty dire and I always remember the selection of buns and cakes to be dry enough to advertise the fact that they were old stock from a baker's shop that would have been bought for next to nothing. I only have the vaguest of memories of the rest of the lodgers there, or how many there were. There was one retired elderly gent who was pleasant enough and certainly one other student. This student was tall, languid and seemed to be pretty well-off. His accent was a drawling, southern English one and he was a member of the University Flying Corps – recruiting ground for RAF officers. My fellow student seemed to fulfill all the requirements for such a task and simply oozed an easy confidence. He made me feel like a clumping uncouth presence on occasions. I recollect the time he asked me what operas I liked and who was my favourite composer. I knew precisely nothing about such elevated art forms in those days but do remember that I did say that I liked Gilbert and Sullivan. There was only a tiny slip in his usual composure on hearing that. But this was as nothing compared with the occasion when I really put my foot in it with him. He appeared one day with a car that he parked in the street outside. It was, as I recollect, a Sunbeam saloon of a slightly rakish aspect but with a rather high mileage. The battery was low and he couldn't get it to start. He asked for help and I leapt to offer. I had my driving licence and had gained my early experience in the pre-war, one and a half litre Jaguar that my father possessed before he traded it in for the splendidly rakish Riley saloon he now drove. I had actually passed my test in the Jaguar and felt that if I could handle that fierce piece of machinery, I would have no problem getting this one to behave itself. One or two of us from the lodgings were to push the Sunbeam along the street while the driver would engage the clutch at the correct moment. I had managed to persuade my fellow student to let me do the clutch bit of the operation, so off we went. As soon as there was sufficient momentum, the clutch was released and the engine surged into life. It was now that my dormant Mr Toad of Toad Hall persona took over and there was no way that I was going to relinquish the driving seat before I had travelled at least to the end of the street. And thus it transpired. I could see the owner gesticulating behind me in the mirror, but I was now in control. I would show him. I would show them all. And I did just that: I showed them all what happened when someone unused to this particular model got his hands on the controls. I steered a vague course along the street towards the busy intersection at the end. The steering was heavy and unresponsive and the brakes were only token. I found myself effectively out of control and heading towards a crossroads with steady traffic flitting across in both directions. It was time to panic, and I did – doing the only thing I could think of, by aiming at the pavement and hoping that the violent jolting along with my hauling on the handbrake at the same time as lunging down on the footbrake would save the day. It did – just. I don't remember anything more except the ignominy of climbing out of the driving seat and giving the car back into the custody of its rightful owner. He was not amused.

CHAPTER 20
The Students' Union

One of the oddest things I found in the press some time ago was the information that the Students' Union building on Broad Street in Aberdeen had been abandoned and was now closed down. The student body had no further use for it. It seems as if their current life style and social requirements had moved on. To what, I found myself wondering? Of all the aspects of university life, to me, the union was the most irreplaceable and indispensable. It was really the first building that we were introduced to. The new first year students were welcomed by the Aberdeen members of the Scottish Union of Students in their traditional short red undergraduate gowns and it was in the main hall in the Union that we foregathered to hear welcoming speeches and to get some basic introductory information about the new life we were entering. Again memory tells me of the deep uncertainties of being unknown in a seemingly vast gathering where so many seemed to know others already, having arrived here in groups from their schools. As hinted at already, I was out of kilter in my arrival in Aberdeen. I was effectively a year late. But the overwhelming impression from this official welcome was that you were not being left to your own devices and the details of the sheer size of the Union building and of its many amenities told us that this was going to be effectively a sort of home from home. The main hall itself was impressive to the initiate. I remember large murals depicting the striving of youth towards various worthy goals on the walls on either side of the stage. In all honesty, I don't actually recollect the precise themes of these murals but they come down to me now over the huge gap in years as redolent of the nineteen thirties. (But I could be very far out here; no possibility of checking it now either. They will no doubt have long fallen to the "ding it doon; it's auld" school of artistic appreciation.)
The front door of the Union was at the corner of Upper Kirkgate and Gallowgate. It was guarded by the most archetypal ex-military man in doorman's uniform who ever minutely and remorselessly interpreted his remit in the face of pleading supplicants begging relaxation of the rules. He never bent or softened. He was implacable. Jack was his name and its

brusque single syllable sums up the man perfectly. But he was immensely popular too. Even when he had crushed you with some refusal or cold act of doorman discipline, there were no really hard feelings. Mind you, one really extraordinary bit of doorkeeper ruthlessness almost managed to ruin a planned evening of bliss with a new girl friend for me. It unfolded as follows. I had arrived early for a dance. With a few pals I joined in a merry exchange of banter with Jack who was in excellent anecdotal form. I looked at my watch and saw that my girl friend seemed to be late. I said, "Have to have a look down the Kirkgate to see if she's coming." And I stepped out the door on to the pavement. A glance told me that she wasn't approaching and I immediately turned around to re-join the small cheerful group just inside the front door.
Jack stood, barring my entrance.
"Could I see your membership card, Sir!"
The word, "Sir" from such uniformed officials always has a chilling ring to it. All the seeming deferential resonance is as nothing when weighed against the sheer power possessed by its user. Well, I didn't have my union card with me that evening. In vain did I slap my pockets and remind Jack that we had just been joshing together a few feet away inside the entrance. He was immovable in the exercise of his authority. It was a "membership card only" dance in the Union that evening and I had stepped outside at the precise moment when Jack decided to start his check on all who entered from then on. My card lay on the dresser in my room in my lodgings, about a mile and a half away. The only tiny consolation as I stood shivering on the pavement was that I had not been singled out for this treatment out of spite. Not even the lordly President of the Student Representative Council would have been allowed in that night if he or she didn't present a membership card. I only did eventually get past Jack when my girlfriend, who was a member, signed me in at the door. Needless to say, that card never left my person after that.
The Students' Union was important to me in those days for several reasons. First of all there were the subsidised snack bars and the restaurant on the first floor where the charges for basic items and food were such that unless you were totally penurious, there was always something to stave off starvation.

There were various lounges with suitable armchairs and tables for either card playing (for the inevitable schools of fanatical bridge players who seem to have been present in every place I have ever worked: a strange breed I have never managed to comprehend.) or for just reading and sitting around. There were rooms with television sets on the top floor. These were the early days of the service when only a modest number of homes would have possessed a receiver. When something like "The Quatermass Experiment" was being shown, the Television room would be packed. During the momentous events in the world during my first year, I remember us crowding into the main hall in the Union where a screen had been set up. A device like a projector displayed a huge image of a televised broadcast by the then Prime Minister, Anthony Eden, telling us about the invasion of Suez. It was around this time that the Soviet Union attacked the people of Hungary in their capital, Budapest, and savagely put down the rising there. The sense of fear and uncertainty abroad in the world then affected us all. There were political meetings and rallies in sympathy with the Hungarians, but there were also counter demonstrations. I recollect one small but energetic one on behalf of the Communist Party who were fighting a rearguard action in the face of the outrage most people felt at the brutality of the Warsaw Pact forces in Budapest. At one point, when a lone speaker was trying to make himself heard above the hubbub, we had to scatter for our lives as a car driven by someone whose critical faculties extended to include homicide ploughed into the crowd. No injuries do I recollect. But it was all a part of those frighteningly uneasy days. It was also, I have to say, exhilarating. Just a few weeks ago, it seemed to me, I had still been a pupil in a rigidly controlled system, and here I was, attending huge angry political meetings against the background of momentous international events. Yes, I was growing up fast.

I can't leave this aspect of early student life without mentioning another institution that was found in the Old Town at King's College. There was a student-dedicated café there called simply "The Auld Toon Café", but better known as "Jack's". That was the name of the kenspeckle proprietor. He was Aberdonian in accent and in pawky humour. He literally knew everybody who came to his café as customer, and that meant the many lecturers and professors who were regulars as well. When I first went there, I was introduced to Jack who made a point of memorizing my name and what faculty I belonged to. For all the years after that, whenever I went in for a coffee and one of his filled rolls, I would be greeted by name. It was a marvellous tradition. The fare was limited. I have mentioned the filled rolls, and there were various biscuits to accompany the milky coffee that was served by two rather put-upon elderly ladies who really did all the work in the café, while the front-man, Jack, provided the banter and entertainment as well as manning the till. Jack's Auld Toon Café indeed, along with the Union, fulfilled the role of "home-from-home" for me. In that role, finally, I have to mention the two pubs that were patronised by the students in my day. There was the already-referred-to Kirkgate Pub, run by its proprietor, I Quirie, round the corner, past the front door to the Union. This pub advertised itself as "The Place where Students meet" and indeed most of its customers during term time would have been from the University. The walls inside had rows and rows of framed photographs of the many sports clubs, which were kept up to date. It was mainly patronised in my day by medical students and there was a sort of rugby ethos about the place. Not my scene at all. But one of its excellent meals was the famed pie, peas and a pint, which was a treat when funds were more healthy. Close by, on the Gallowgate, was the Marischal Bar, with its eccentric proprietor, W B Wilkie. Occasionally, a selected few (when closing time came at its untimely hour as it did in those days) might be invited back to the proprietor's home in up-market Aberdeen. On one occasion, I tagged on to one of those invitations and marveled at the opulence of the premises into which we were ushered. It was a loud and confused evening and only the vaguest of memories remain, but there was a sense of having been part of a rather select social grouping. This only occurred on the one solitary occasion, I have to confess.

The Union was the natural base from which many activities in the student year were launched. There was a distinct sense that students were a privileged group within the community and this was particularly so during the annual Charities events. These still survive, but my memories of the huge parades in fancy dress with collecting tins being rattled violently in front of the

Aberdeen citizens lining Union Street during the main official procession, the Torcher Parade, when all the normal traffic was simply stopped or diverted - these memories always accompany the notion that the community tolerated a level of behaviour from the student body that it never would from any other. The wilder activities could sometimes go over the top, as I have described elsewhere. An outstanding memory of the last Charities Campaign I experienced had coincided with the appearance in cinemas of "The Bridge on the River Kwai" with its interpretation of Japanese prisoner of war conditions that would have had real survivors of these events incandescent with fury at its wild inaccuracies. The music track of the film was a whistled version of "Colonel Bogie", and one of the decorated floats for the actual parade had a hugely amplified recording of that music playing as it cruised through the streets of the city to raise awareness of the imminent charities events.

The other occasion when the community permitted what could be termed outrageous behaviour by the student body was during the rectorial campaign. This was the uniquely Scottish system whereby the students vote for an eminent individual who will represent them during meetings of the University Court and would chair the proceedings. In 1957, the candidate favoured by such as I, a Highlander and member of the shinty club , was John MacDonald Bannerman, a prominent Liberal politician and also legendary Scottish international rugby player. One of the traditions of the campaign was the rectorial battle, which took place in the quadrangle of Marischal College. It was basically a crude affair in that the opposing armies of supporters would face each other in the quad, and guard their standards which were fixed to wooden frames, with each side trying, by whatever means they could, to capture the standard of the opposition. Bannerman supporters wore blue and white favours on their lapels and that would have been the colour of our banner. As we gathered in the quad and looked around, we saw that the university authorities had boarded up all the windows which might get in the way of any missiles that would be hurled by the opposing armies. One of our side came from a farm and drove up with huge numbers of eggs in boxes that we were assured were well past using date. What primitive urges were being catered for. Here was the chance to hurl as many of these ideal missiles without any reprimand and not have to clear up the mess afterwards. (I found out a basic problem immediately hostilities commenced. If you hold an egg and try to throw it with any force, it will explode in your own hand before it leaves it. You find that your fingers tense just before the act of throwing and all you do is see that your throwing arm is drenched in rotten egg. You have to lob the egg projectiles so that they fly through the air intact. I trust that information will stand you in good stead should you ever require it.) In the surging confusion that followed the signal to join battle, I found myself with a group of my shinty fellow members forcing ourselves towards the enemy standard. When we got just below it, I was grabbed by a few of the more robust of my colleagues and someone yelled at me that they were going to lift me up and I was to grab hold of the wooden pole that carried the standard and hang on to it – my weight presumably would do the rest. That was what happened. I was thrust up violently and grabbed the pole. It was nailed on to a wooden panel and it came away fairly easily and unbelievably, I saw it dipping down into the massed ranks of the Bannerman faction. That was the last I saw of it as other hands grabbed it and with more violent surgings, it eventually made its way back to our side of the quadrangle. Now, as this is being read, I have little doubt that by recounting that I had played a small but sort of pivotal part in this long-ago rectorial event, the reader may experience just a creeping sense of doubt. I have absolutely no proof to back this up. I have searched and found my small blue and white lapel favour in an ancient wallet, but that isn't much help. There were a few photographers in the quad who wanted pictures for the evening press and I do remember flash bulbs going off when I was being heaved aloft. However, the evening paper's photograph showed a mass of egg-besplattered shapes with no distinguishable shape that I could have triumphantly claimed was myself. No, you will just have to take my word for it. Afterwards, many of us made our way across the street to the Student Union to get ourselves cleaned up in the basement. Oh yes, John Bannerman later won the vote for Rector as well, and held the post until 1961.

And one other tale of the rectorial fever that gripped our student community in 1957. In an effort to head off any of the more potentially violent groups who might cause disturbance during the period, several of the university sports clubs were contacted by the Chief Constable of the City of Aberdeen. The shinty club was one of them. I remember entering the solemn wood-paneled sanctuary of the Chief, and us sitting on the chairs provided while he surveyed us from behind his enormous desk. He didn't actually read us the riot act, but we had what seemed more like a friendly chat about the risks of over-exuberance during charities and how we should temper our youthful urges. We trooped out afterwards slightly bemused, but also slightly flattered that our club could ever have been considered as a threat to the community. The report in the Evening Express that night had us mightily amused when we saw ourselves described as the "burly members of the university shinty club" being warned by the Chief Constable about our behaviour. A pretty far from "burly" gathering we were, I fear.

I think that the disappearance of the Student Union from the university experience of students in Aberdeen marks just one of the many outstanding changes that have occurred in the evolution of student life over the past half century. I have to confess a pang of sadness.

CHAPTER 21
Time To Move On
The Groves of Academe

It's a strange thing, but when I was setting up some notes with which to write this material, I found it problematic recollecting the other lodgings I had in Aberdeen during the four years I was there. Every time I set down the several addresses, I would have a moment of doubt and a re-drafting. Well, it is almost a half-century ago now so I might be permitted a little wooliness of memory.

I became friendly with two students in different faculties who were able to tell me that there were better places than Ashley Road in which an impoverished student could find better accommodation   Johnny Fraser I had known some years previously when I had been, for an unhappy spell, a pupil in Inverness Academy. Johnny was studying History. The other pal was Jim Barclay. Jim came from the Borders and was the son of a banker in one of the towns there. Between the two of them, I got a place in Crown Street – a lodging far removed from my present one in ethos and conditions. It was a tall house quite far down that street – four floors from basement to the top. My room was right at the top and the only drawback was that I had to share initially with an elderly commercial traveller. The name has long gone, but he had one characteristic that did tend to blight my nights. He snored remorselessly. This did cause some initial despair, but I seem to have discovered that if I made some sudden noise like clapping my hands, it would shut him up quite effectively. Anyway, it faded away as a source of irritation. However, it is with the advantages of Crown Street that I must dwell. There was a large number of lodgers – mainly, but not exclusively – students. And there were girls there. Not only that – attractive girls. Two student nurses I remember, from Orkney, with to me the strange lilting accents of these Islands. To be asked to "pess the chem" at the table always remained with me. Jackie and Ruby were their names. And occasionally others would take up residence and move on in the ever-changing household - of which more later. The food was much better and there was more of it. It was mainly the landlady that we came in contact with – her husband was a vague and shadowy presence glimpsed occasionally through the door into their own living quarters. He was said to be Irish. There was also a daughter who was a quite distractingly ravishing looking young woman. To make her even more of a disturbing occasional presence, it became known that she did photographic modelling to help her with finances. I seem to recollect that she was separated from her husband. I had first hand knowledge of this in the following manner. I have to emphasise here that we are talking about the year 1957 when censorship in all of the media and in popular literature as well as the cinema was like living under a Taliban regime when compared with nowadays in the early 21st century. This I mention to give some context to what happened when I was back in Crown Street one autumn for my resit exams. I was still fumbling with the demands of the world of academe and the resits were always the last chance saloon that saved me from disaster. Anyway, the boarding house was quiet and the atmosphere – apart from the frenzied study before entering the examination hall – was actually quite pleasant. I was temporarily in a large downstairs room near the front door sharing with a young, laid-back, worldly photographer who had expensive cameras with him. He did work for magazines and newspapers and once told me that he also was a member of the Aberdeen Photographic Club or Association. This meant that he could process all his own photographs. You can see already where this is going. One evening, he mentioned that he had been doing a photographic session with the daughter of the household and asked me if I would be interested in seeing some of the results.

Would I be interested!

I can remember the sheer stunning effect of holding up colour slides to the light and then afterwards seeing them in a battery-powered viewer, of the red-haired and totally undraped beauteous creature who sometimes helped her mother with serving in the dining room. I was sworn to secrecy, of course. I suppose this is the first time I have ever put this down in any detail but with the vast gulf in years since those amazing images were shown to me, I think I can safely say that I won't cause any offence to anyone. A confidence might have been broken but time will have expunged any fear of offending.

Crown Street had no room in the house where you could study. The tiny bedroom up at the top simply was too cramped. These were the days long before central heating and in winter it was grimly frigid up in the heights. This meant that it had to be a library for this purpose – summer or winter. The choice was King's College Library or the Public Library beside His Majesty's Theatre. This latter was the choice as far as I was concerned if only because it was a very long way up to Old Aberdeen. So the Public Library it was and since in my early years at the university I had most afternoons off, I found myself with several like minded pals, heading from the Students' Union down Upperkirkgate, up Schoolhill, past Robert Gordon's and then past the magnificent theatre to the flight of steps that led up and into the gloom and silence of the library. It all sounds so scholarly and worthy, doesn't it? This was the whole reason for me being in Aberdeen and here I was comporting myself as any earnest seeker after truth and learning should comport himself. But that was not the complete picture. Another ritual overlaid that worthy intention and latterly became the true pattern. You see, not too far from the sweep of the stone steps, along Union Terrace, there were at least two very pleasant, snug cafes. This was established early on and the real procedure was as follows. The books and folders would be placed on the chosen desk or alcove and a preliminary shuffling of paper would take place. Then the eyes would be raised to take in the other people in the vast room. A spell of reading of lecture notes or text books now. After that it would be towards the high windows that the glances would be turned – especially tempting if it was a sunny day out there. Soon eyes would be locked on those of one of the pals who might be in a similarly restive frame of mind. A raised eyebrow and a tipping back of a cup gesture would receive a positive acknowledgment to be followed by a discreet scraping back of chairs leading to a procession to the exit. Soon we were round one of the tables in the nearest café ordering a round of teas or coffees and buns and biscuits. The inevitable lighting up of the cigarettes rounded off the bliss completely. Time would drift by and eventually there would be a leisurely return to the long-ago abandoned desks. A glance at watches or the large clock high on the wall would presently tell us that it was rapidly approaching tea-time. Time for a game of snooker back at the

Union maybe? Why not? And that would be the all-too-frequent self-delusion that marked out student life for me and quite a number of my companions during much of the first and second years of my university education. Much I might have rued it all when the agonizing study of the pass lists took place in the quad at Marischal College or Kings College and the realisation that the impending summer would have to be one of remorseless study in order to pass the various failed subjects in the October resits. Whenever I might be asked by those at home about how I passed my day when I had no lectures timetabled, my answer was always, "at the Library catching up with stuff." And I think I actually believed it myself. All a little bit sad – even at this very far remove.

My digs in Crown Street were the background to an eventful period of my student days in the Fifties. As already mentioned, I was lodging in a large establishment run by a singularly impressive Aberdeen landlady. Amenities for the large compliment of tenants were not too bad. There were bathroom facilities on each floor, and downstairs in the basement, was the dining room/sitting room. It was also the level where the family lived. Catering was also adequate. Two meals per day. Standard breakfast and evening fry-up with bread and various cakes and buns etc. The student lodgers were predominantly male. Some were studying History, others Physics and Chemistry and Engineering. So far as I can remember, I was alone in being a humble MA Ord (Ordinary) student, studying (mainly) English. The Scottish MA Ordinary Degree in those days was a unique qualification. Its collection of subjects: in my case, two studied in depth like History and English, along with a language (French) and a science subject. Geology in my case.

There was also Moral Philosophy. This was a quite extraordinary experience. The Regius Professor of Moral Philosophy in those days was a truly amazing man. He was Donald MacKenzie MacKinnon who was born in Oban in 1913. He was the head of the philosophy department in Aberdeen from 1947 till 1960, after which he moved to Corpus Christi College in Cambridge. He had an enormous influence on generations of students in Aberdeen, Oxford (he had been a lecturer there from 1945 to 1947) and Cambridge. His obituary on the 9th March 1994 described how he had 'bewitched' generations of students both with content and his 'quite unique style of lecturing'. His obituary also refers to his 'breathing inspiration into the Ordinary Moral Philosophy class in Aberdeen at 9am on a February Monday morning'.

Well, I can vouch for that. I was at that lecture on that February Monday morning. It was one class that you just didn't miss. Ever. As to him being 'bewitching', a word I might use to replace that would be 'terrifying'! He loomed over and totally dominated the lecture theatre. He was an enormous brooding presence and his voice and deportment were like something booming across the parted Red Sea in the Old Testament. His arguments as he threaded through the thickets of Plato, Socrates and John Stewart Mill and others were detailed and to me often dense and unfathomable. He let you feel that his subject was of vast importance to the human condition. When you were given an essay, it could be handed back to you by the great man himself in his utterly chaotic office at a corner of the quadrangle in King's College. This could be a frightening experience, as he was on an intellectual plane so far removed from the one that you inhabited. But he was not condescending either and really tried hard to get your dull intellect to join his on the sunlit meadows of academe over which he moved so effortlessly.

To indicate his concern for even the humblest of his students, I give the following example. For some reason or other, I had not been able to attend the return of an essay, and had headed off back home to Fort Augustus one Easter holiday. A large envelope arrived through the post and I saw the Aberdeen postmark. Inside was not only my essay, with various corrections and observations in red ink written over it, but an accompanying sheet of close-typed text. It was an exposition of an answer to the basic question that had been posed in the original essay title. And it had been sent by, and signed by, Professor MacKinnon himself. All that effort for a very unspectacular and humble ordinary student of his subject. The best part of it all was that I kept this letter and not only read it closely, but all but memorized it. One of the main questions in the Moral Philosophy final examination that year chanced to be the topic of that essay theme, and in reproducing it in the examination hall at King's College, I was a third of my way to passing that difficult subject. I had good reason to think highly of this eminent man.

He was the quintessential eccentric and absent-minded professor and the tales of his odd behaviour were legion as they were often no doubt apocryphal. One of them concerned the timid first year female student who knocked on the door of his shambolic office at King's to get an essay returned.
"Come in," boomed the familiar voice from within.
She entered. "Sit down, Miss Fraser," the voice instructed.
She did.
And from that point, the still-disembodied voice continued the colloquy with questions and hesitant answers following until the session was drawn to a close. Still not a sign of the professor.
"Good bye, Miss Fraser," came the valediction as she opened the door to depart.
It was then that the clank and rush of cascading water brought the familiar sound of flushing. The professor had conducted the tutorial from his adjoining toilet.
And my own, not-so-spectacular, experience. One day, I got on board the bus to take me back down to Marischal College and the Students' Union. It was quiet and the top deck was empty. I sat about half way down and prepared to look into the upper windows of the houses that lined the narrow bus route, which was often a mild form of entertainment. I became aware that I was not to be alone. I glanced round and saw the swaying, bulky looming shape of Professor MacKinnon. He hunched into the seat directly behind me. I became aware that he was muttering to himself. At first, it was very quiet, but soon it was impossible to avoid picking up the occasional word. It was all very embarrassing. Why on earth, with all the many other seats available, had he chosen to sit where he did? Then the words became clear. It was a continuous repetition of the sentence: "My mother is dead". It was whispered, then uttered quite clearly, then quietly again and it almost had my hair stand on end. So odd, so personal, yet it could have been some philosophical conundrum that he was turning over in his mind. And that really was it. I would have told people and we would have laughed at further confirmation of the "nutty professor" syndrome.
But to get back to the Ordinary MA Degree. This group of subjects was studied over three years. I can remember the look of utter incomprehension when I was telling this to students from

English universities I met on a holiday job in Norfolk. Without exception, they were specializing in their chosen subjects from the day they entered university. The notion that you could study such diverse things as Philosophy and Geology in the same year to them seemed absurd. A deep cultural divide became apparent to me in those days. The Scottish MA was originally meant to be a preparation for specialisation, later leading towards an honours degree. However it had for long been a degree in its own right in my day – an ideal one, for example, teaching. It was the result of a Scottish belief in the "Democratic Intellect": the desire to open up the mind to different disciplines. The belief in width of knowledge in the educated person. Specialisation from the earliest years of study was considered to be harmful and would lead to a narrow, hemmed-in intellect. So, I can pride myself in my broad, all-encompassing educational base provided by Aberdeen University in the three years I spent there in the late Fifties. Thus it was that I, who had little leaning towards science subjects, found myself studying Geology and going on field trips to places like Stonehaven to chip away at deposits of porphyric rock by the shore. It couldn't be further away from struggling with Plato and Socrates in the challenging lectures of Professor MacKinnon in the Moral Philosophy department, but it was a splendid shaking-up of the mental faculties. Yes, in retrospect, the Scottish Ordinary MA Degree had a lot to commend it. Not least, it has to be confessed, afternoons free during some years to live a stress-free life in the Students' Union, looking along the length of a cue on the perfectly tended snooker tables.

It was in Crown Street that I first became drawn into politics. Liberalism had been the orthodoxy of our household at home and I had actually joined the Young Liberals at one point. But it was in Crown Street that I became drawn into the more radical embrace of the Scottish National movement. My sympathies lay in that direction already from the history lessons in primary school in Fort Augustus taught by my mother. She, as a student in Edinburgh, had been right at the epicentre of the formation of the modern version of that movement as secretary of the University branch. She had actually rubbed shoulders with the giants of those days: C. M. Grieve, Compton MacKenzie and Cunningham Graham – indeed a close friend of hers had actually married Compton MacKenzie. It was the history students in Crown Street who were the crucible of nationalist fervour and soon detected my own sympathies. They were much motivated in their beliefs by their reaction to their professor – Professor George Osborne Sayles. His Anglo-centric interpretation of the world was a source of much wrath to them. His most notable publication was "The King's Parliament of England" which was published in 1974.

I quickly became a card-carrying member of the University Nationalists. It initially meant attending meetings and even taking part in debates. In the latter activity, my contribution was mainly that of a voting presence. I never had the courage to stand up and deliver orations. It was all quite exciting, however, and one of the highlights, I remember, was an inter-University conference in Edinburgh to which our Aberdeen branch intended going. For some reason, public transport was not chosen, but hiring a car was suggested by someone. Since I was the only one at that juncture who had a driving licence, I was left to organise this. As I recollect, it was a Ford Consul – then a new model with pleasant driving characteristics including the, then, daring steering-column gear lever. All went surprisingly well and I was buoyed up by my pivotal role in this adventure. Until the journey home, that is. We were all piled into the car after the meeting in the Edinburgh Students' Union and were heading down Princes Street. I am sure the trams had gone by this time but the street was churning with traffic. Suddenly I found that we were isolated in an eerily empty part of the street. A movement at the corner of my eye reared up and took the form of an enraged traffic policeman whose presence and halt signal I had failed to see. Humiliation was total. The wound-down window, the crimson sweat drenched features and the withering scorn of the uniformed authority figure. No, it was not my finest hour.

CHAPTER 22
Politics, A Narrow Escape and A Welcome Windfall

By far the most traumatic event in my political life at Aberdeen University involved a significant anniversary that fell in 1957. It was the 250th anniversary of the Act of Union of 1707. To mark the occasion, it was decided that the University Nationalist Club would hang a flag – a large Saltire with a black border - from a prominent building in the city. The building chosen was the Music Hall, right in the middle of Aberdeen's main street, Union Street. I have dim memories of intense planning meetings for this act of political bravado. In the early stages, I was simply "among those present". It began to assume more serious implications when I was marked down as one of the main assault party. A front-line storm trooper. It was unreal. But terrifying. We carried out reconnaissance sweeps of the building, inside and out. It became clear early on that there was no practical access to the roof of the Music Hall from the inside: it had to be an assault on the outside of the building. As I recollect, there was a flagpole in those days on top of the main classical pillared front entrance. It was mainly flat there, and we had identified various service ladders fixed to various walls that could just allow eventual – but desperately risky – access to the parts of the roof leading to the actual flagpole. To add to the total insanity of this crazy plan was the fact that the whole operation had to be carried out at dead of night. All the surveys were completed. The team to make its perilous way on to the roof with the symbolic flag was picked. I was one of that four – though not, as I recollect, one of the final two who would affix the flag to the flagpole and see to its successful unfurling over an unsuspecting Union Street. Then followed a dreadful week of countdown to be got through. Details were gone over again and again. Appropriate footgear – sandshoes, in those days – and they had to be blackened. As had our faces. Did we have balaclavas as well? I really cannot remember. I think I can still feel echoes of the liquid terror that suffused my whole system as the minutes, hours and days dragged agonizingly by to the dreadful May 1st. The day in 1707 when Scotland signed away its independence. I could not believe that I had got myself into this madness: I suffered from a fair dose of vertigo for starters (something concealed from the main plotters for all too obvious machismo reasons) and I continuously and ponderously dredged the innermost recesses of my mind for some credible excuse that would get me out and not leave me exposed as a cowardly milquetoast.

But the symbolic raising of the black-bordered Saltire from Aberdeen Music Hall never took place. For a reason that none of us could have foreseen. It happened as follows. In those far-off days, student excesses during Charities Week were becoming rather more than the staid authorities (be they civic or university) were prepared to tolerate. There had been a spate of highly dangerous stunts during that year's Charity campaign. Banners had been hung from Redmoss wireless mast, Marischal College spire, the scaffolding on the newly-constructed C&A branch on Union Street. An effigy had been hung from the dizzy heights of the cables across the terrifying granite quarry at Rubislaw and the Aberdeen star footballer, Harry Yorston had been kidnapped and held to ransom. But most shocking of all, to the sensibilities of those times, was the sacrilegious hanging of a white flag from the main flag mast on Balmoral the royal residence. This latter caused an outcry – mainly from residents in Deeside who tend to be more royalist in outlook than the rest of the land. Such indeed was the wrath of these loyal citizens that the student newspaper, Gaudie, published an editorial that defended the actions of the students while taking a swipe at the attitudes of the people in such communities as Ballater. Much better, said the editor, to attack the behaviour of the "yellow press" who spend their lives camped around Balmoral in order to catch any crumb of information that can be inflated into some pointless story or other. But tucked away in the press of those days was an item that really drew a curtain finally over our brave nationalist escapade. While the police in Aberdeen tended to take a grudgingly neutral approach to the charities follies of the student body, those in Edinburgh were showing a sterner attitude. These were the days when Scotland's uneasy evaluation of its identity and place within the Union tended to manifest itself in attacking Post Office letterboxes which bore the historically inaccurate E II R (which actually negates Scottish royalty: denying any of ours ever existed) on them or whitewashing slogans on public buildings in the capital. Several students, including three from Aberdeen, were hauled up before the courts and fined. Now, I would have known who the three unfortunates from Aberdeen were at the time, but have no recollection of their names now. But what I do recollect was the stern injunction that came down from on high: from the god-like University Principal himself: Sir Thomas Murray Taylor CBE, QC, MA, LL.B, DD, LL.D, FRSE, FEIS. It stated tersely that in view of the excesses of recent weeks, be it known that the very next stunt or outrage carried out by members of the student body would result in the instant "rustication" (expelling) of said members.

A swift summit conference was called and to my utter and total relief, it was decided that the risks of discovery were much too great. Even the actual gesture itself – the significantly altered Saltire – would be a dead give-away. As well as the surge of relief, there was a slight but distinct under-tow of elation. To even hint that you had been involved in the final stages of such a daring act had more than a slight cache about it. It could be a brilliant conversation stopper in the student union.

I mentioned a third role I played in the Nationalist group. This was a rather shifty one and nothing really to be all that proud about in retrospect. The University Debater was the formal stage for the strutting of embryo politicians. Here they could let rip all their artificial fire, outrage and stage fury – but all within the bounds of the strict code of formal debate. One such clash had been advertised and the big publicity in "Gaudie", the student newspaper set the scene. The main protagonists were to be the Nationalist and Labour parties. Some kind of deal had been worked out beforehand regarding voting intentions and deals had been made. However, just before the debate got under way, a hasty cabal was convened and the decision of one of the more Machiavellian of our leading figures was that, at a given signal, the entire Nationalist group would announce that it could play no further part in the flawed proceedings. At that point, we were to stand up, and in dignified silence, leave the debating chamber. I can just recollect the event and the wave of jeers and heckling that accompanied our rather silly gesture.

Subsequent reports in the student press made it clear that we had scored a pretty decisive own-goal.

Crown Street was, on the whole, a happy place. The students staying there found themselves in as near the conditions they might have experienced if they had been living in a rented flat. This latter was the ultimate and much envied state then enjoyed by only a tiny few from privileged backgrounds. They were the only ones who were totally free of the chilly mores of these buttoned-up fifties days. Parties of the more licentious kind were reputed to take place in such places and the illicit booze (I seem to recollect the odd-sounding word "feek" as the name of that forbidden elixir) was reputed to flow freely. The family who ran our boarding house rarely emerged in any supervisory capacity over our occasional revels. On my birthday in January, I was the epicentre of a fairly spectacular hurricane of revelry. For some reason, my parents had thought that I was due a financial leg-up beyond the normally modest weekly allowance. I was stunned when I opened the envelope with my mother's distinctive handwriting and slid out the cheque it contained. It was for the astounding sum of (I think) £30. A tiny sum today, but in 1957, a statement of potential luxury and social extravagance. The accompanying letter contained homilies about opening a bank account and husbanding my riches wisely. I set out doing just that – immediately – in what I dimly recollect was then called the Aberdeen Savings Bank on Union Street, near the Grosvenor Hotel. With a name like that, the rectitude of the institution and the equally solemnly sensible character of its clientele were self-evident. O, if only, in my case, it had been so! The moment I had the small black pass-book in my hand and had looked at the date and the stunning sum of money on the top line, I instantly slid the book back across the counter to the teller and, "I'd like to withdraw five pounds," I intoned.

It was the opening of a door into a brief and hectic surge of celebration that drew in most of the household. Cans of beer in those days were built in shipyards of high-tensile steel. To open them you had to come equipped with a special dedicated implement with a sharp, pointed triangular piercing tip. These openers were much in use for the next couple of nights and I slipped quickly into the oblivion of the enthusiastic but inexperienced toper. One of the few memories that have survived is my decision to make acquaintance with a tall, silent Swedish female student who had recently joined us. I sat on a small landing, trying to keep my eyes open, intending to ask her to join the raucous nearby party. I saw the top of her flaxen head as she climbed the first flight of the stairs and galvanized myself to make an offer she could not refuse. But the words would not form. Not a flicker of recognition or acknowledgement moved her distant, impassive features as she delicately stepped over me and merged into the gloom. The finality of her door snapping shut ended any foolish dreams I might have harboured.

Not much more do I remember, except that a day or two later, I woke up lying, fully clothed, on the bed in my room. My eyes focused on a dark brown zipper jacket lying at my feet.

"Whose is that?" I asked my roommate.

"It's yours," came the reply. "Don't you remember? You bought it in C&A's yesterday afternoon!"

And indeed it was so. Actually, it was a smart enough garment and it did me for the next couple of years or so. But it tore a huge hole in my rapidly-disappearing bank account. What pathetic testimony to my fiscal uselessness that sad little book provided. I would look shamefacedly at the steady descent from the powerful initial statement of Thirty Pounds Sterling, as the hand-written withdrawals – latterly more meagre sums of ten and five shillings, followed each other steadily downhill into the finality of the black abyss of zero. I don't remember how long this episode lasted but it was painfully brief. Then it was back to the weekly dismal allowance with all its attendant privations.

Just a final word about memorable fellow-lodgers in Crown Street. There was the cocky little corporation bus driver – a native Aberdonian - who was always seeking to impress us. The students, that is. The municipal bus fleet in Aberdeen in those days was equipped with the green and white double-deckers with the traditional open rear platform. Our new pal was one of the regular drivers. One day some of us were walking up Crown Street heading for Union Street, when a double-decker suddenly pulled in by the kerb beside us. Waving energetically from the cab was our jovial fellow-lodger. The bus was empty and was heading back to the depot. He shouted to us to climb aboard and he'd give us a lift to where we were going. As it happened, we

were heading up to King's College in Old Aberdeen. "Nae bother. Climb aboard".
And off we lurched and sped. He was out to impress us with his handling of his immense tower of municipal machinery. The transmission in the buses in Aberdeen was by pre-selector gearboxes in those days. The driver did not have a clutch in his cab to disengage the drive while he changed gear. Instead there was a gear selector lever, which was slipped into the position of the next gear he wished to engage. When the moment came, the driver merely dipped a pedal and the gear was automatically engaged. It made the task of the driver much easier than the traditional clutch method. But it had to be done smoothly. If you tried to rush things, it could result in huge surgings, lurchings and lungings in the progress of the vehicle. Our cheerful fellow-lodger gave us a truly scary performance in the driver's cab. He kept turning around to wave to us as we were swept along Union Street on our illicit joyride. It was with the most immense relief that we were swept up to a road end on King Street which was as near King's College as he could get without being detected by an official of the corporation transport company. But it was great fun too. A final memory of Crown Street has to be the splendid fish and chip shop away down at the bottom. This was a fairly regular place of delight when funds were adequate. In those days, I had homed in on white pudding and chips as the most delectable evening meal imaginable. The white puddings (mealie puddings) were quite enormous and the pile of chips sharing the plate was equally heroic in scale. It was about two-thirds towards the end that doubts began to form about the ability to finish the whole portion. There were tables in the premises and we'd usually eat there instead of taking the meals back up to the lodgings.
Yes, rather basic stuff, but happy memories for all that.

CHAPTER 23

Aberdeen Trams
And the Final Lodgings

Another of the enduring memories of Aberdeen city in the fifties is the tram cars.
During an early visit to the city with our parents on a holiday, we had stayed in a hotel on Great Western Road. An already exciting experience had been made even more magical by the sound of these trams as they made their way up and down the street close to the windows of the hotel. The rising hum of the electric motors and the unique noise of their wheels on the steel rails from then on became associated in my mind with the essential background sounds of the big city. Any big city. By then, I had already had experience of the majestic system in Edinburgh with its cream and maroon cars and the comparison between them and Aberdeen's different designs and livery was an added excitement.
But the tram system in Aberdeen was already doomed in 1956 when I started student life there that year, but I had over a year of travelling on them before their obliteration. When I was lodging in Crown Street, my usual morning walk by short cut to the Student Union on Broad Street took me across the railway on an iron pedestrian bridge from which you could look up towards Union Bridge on Union Street, which was clearly and unambiguously a bridge in those days before shops had been built on one side of it. The slow, dignified progress of trams across this bridge was such a quintessentially a city scene – especially if it happened to be one or other of the splendid streamlined latest models the city had bought. These were much more comfortable than the old, square traditional ones. They were more weatherproof and didn't have the open platform at either end for boarding and descending. They had an electrically operated door in folding sections that was worked by the conductor. When the tram was stationary, there was a busy clicking sound from the motor that operated them. The best and most sought seats were upstairs – right up at the front where the curved glass of the window, almost down to your feet, afforded

an unparalleled view of Union Street or King Street as we were eased out to King's College. A regular Saturday treat would be taking the tram from one extreme outpost of the city at Bridge of Don to the other at Bridge of Dee. It was a smooth and graceful way of seeing the city go gliding past. Subsequent generations who have only known the heaving and surging progress of city buses, however competent the driver, can never understand the stately elegance of tram cars as a means of urban transport – their pre-ordained progress on smooth steel rails and propelled by the equally smooth propulsion of electric motors.

I still have the ticket I bought for the last trip on the Aberdeen tram service on May 3rd 1958. The ruthlessness of the changeover to buses was characterized by the vast funeral pyres of trams as they were burnt on the Beach Boulevard. Smudged photographs of this destruction appeared in the local press the following day. Soon the tracks were torn up and an era was abruptly brought to a close. Not even a single one of Aberdeen's tram fleet has survived in a transport museum. One had been kept for that purpose, but lack of funds meant that it too was scrapped.

My last lodgings in Aberdeen were in Carden Terrace. This was probably the best of the lot and I spent my third year in University there as well as my year in the College of Education, which I attended in order to get my teaching qualifications.

Carden Terrace (the number has completely vanished from my memory) was a solid and substantial detached house with three floors – one of them a basement. This latter was where the family who owned the house lived and where the large dining room and kitchen were situated. The ground floor had a large sitting room and a number of bedrooms, while the upstairs level had bathroom facilities and the rest of the bedrooms. Unlike Crown Street, there were no female lodgers, but it was mainly students who stayed there. In addition there were two teachers who worked in local schools. There were also office workers. It was a large group of lodgers and we all got on pretty well. I shared a large upstairs bedroom, looking out on to the street, with a young photographer who worked for the local "Press and Journal". His name was Fiddes Horne and he had such a totally relaxed attitude to life that he appeared to spend an enormous part of it in his bed. I always envied the large and, in those days, the Rolls Royce of cameras with which he was equipped: the twin-reflex Rollieflex. This was the standard camera used by newspapers and the quality of its pictures was amazing.

I might mention here, by way of parenthesis, that when I got married the year after I had left Aberdeen, I kept my promise to Fiddes, to hire him as the official photographer at our wedding. He was there, with Rollieflex to hand and the shutter clicked industriously at the appropriate times in the proceedings. He said something about having to rush away immediately after the event, and that he would have the prints in the post immediately. It was some time later that we realized that nothing was forthcoming and we became a little alarmed. When I got in touch with the telephone number we had been given, I found myself talking to Horne pere. He said that he had no idea what I was talking about as his son Fiddes was away somewhere in the Caribbean on an ocean liner as the official photographer. I was aghast and made such spluttering noises that Horne senior said he would have a look to see if he could find any evidence of our pictures. When he got back, he was overwhelmingly apologetic on behalf of his son. He had found the negatives and set about converting them into the albums of photos that mark that rather important day in our lives.

Oh, and while I'm at it, I might mention another bit of misplaced faith in the skills of young Fiddes on that day. I had my own Voigtlander camera with me (about which I waxed lyrical in my first book on the amazing quality of its pictures) and I asked him if he would take one of us cutting the cake in the function room of the hotel in Montrose where our reception was being held. "Sure thing", he replied and the complicated gantry of the flash equipment was set up and all the complex preparations required of slightly more sophisticated cameras in those days appeared to be being seen to. We had been looking forward particularly to this picture as it was to be in full Agfacolor brilliance. Oh dear. When the large transparency was eventually delivered, the most basic fault on the part of the person in charge of the camera became apparent. It was out of focus. The fine grain on the wooden panelling behind us is etched in needle-sharp detail, while the two of us are misty, wraith-like shapes in the foreground. It would never have occurred to me that a professional photographer would have made such an error.

Probably the best thing about the Carden Terrace lodgings was that for a slightly more expensive weekly tariff, we got three meals in the day. Yes, lunch in the middle of the day as well. It was quite amazing and other students I would tell about this were more than a little envious. My younger brother had by now joined me as he was starting his civil engineering course, and it was due to a lucky contact that we were both able to get into that highly desirable lodging house. One of the lodgers was a son of a wealthy farmer somewhere in darkest Aberdeenshire, and he would occasionally turn up with startling treats to enhance our evening tables. Quite early on, we came down for the evening meal to find that we were being treated to roast pigeon. Our farmer fellow-student had been shooting on his father's land the previous day and we were able to share in the spoils. Since he had his own car, there were no problems of transportation of the large number of pigeons. Yes indeed, Carden Terrace was a real find.

I did stumble across a down-side, however. One of the marvellous extras provided for the lodgers was the free run of the kitchen in the late evenings. After we had got back having been out at a dance or something, we could head off down the stairs, through the dining area and into the kitchen where there was always a single light switched on. There was a kettle ready for action, a sliced loaf and a toaster. Cups were laid out and a late-night snack of toast and tea was often the perfect end to a night of excess. One night, I got back in on my own, and thought that the cup of tea was an excellent idea. When I passed through the dining area, I noticed that the usual light in the kitchen was not switched on. No matter. I reached in and turned on the main switch. The room flooded with light. It took a tiny fraction of a second to realize that things were not as they should be. There was a disorientating sense of febrile movement in that ordinary looking room. When my eyes locked on to the cause, I felt such a surge of near-nausea and fear that I was locked motionless. The whole of the floor was a carpet of black scuttling shapes. They made a dry rustling noise. Their shining black carapaces and waving antennae identified them as cockroaches, and they were speeding as fast as their instincts told them to get out of the direct light. In a brief moment, they had gone – apart from a few of the more sluggish who had fallen victim to the sweeping armed paw of the lazy household cat that had its bed in the kitchen and would augment its diet on these grisly creatures when it got the chance. I don't think I had the appetite that night for tea and toast, and when I mentioned this to some of the other lodgers, they all knew about this nightly invasion, but as long as the light was on in the kitchen, they kept away far out of sight. I was just unlucky to have chanced on the evening that the bulb in the small lamp had failed. It sort of modified my estimation of the meals prepared in that kitchen from then on

I always yearned, one day, to attend a dance in Marischal College on a Saturday evening and to turn up with a car which would be parked in the dark quadrangle. A few of the impossibly well-off among the student body regularly did that, and drew glances in which envy was laced liberally with hate. Well, I did manage that once – but just. My girl-friend and I decided to rent a car for a day one weekend in the third term. It would be for just the single day, so that we could go for a run up to Deeside, head back to Aberdeen, go to the dance and home again to our separate (alas) lodgings – making sure that the car was back at the garage early the following morning. The trip to Deeside was somewhat spoiled by the fact that severely limited funds meant that when the rental of the car had been covered, there was scarcely anything left for petrol. I remember us calculating out the mileage each way, allowing a little surplus for the extra run to and from Marischal and the dance, and then plotting out exactly how far we could go for our run. All worked out well, and the supreme delight of leaving the crowded dance hall, stepping out into the quadrangle and into the car in front of the massed crowd heading away on foot, brought out all the worst in us in terms of haughty superciliousness.

CHAPTER 24
College of Education

When the vast relief after graduation had subsided, the pleasant thought took hold that there was yet one more year as a student ahead before the realities of a life of gainful occupation were to be confronted. I never had the slightest doubt about the next stage – I was going to do my year's training and gain my qualifications to teach. This was also to be done in Aberdeen, the city to which after three years as a student, I had become rather attached. Aberdeen College of Education was situated fairly centrally and would not involve travelling too far from the Students' Union and the Kirkgate and Marischal Bars. The life of the student could continue – this time without the fear of the dark clouds of difficult final examinations. The courses in the "TC" (Training College) as we called it were considered to be a bit of a doddle and not too likely to strain the intellect. Just do the minimum required by the syllabus and pick up the scroll at the end. Then it would be time to start to worry about where the first teaching job was going to be. I imagine from this vast distance in time, that the yearly influx of graduates from the University, who intended to train to be teachers, must not have been a very pleasant prospect for the teaching staff in the College. As a group, I think we must have been fairly intolerable. We had our recently gained degrees of which most of us were extremely proud, and we did not try hard to hide our patronizing hauteur towards the College and its entire staff. During my year, there were quite a number of minor rebellions among the graduate intake that sprang from this attitude. Of which more later. Many of the classes seemed to be quite absurd and a total waste of time. Soon they began to be dodged and gaps would appear in the registration records. However, the looming threat to our peace of mind in the College was approaching ever more rapidly. This was the first-hand teaching experience that we all had to undertake in local schools. A brief word of explanation here. The Scottish Ordinary Arts degree, which I had gained, in theory, only qualified me to teach primary pupils. Honours graduates in those days were the only ones who could teach in secondary schools. Well, that was the theory, but in practice that was quite unmanageable, simply because there were not enough honours graduates around then to supply the secondary schools' needs. A category called Article 39 allowed Ordinary graduates to teach in secondary schools, but only up till third year. After that, the task was restricted to the honours graduates. Well, that again was the theory. It was not too long before ordinary graduates were filling all of the teaching roles in Scottish schools at all secondary levels.

But to return to the teaching practice, the day eventually came when we crowded round the notice boards to see where we were to be sent for the weeks at the front line. The grapevine already had informed us of the fact that there were good schools and ones that were to be dreaded. This latter could be either the nature of the pupil-intake – tendency towards urban jungle – or the atmosphere created by the staff who worked there. On the whole, students were not really welcome in many of the schools. Teachers just did not like to have a total stranger standing or sitting at the back, listening in to what was happening. My girl friend and a friend of hers were sent to one school that at first seemed to be all right. The welcome was reasonable and also the introduction to the classes. It was only when the first morning interval arrived that they were made to feel like lepers. When they nervously approached the staffroom, they were told firmly that students were not admitted. If they wished a cup of tea or coffee, they could bring their own cups and they would have to have it in the corridor. It was nothing personal, it was just the way that the staff in that school liked things to be organized.

But many of them were patient and helpful. Some also could take advantage and tell you to your face that the best training was to be thrown in at the deep end. Then would follow a perfunctory explanation as to what was being taught, and the instruction to "carry on". Meanwhile the teacher would head off to the staffroom for a cup of tea and a fag. This could be quite terrifying, and only happened to me once that I can recollect. You knew fine that you were being exploited, but what could you do about it? One of the primary schools to which I was initially sent almost saw the abrupt ending of my prospects of making it into the ranks of the profession. The teacher of the class was ex-forces. He had been in the RAF and looked the part, down to the handlebar moustache and the raffish sports car he drove. He was cheerily confident with his pupils – a huge mixed class of

Primary 6 or 7. He was fairly easy to get on with and all seemed to be going not too badly. But the worm in the bud was a pair of totally obnoxious boys who quickly exploited my lack of experience and rapidly had me lose my temper explosively. I spoke to their teacher about them, but it soon was clear that he did not reckon I had any case against them. "Just high spirits. They don't mean any harm. They'll settle down. Just keep them interested" - and other useless advice.

Well, they did settle down: into a pattern of behaviour that became corrosive and began to undermine my already shaky confidence badly. They knew well that their teacher was effectively on their side since they saw I had been reporting them and nothing had been happening. Until one afternoon when I had been striving to complete some task or other while their continuing threnody of subversive asides had me finally erupt. I grabbed one of them – the smaller of the two for obvious reasons – and dragged him first, then carried him under my arm along the corridor to the staffroom. I hurled open the door and deposited the now-silent, beastly child on the floor and addressed his startled teacher along the lines that until something was done to sort out the problem, no teaching was possible in that classroom. I cannot remember precisely what happened immediately, but I had broken every rule in the book of those days. I do recollect that at one point I was sitting in the head teacher's office, across his desk, and he was suggesting to me that teaching really was not the best profession for me to be contemplating. He also said that he would have to report my behaviour to the college.

What really finished me, as it were, as far as that school was concerned, happened in the following fashion. This was really weird. During one of our lectures at the college, we had been told about the various students in the past who had excelled in various ways in their responses to the courses and subjects. It was the geography lecturer as I remember, and she had been telling us about one particular student from several years ago who had made models for his classes to illustrate his lessons and who had been quite outstanding. One of those models had been of Aberdeen harbour and had been made to demonstrate aspects of the fishing industry. It had realistic waves, the harbour buildings and ships and fishing vessels and must have taken an immense amount of time and application. In conversation afterwards, the general reaction among us, the students, was "What an idiotic waste of time and energy!" and others were even more dismissive. We just thought it was absurd to hold up such preparation for a series of lessons by a teacher as preposterous and set an impossible standard. The matter slipped away and was forgotten.

One day, in the school where I had lost my temper so spectacularly, I had been talking to the raffish teacher and speaking about the college and how I was finding it. He had just been asking me how I was finding the TC experience. (This was before the incident, by the way. There was little by way of light conversation after I had laid hands on one of his charges.) He had been asking me about my impressions of the lecturers and the various classes. It was then that I launched into a diatribe about the kinds of impossible standards and role models they were holding up for us to emulate. I then gave a fanciful and scornful description of the model of Aberdeen harbour made by a student to teach a lesson about fishing in the North Sea. I exaggerated the scale of the details and even said that this student had wee seagulls suspended by threads all over the place for increased verisimilitude. I did notice at the time that he had not joined in the hilarity as I had expected, but just let it pass. When my last day in that school came round and it was time to return for the next spell of lectures at the College, I found myself in the small storeroom adjoining the classroom. I had been looking for some piece of equipment the teacher had told me was on a top shelf. I got hold of a stepladder and reached into the dusty depths. The light was rather faint, but after scrabbling about for a while, I found to my horror that one of the items on that dim shelf was a very large model of a harbour, with buildings and waves and ships and fishing boats meticulously glued in place. I knew that I was now doomed, and why there had been the neutral response to my gales of ridicule at the achievements of former students of the Teacher Training College. I had been all this time under the care and tutelage of the prize-winning model maker himself and he was pretty certain to have that colour his report when he came to write it up.

After the solemn talk by the school's headmaster, I had another at the College when I had to account for my sins before a senior member of staff. Again I was asked to consider the wisdom of continuing with my teacher training, but was not actually threatened with being booted out. Much relief indeed.

My secondary school experience was rather better. It was in a Roman Catholic school, called, as I recollect, St Peter's. The teacher in charge of my class (a large third year mixed group) was a middle-aged, tweedy Highlander with strong accent of the Western Highlands. He was also a Gaelic speaker. I felt much more at home with his easy-going approach as well as his practical evaluation of the job of teaching. He also was more redolent of home. He was in command of his pupils and made it clear to them that when I was left in charge, he would not expect to hear any adverse reports about their behaviour. It was clear that he meant it and that they believed it. What a huge difference it made to the uncertain student when that atmosphere prevailed in the classroom. Apart from the unease stirring within my Presbyterian soul caused by the strange Roman Catholic icons in their alcoves with their candles throughout the building, my stay there was reasonably productive. A vast improvement on the previous experience.

My last hurdle that I had to surmount before the graduation at the end of the session was a rather absurd one. It happened thus. One of the classes that caused little strain was Geography. Remember again that although our year group were graduates of the ancient University of Aberdeen, when it came to teaching, in theory, we were only to be allowed to teach primary pupils. Except for the existence of the Article 39, of course. As a result we had to be prepared to teach our charges the whole wide range of primary subjects. Our final task for the Geography class was the preparation of a project with notes on methods and presentation as well as some form of illustration. Now I had decided to do something on my own part of the world: the Great Glen, of course. It was to deal with the employment and the sort of lives the people lived in that part of Scotland. I spent a ridiculous amount of time in drawing a huge map of Loch Ness in the middle of which I had a magnificent Monster, with tartan toorie on his head. All the other stuff was there and it was, I felt, a fitting way to round off that part of my course. It was a condition of the granting of our final certificate that all projects and assignments were handed in by a certain date. I

remember the irritation I felt when I consulted my name on the results list pinned up outside the Geography Department door and saw that there was a blank. No mark. Why? I caught up with the lecturer and asked.
"Quite simple. You didn't hand in anything."
This was preposterous. I had really worked at this stupid thing and knew I handed it in.
What followed was a lengthy period in which I strove to convince the lecturer that I was not to blame and that the thing could have gone missing in her department. I described in the most minute of detail what my assignment looked like and I waxed indignant and hurt and eventually managed to convince her I was not to blame. She relented and I was granted the equivalent of a DP ("Duly Performed") for my project. Vast relief and now my final graduation would be taking place after all.
When I was leaving Aberdeen after my student days were over and was clearing up my things for the last time in Carden Terrace, I had a very last check-up of my room for any scrap of mine that might be left behind and, for some reason, I pulled out the wardrobe and peered into the dusty space behind it. I saw a large piece of paper jammed low down towards the floor and reached for it. And, you've guessed it: the missing Geography project. Quite simply I had placed it up on top of the wardrobe at some point and it had fallen down. There it was, in all its splendour and the cartoon Monster with his green humps and coils was smiling back at me. No, I have no idea how I could have convinced myself that I had handed the thing in, but no harm was really done by the innocent deception.
I mentioned earlier that there was a degree of tension between certain elements of the graduate intake the year I was there. I can't say that it bothered me too much, but there were some of my fellow graduates who held a rather lofty attitude regarding the institution in which they now found themselves. A few years of difficult academic work lay behind them, and here was a place that taught pretty mundane subjects, and had the occasional member of staff who was not even a university graduate. It came to a head towards the very end of the session and it was the graduation ceremony that was the catalyst. A directive came from the Principal, instructing all graduands about the garments

to be worn for the occasion. Gowns could be worn and faculty hoods, but mortar boards (trenchers) were not included.
Some of the graduates claimed to be insulted by this. It was an outrage. We were entitled to wear this traditional head-gear and suspected that the ban was in place because some of the members of the College staff, who were not university graduates themselves, were not entitled to wear it. As I said, this matter really didn't bother me and I just wanted to get the whole thing over and done with quietly. It was good to be collecting another certificate rolled up tight in a cardboard tube. The one from the university was extremely impressive, written in elaborate longhand, in Latin and on expensive vellum. But the agitators were not to be placated easily and there was much negotiation between their spokesmen and the college authorities before the matter was resolved. And, to tell the truth, I have not the faintest idea as to what this resolution was except that it showed how trivial matters could be raised up to absurd heights by determined agitators.
When I had been accepted by the Director of Education for Inverness-shire as a suitable replacement for a teacher in the English Department of Inverness High School, I little thought what kind of experiences lay ahead in what was then the largest school in the Highlands with a quite enormous roll of pupils and a huge staff. The building itself had been of an inspirational design when it was opened, but its resemblance to the shape of a German pocket battleship in outline was testimony to its nineteen thirties design. It certainly was intimidating to me and I would be at least two years into the job before I actually came to accept that this would continue to be my chosen profession. There were occasions during that initial couple of years when I contemplated giving up and finding a job that did not lacerate the very soul by its demands.
I stuck it out, though.
And truth to tell, I have had few regrets.

CHAPTER 25
The Lothario, the Duffel Coat and The Cracked Library Window

Shinty Days In Aberdeen

When I boarded the train at Inverness station in September 1956 to head off to Aberdeen University for the start of the Great Adventure, I already knew that there was only one sports club that I would ever contemplate joining. That was the shinty club.
I already knew from the advance publicity the university gave to all the new students that such a club did exist.
Fort Augustus was solely shinty-orientated as far as sport was concerned when I was young. The local team, Fort Augustus, had morphed into Inveroich in the late forties by linking up with neighbouring Invergarry. I have already elsewhere told of the embarrassment visited upon me and fellow village lads when we went to play a neighbouring village at football and had it brought home to us in cringing fashion that we were totally clueless about the rules of that game. The reason for this gap in our basic knowledge was just that these were pre-television days and none of us had really seen a full game of football played – only snippets on old Movietone Newsreels.
But back to shinty. I recently unearthed a miraculously-preserved Aberdeen University Athletic Alma 1957-58. This was my second year and after my name under the official team photo of the shinty club is the word "Secretary". I did indeed bear that responsibility for that year, though all I can recollect of my term of duty is the stuffing of mimeographed begging letters into

envelopes to be posted out to the various sponsors and patrons of the club from whom we hoped to wheedle some cash. There were some rather grand names on that list, but for the life of me, I cannot remember a single one from this vast distance in time.

A small puzzle has emerged from the shinty entry in the Athletic Alma of that year. All the members of the team are listed and each has a quote after his name – obviously to encapsulate his main characteristics either as a team player, or a player on the wider stage of life. As the secretary that year, I would assume that I would have been put in charge of the task of trawling through dictionaries of quotations to seek out the most suitable and apt. But I know for certain that I did not. Indeed I have no idea as to who made the selection. Do I recognise myself in the following quote?

> *"Hunger, perhaps may cure your lust,*
> *Or Time your passion greatly alter.*
> *If both should unsuccessful prove,*
> *I strongly recommend a halter."*

Is this a true reading of the persona I projected in those days? Some heavy-lidded Lothario with a string of conquests? Despite the fact that deep down I might not have been too offended at being thought of as a bit of a jack-the-lad, the brutal reality is that I most certainly was not. Oh yes – that quote. I thought that I would try to track it down since it had a sort of ring of authenticity about it. The first two lines could almost be said to have the feel of some classic source although the final two obviously lacked the gravitas. The dictionary of quotations yielded nothing so all that was left were the infinite wastes of Google. A blank was drawn there too.

Since I was secretary that year, then the brief summary of our activities on the field of play had to have been written by me. Succinct is a euphemism for its brevity. The most important information and our crowning achievement was the winning of the Littlejohn of Invercharron Challenge Vase. This was the inter-university annual competition, which we won by beating Edinburgh 2 – 0. The only game we lost that season in this competition was away to Glasgow by 5 goals to 4. I do not record the scores of the other matches. Strange. You would have thought a little more triumphalism might have been the natural response. I was carrying the true Corinthian approach to sport a little too far I think. Our run in the Sutherland Cup was brief after having been drawn against Newtonmore the previous season's champions. We were beaten by them 2-0. We won our friendly matches at Kings, though irritatingly, no details of them are given either. At the time of the writing of the piece for the Alma, we were due to meet the other Strathspey giants, Kingussie in the Strathdearn Cup at Inverness on March 15th that year. The Alma account somewhat naively suggests that we were eventually hoping to bring back that trophy to add to the Littlejohn. Not very likely, I fear.

In the pages of the Athletic Alma, the Challenge Vase doesn't stand in the foreground of the team photo (as it did on the two other occasions I was in the winning team during my spell in Aberdeen). It was an extremely handsome trophy and not only brought its own accolade, but also there were medals for each of the winning team. I remember that I arranged for all of them to be inscribed with our names – and I still have mine. There was an occasion when I showed it to my father with a flush of pride, only to be upstaged by him when he showed me the one HE had been awarded in the same competition in the twenties when he played for Edinburgh University. His was made of silver and was nestling in plush blue velvet in a beautiful presentation box that snapped shut. Ours were bronze and in a small cardboard box. Ah well. Do they even exist nowadays? I have the original photograph of the team that was taken that year in front of me as I write this. If I hold it sideways to the light, I can just make out a small square slight indentation in the centre front of the picture. This was where we had arranged with the photographer, Strachan of Aberdeen (*A.J.B Strachan of 130 Union Street "A Graduation photograph is a life-long memento of an important and very proud occasion"*) to paste on a small photo of the actual trophy. For some reason, we were not able to get hold of the Vase that year for the photograph, so this was to be the next-best thing. That little photograph-within-the-photo remained in place for many years, but at some point it dropped off, just leaving its faint outline.

And there is another tale behind this team photograph. On the appointed day, we all turned up at the sports pavilion at King's

College and got changed into our kit. The actual photograph was to be taken at the imposing Library door.

It was a cold wintry day and some snow lay on the ground. But two of our number were nowhere to be seen and we began to get a little bit uneasy. The camera was on its tripod and the photographer was starting to fidget. Johnny Sutherland from Portree, the grand old man of the team and John Alec MacKenzie from Torgoyle, Glenmoriston were still missing. Then we became aware of raucous voices echoing around the outside of the archway into the quadrangle of King's College. Through it then swung our two missing team-mates. Clearly they were in an advanced state of swaying inebriation and their bellowing laughter shattered the hallowed precincts' normal scholarly calm. All attempts to get them into their kit failed. It was as if they were made of rubber. Eventually, we managed to get Johnny Sutherland into a pair of boots (though why we bothered is beyond me) while John Alec was eventually forced into a jersey.

Now as you read this, you are lacking one vital item: the actual photograph. My powers of description will have to suffice. In that team photograph, John Alec is being propped up between Donald "Prof" MacLeod and Iain Finlay in the back row. If you were looking at the razor-sharp quality of the original print, you would see some extra details that are evidence of further drama that occurred on that day. John Alec had grabbed a caman while we were being lined up by the photographer and was reluctant to give it up. As he was standing in the back row he didn't require one. Before he was disarmed, he swung it over his head. A loud crack rang out. He had broken the window immediately behind him, beside the University Library front door. The evidence is clearly visible on the original picture. He had to be firmly propped up by his two team mates for the shutter to click and record that small drama for posterity.

Most of our away fixtures in the south depended on rail travel – to Edinburgh and Glasgow. These trips had a special quality about them – adventure even. I will refrain from foolish braggadocio about our behaviour on some of these return journeys through the pounding soot-flecked blackness – but it was occasionally far from exemplary.

On the way south, there was the excitement of the game ahead as well as the post-match in the student unions. Unlike liberal, enlightened Aberdeen, the student unions in Glasgow and Edinburgh in those days were men only. The women had their own ones and we never saw the interiors of them. It all seemed odd to us, but it all added to the sense of the foreign-ness of these large and dark cities. Glasgow, certainly, was dark and frantic of pace. Trams were still running there and were impressive for their speed and the reckless way they hurled themselves into the tight bends in the tracks that had us lurching and swaying in the dim flickering lights inside – even more so if you were on the upper deck. They were so unlike the graceful and handsome ones that Aberdeen had only recently scrapped and burned in a foolish act of civic vandalism. We had our pies and pints in the students' unions before heading back to the station for the journey north again.

When it came to hiring buses to take us to play fixtures in Badenoch or Inverness, we had a regular firm to contact. I have no recollection now of the name, but it was cheap and rudimentary. Our regular driver was a silent, patient man. He had to be. The return journeys were punctuated by frequent requests for comfort stops as the cans of beer began to have their effect. There was one occasion when my frantic beating on the window behind the driver (drivers were isolated in their own small cabins to the right of the engine casing in those days) didn't achieve the desired result of the heavy grinding of crude brakes being applied. Clearly he had had enough and was just going to ignore me. What I could not ignore was the deadly build-up of pressure inside me. Someone suggested that I should lean out the door of the bus and just – well, you get picture. So the big chrome door handle was hauled back and the icy blast tore into the bus. Someone gripped hold of the hood of my duffel coat (standard student uniform of those days) while I leaned out into the numbing slipstream. With complete trust, I hung, buffeted by the force of the wind until I managed to signal completion and was duly hauled back into safety and the door slammed into place. The slender gossamer thread that binds us to life was never more evidenced than by those insane few minutes in that bus, bucketing along a black winter road with telegraph poles whipping past my head. I can still get nightmares over it.

A glance at the photograph I have been describing will reveal another feature – the fact that no fewer than four of those posing for it are wearing spectacles. The clichéd student image, you might say. Actually, there were two other members of that team who required specs. One of them was Iain Matheson MacLean from Dunvegan on the Isle of Skye. He didn't wear his glasses on the field because he used contact lenses. Now you have to remember that we are back in the mid to late fifties here, and the technology of these things was still pretty crude. I can remember the first appalling glimpse I had of Iain inserting his lenses. We were on a train speeding south for a fixture and I was sitting opposite him in the compartment. I saw him leaning forward and pulling back his eyelids while holding a shallow transparent concave thing on the tip of a finger. He slowly placed it on his eye and then allowed the lids to slide back into place. He was clearly in great discomfort (as I was with near-nausea at what I had just witnessed) and it was some time before his eyes had stopped watering and he had returned to normal. I had seen the insertion of nineteen fifties contact lenses. It was a seriously unpleasant sight. And the other member of the team who needed specs? Well – I was that man. I had been wearing them since my first year in secondary school and by the time I was at university I really needed them. I was short sighted and it was only the fear of getting them broken by a caman that had me leave them in the dressing room. This had the very obvious disadvantage of reducing my effectiveness on the field of play. It wasn't too bad a problem if the weather was clear and bright, but if the match was taking place on a dull, grey afternoon drifting towards the encroaching evening, it could be little short of disastrous.

One such occasion was a match we played at Newtonmore. Light conditions were bad enough at the start, but as the game progressed, it became more and more farcical. I played left wing forward in those days and would look up the field and try to guess the drift of the play – attempting to anticipate where an incoming ball might strike earth, by the flow and drift of the two sets of players. I have to say that I had become quite adept at this skill, but I was always that nanosecond too late to be able to play anything more than a decorative role in the actual action. A spectacle of ferociously energetic running, but little else. It did, however, go badly wrong sometimes. On that day, two events stand out. My judgement had anticipated the incoming projectile heading towards my right, just a little ahead of me. I set off at full power on my lonely trajectory towards an empty sector of the field, while the actual play was taking place far away in the opposite direction. My embarrassment was compounded by the advice from the Newtonmore spectator who called out, "The toilet's behind the garage, that way ...!" God! The embarrassment. Nothing could hide the fact that this Aberdeen forward was as good as blind in the dim light. One last detail on this matter, which compounded my problem, is that shinty balls in those days were jet black. They didn't become white till many years later. The conclusion to this inauspicious day was that a tussle with one of the Newtonmore full-backs had me stop a ferocious blow across an ankle and saw me carried off the field. My trip back to Aberdeen in the freezing bus ended in Woolmanhill hospital X-ray department. There was a slightly chipped bone, but no treatment was deemed necessary. It was to be my only real battle scar from four unremarkable years as a member of the Aberdeen University Shinty team.

The insecure position of shinty in the gallery of Scottish sports is evident in the reference to the membership of the club. The report in the Alma says: "Our club membership, now at 18, is low and we hope to see some new faces next season."

Membership indeed was always on the low side and perhaps the fact that I held my place in the team for four years when I was, at best, a workmanlike player is indication of that.

One of the "new faces" that joined us the following year was that of my younger brother, Gregor, who began his Engineering studies, which were to lead to him becoming a civil engineer. He was, I have to confess, the talented shinty player in the family and not only went on to be selected for the University's team but also played for many years for Glasgow Kelvin after qualification. He also was awarded a full Blue.

On a visit to the Kirkgate Bar in Broad Street, Aberdeen, in February 2005, to retrace steps taken so many years ago when I was a student, I was astounded to see not one, but two official photographs of the nineteen fifties University Shinty Club hanging on the wall – and both of them had me in them. It had been customary for the various sports clubs to have their photos hung there in the days when that pub was a very popular student haunt. It no longer is, of course. Changing social habits have seen today's students abandon the nearby Students' Union in its handsome building at the top of Broad Street, opposite the imposing granite spires of Marischal College. In my day, life as a student without the comforts and subsidised facilities of the Union would have been well-nigh unliveable and unthinkable. It was indeed a home from home. What supplies these essentials for the students of today, I wonder?

I have to confess that I gave up playing shinty shortly after I had left teachers' training college in 1960. I did assuage my conscience, however, by serving a stint of several hectic years as a shinty correspondent with the "Scotsman" and "Scotland on Sunday" in the late nineties.

CHAPTER 26
The Great Norfolk Adventure

The Great Norfolk Adventure began towards the end of my second year at University. I had assumed as the break approached, that my summer money would be earned through a job at one of the Hydro schemes or with that reliable default employer, the Forestry Commission. Then someone drew my attention to a notice in the Students' Union to the effect that fruit canning factories in England were to be paying very acceptable rates for jobs for students. They were either for picking fruit or for working in canning factories. A discussion among some of us came to the conclusion that it could be a useful money-spinner and it could also be a bit of an adventure as well. Along with Roddy Whyte from Inverness and Alistair MacLean from Aberdeen we looked into the details. Applications were filled in and dispatched and soon the details of where we were to report and when – as well as what basic requirements we had to bring along with us – were received. Accommodation was to be provided by the company, Duncan's Fine Food Products (a well-known brand in those days) in what was termed a "hostel", and catering was to be provided for a reasonable fee, by the factory canteen. The accompanying pictures showed an almost idyllic scene of rural bliss and the impression was given that we were in for what would be a summer holiday in Norfolk with some factory work thrown in. How easily is our gullible species taken in by such blandishments.

My parents were somewhat concerned. Travel on such a scale was not so commonplace in those days and East Anglia was a vast distance from Fort Augustus and would require complicated train timetables to unravel. But the spirit of adventurous youth was not to be gainsaid, and at a prearranged date the three of us met at the station in Aberdeen and set off into the seriously scary unknown. By this time, we had found out that we were not to be the three only representatives from Aberdeen University: quite a sizeable number of others had signed up for the Duncan's Shilling as well. In fact when we had settled in in North Walsham (the Norfolk town where the large Duncan's canning factory was situated) the Aberdeen contingent was the largest. But back to more of the early details first. The complexity of the pre-Beeching railway system had us change on to several other branch-line trains after we had left the main south line and memory is chiefly of puffing laboriously through dark leafy countrysides in muggy, moist temperatures. We eventually found our way from North Walsham station where we had alighted, to the "hostel" that we were now aching to get to. Exhaustion and the sheer uncertainty of our new situation had us very much on edge and hoping to find somewhere we could gather our faculties and take stock. After all, there was still the huge uncertainty of the factory itself. What shocks and problems would it throw at us? But there would be the comfort of our accommodation to cushion us from all of that. We had been provided with a sort of map to help us to find our hostel and we followed it through the streets until we found ourselves standing in front of what appeared to be the brick extension of an abandoned factory. It had grubby windows and looked totally derelict. We spoke to a figure who materialised at a small door and asked if he could tell us where the factory hostel for the students was. And it was here that one of the biggest problems we were to encounter in Norfolk first raised its head. The man we spoke to looked completely baffled and it was obvious he could not understand a word we were saying. And the corollary of all this was that what issued from his mouth was almost as unintelligible to us. There was a huge language barrier between North Walsham and the north of Scotland that was to be a source of mirth and frustration for the couple of months or so that we were to be in that part of the world. But by application of some patience, we did begin to get the drift of the strange almost sing-song swooping of the Norfolk accent. And the news it imparted to us was far from pleasant. The shabby crumbling brick building that we were standing in front of was the hostel that was to accommodate us. Had we been nearer home, we would have turned around immediately and headed back. But we felt that we were a continent away from our own familiar land and accents and had no choice but to make the best of it all. We were shown into the dingy building and found it was even less pleasant inside. The only furnishings were rows of basic metal bedsteads that had khaki-coloured blankets on them. They were on two floors and would clearly accommodate a fair number. It was also clear that there would be absolutely no privacy. The only advantage in being the first there was that we could have first choice of beds. I chose one on the first floor up and right next to the stair – or rather ladder – so that there would be least problem should an emergency necessitate a rapid evacuation and also provide some protection from the possible thieving intruder at night. Our ablutions and other facilities were some distance towards the back of the building. There were toilets and crude showers. And that was it. It really was a profound shock to us and we were dispirited by the deception that lay behind it all. Perhaps the working conditions in the factory would be just as bad. We met in a small downstairs room that we had decided would be the main office for the student contingent and where our representative (after he had been selected) would have his base from which to work. And it looked as if he was going to have a lot of hard work ahead of him. There was no problem with the choice of Student Representative as another early arrival from Aberdeen had been Neil MacLeod. He was a prominent member of the student body and noted for his fiery political speeches in the debating chamber at Marischal College. He was just the sort to see to it that the management of this company were held to task for luring us such vast distances on such a deceptive prospectus. His skills as a pugilistic tribune of the people (us) were to be called into operation on several occasions – though he did not always prevail against one fearsome adversary on the factory floor.

But before that theme is developed, a word about the exact nature of the employment that Duncan's Fine Foods had lined up for us. The factory in North Walsham was the main employer and had a large workforce – hugely swollen by the numbers of students who flocked there over the summer months. Seasonal work, for obvious reasons, and one of the most delicate and skilled operations was the canning of peas, which were farmed over a large area of that part of East Anglia. The harvesting of these was all done by machinery and truck-loads of them, still in their pods and attached to their stalks, were delivered to the back of the factory. We were told that the choosing of the precise moment that the peas were to be harvested (you can't say "picked" because whole rows of them were scythed just above ground level) was a stop-watch operation. There was a precise moment when they were the correct texture for the cooking and canning process and this was where the skill came in: specialist members of the staff from the factory were on hand to give the signal for the crop to be gathered. Anyway, the crop was loaded into the hoppers and was then churned around till the peas came tumbling out of their pods. Then it was into the vast cooking vats and afterwards to the cans where they were sealed in hermetically. Now it was time for the cans to get their distinct "Duncan's Fresh Garden Peas" labels slapped on them and that was where I came in. I have mentioned that being among the early arrivals meant that our Aberdeen group managed to get some of the most desirable jobs, and that was why it was that someone pointed at me and told me to report at the labelling machine. Yes, I was to be a machine operator. No boring details, but the briefest of sketches as to what this entailed. It was a hefty-looking Heath-Robinsonish device which was set at the end of a vast and seemingly endless conveyor that ribboned across the upper reaches of the factory roof-space, carrying a shining stream of clattering cans of peas that finally swooped down and into the maw of my machine that saw to each one having its label glued in place. My task was to see that the pot of hot glue at my left hand side was kept full and that the packet of labels was slotted exactly in place so that each can, as it rolled in front of me, picked up its two spots of glue which in turn lifted the label which now became attached and by just continuing its rolling, affixed said label completely round the can. This was all happening at some speed and it does not require too much imagination to see that quite a lot could go wrong here. And in the early stages, it certainly did. If there was a hold-up at the labelling machine, the cans would stop and a break in the production line might occur. But that did not mean that they stopped their progress high above the busy factory floor. A clattering chilling cacophony of metallic protest then began which, if I didn't manage to get the fault sorted, would cause a hooter to sound and the whole production line to my machine would have to be halted. Mine was not the only labelling machine, of course, but any such hold-up meant the rapid appearance of the Ogre – the Foreman. A truly terrifying creature and more frightening than any human being I had yet come in contact with up till that point in my life. I have no memory of his name, but it could have been something monosyllabic and innocuous like "Alf". He was fairly bulky and wore a shabby grey overall. He leaned slightly forward when walking and had a large, lumpy head, sparse hair and what can only be termed knobbly, brutish features. He had a deep dislike of all of the student intake. One of his favourite aphorisms summed it up for anyone who came within earshot of it. I just cannot reproduce it here in all its blistering venom and crudity, but you can, if you like, fill in the blanks: "F*****g students! Oi **** 'em". It was spat out into the clamour of the factory floor on each occasion that one of us failed to live up to his standards. Often it was the accent of North Walsham that could be the root of the problem. I remember finding one of the African students wandering around with some piece of waste material. He was looking fearful and asked me if I could help. He was on a last warning from Alf the ogre. He had been told to put the item in the "pile" and he was looking for just that. I suggested that it might be a "pail" that he should be looking for, as I could see one against a nearby wall. Problem solved. I had been there a few days longer than the innocent newcomer and had that little bit of extra experience with the local demotic.

It was while working at that labelling machine in North Walsham in the late nineteen fifties, that my education in matters pertaining to the basic realities of life and our species – in particular, the true nature of the female of our species – was expanded exponentially. Up till then, my experience had been with my contemporaries and the females of my parents and grandparents' generations. With my contemporaries, it was the cautious testing of the waters that typified the buttoned-up fifties and with the older generations all was of the most severely formal. Here, while at my bulky machine with the constant stream of shiny metal cans clattering past me, a whole new dimension to the female psyche unfolded itself before my startled and sometimes aghast eyes. Down to my right, was a bench with rollers on to which the freshly-labelled cans would march. They were lifted from the roller bench and deftly packed into cardboard boxes by teams of women, half of the team on the one side of the roller bench and the others opposite. I cannot remember how many there were in the team, but it could have been eight. From the word go, when I first sat in my place, in a highly nervous state, waiting for the river of metal to sweep from the high regions of the factory, it was clear that I was to become the butt of humour as far as the team of female packers was concerned. Their ages ranged from the sonsiness of middle-age to the lissomness of youth. All seemed to find the presence of a lone youthful male with an odd accent from a faraway land and with a nervous disposition to be the catalyst for a surge of innuendo and downright lewdness to be directed at me. It was initially quite frightening but I have to admit that it became quite entertaining after I had got used to it and they got the message that I was not going to stalk away in outrage. Most of the cruder details of the gossip about the factory and the personnel came to me in torrents and it helped me to adapt to this strange and unsettling environment. They could be ruthless as well when they found a victim. The following will illustrate. One of the packing team members was rather stunning-looking and knew it. A student from among the contingent from an English university very quickly made it plain that he had eyes for her. He was a tall, floppy-fair-haired sort of Rupert Brookish type and he was soon seen in the company of the busty packer from my team. The poor fellow was soon to regret it. The following day, I saw that the busty one had gathered the rest of the packing team around her and was regaling them with energetic anecdotes that were bringing huge waves of coarse laughter. There is a special quality about human laughter that denotes heavily sexual content in its source. And that was what was behind all this ribaldry. All the details of that date she had with the unfortunate golden-haired one were being shared with her eager fellow- packers – and I mean, every detail. When he happened to drift past our part of the factory, a chorus of mocking jeers flowed over him and his discomfiture was painfully obvious to all of us. It was not a very edifying sight.

CHAPTER 27
A Picnic in the Park

Since I was a second year student in Aberdeen University at this time in the Norfolk Adventure, I probably felt that I had had quite a bit of experience of life, what with the intrigue of the activities at the student dances and other gatherings, large and small, and had assumed that this sort of thing would just continue in its haphazard way while we were in this really strange community so far down in alien England. I am referring to the opposite sex, of course. What we had not expected was the response that we found among the local girls. We were really quite strange to them and apparently the first lot that had come down from Aberdeen University. It was our accents that had us stand out and provide that little bit of mystery and we were not slow to take advantage. It was quite amazing to find that there was not too much problem in making satisfying contacts. Back home on my own turf, it was not all that straightforward, but here – well, it was quite startlingly different. A local meeting place for youth, this being the fifties, was the coffee bar. North Walsham had one and it was called simply "Brian's Coffee Bar". Nothing flash about the name and inside it was pretty basic with the main features being the juke box with its shimmering lights along with the garish chromium dazzle of the Espresso coffee machine. We were well into the age of Elvis at this time, but for some odd reason the tune that sticks in my memory and is forever associated with that place, is "The Whistling Gypsy". Brian, the owner of the establishment, was a youthful sort of laid-back presence and the atmosphere was friendly enough for the café to become one of our natural meeting places. And it was where the local girls congregated also. More about that later. Meanwhile, I had become affected by the atmosphere in this strange new environment enough to make a few changes in my rather staid appearance. I was more or less a "tweed sports jacket and flannels" sort of bloke at this time, but one day I was drawn to the window of a department store with the latest line in jeans on display. I fancied a pair of black narrow ones with green stitching on the seams and overcoming all my natural reservations, I strode in and bought them instantly and decisively. My next fashion epiphany involved a pair of pointed black shoes which in my mind transformed me, along with the jeans, into the fifties equivalent of "cool". Certainly my next visit to Brian's Café seemed to show I had made a smart sartorial move. Two girls in particular stood out. One was small and dark-haired and worked in the local Boots, while the other, Brenda, worked in a small corner shop. I made a date with Brenda to meet in a local pub. Things were really moving.

But first, a word about the pubs in this part of England. They were truly odd places to us from the north of Scotland and used to the crude amenities that were deemed suitable for us by hotels and landlords and publicans. Our habits had already been drummed into us in that a night out consisted of nips of whisky with chasers of beer. And that was the order. The whisky was hurled back (usually neat) and before the tears blinded the eyes in reaction to the scouring of the delicate throat tissues by the spirit, the beer was sluiced down (it "chased" after the whisky) with heavy gulps and gasps and the stage was being set for fairly swift inebriation. In the North Walsham pub that we decided was to be our regular drinking place, it took a little time to get a routine under way. The pattern of the nip and pint was totally alien here, mainly due to the fact that instead of a gantry with a vast selection whiskies – blended and malt – this one had one solitary bottle so that the barman had to get a ladder in order to take it down and dust it. The beer was so different from the Export that we tended to go for on our home patch. It was flat and dull and one brand carried the strange name of "Starlight Special".

Now back to Brenda. The first date of our brief relationship was pretty unremarkable. While I threw back my usual pairing of whisky and chaser, she opted for the fashionable women's drink of those days: Babycham. Several of these and we drifted into the warm evening till we eventually ended up at her house back door. A further date was made for the following day. I had the whole day off from my labelling machine, and I had a notion to explore the enticing looking local park with its well-tended meadows and shady woods. Much potential there.

Little did I guess the weird events that were to unfold.

Brenda appeared in her billowing, frothy fifties dress, with her spiky high heels. She looked mightily attractive and I felt a sort of surging rush that fortune had selected me on this occasion for some really special treatment. We drifted through the hazy summer afternoon and I guided Brenda towards a more remote area of the park where the grass was longer and we could be safe from the eyes of the prurient passer-by. This was just too good to be true. She gave every sign that she was more than happy with my company and the runes all were saying that this was IT! We had just settled down into the tall, lush grass, (magically free of that abomination of the Highlands: the vile midgie) when Brenda suddenly sat up and looked into the distance, towards some houses beyond the park boundaries.

"Ooh look. It's me mum. She's heading this way!"

The sky turned red.

The veil in the temple was rent in twain.

No force in nature is more deadly, more terrifying, than that of the mother who sees her progeny in danger from the predator. And no mother could have harboured the tiniest smidgen of doubt about what my plans were for that long-ago East Anglian afternoon. They were certainly not honourable. I was scrabbling to heave myself upright in preparation for a desperate sprint towards the distant horizon, when I heard Brenda's completely angst-free voice cheerfully announce:

"Ooh look. She's got a basket. Oi think she's brough' us a picnic."

A picnic! What in God's name?

Through the summer drowse of that Norfolk afternoon hove the mother of my companion. She was all that a caring mother ought to be in terms of appearance and deportment, and hanging from her arm was a basket with a blue and white checked cloth draped over it.

She was comfortably bulky and was puffing slightly as she reached us. I was still staring in disbelief. Perhaps it was some kind of trap. After all, I was in a very foreign country and the arcana of the mating rituals were unknown to me. But no. Brenda's large mum in her mum's kitchen overall, knelt down and placed the picnic basket on the grass in front of us.

"Oi just thought the two of you would loik something noice. It's a lovely day for a picnic." Then with a cheerful, "Ta ta. See you back for tea," (addressed to Brenda) she was surging back towards the distant houses.

Well, that was truly the end of the plans I had for that afternoon. There was no way the pounding anticipation I had been experiencing could survive anything like this. It was total and utter collapse.

The surreal picnic was duly disposed of and the things were packed away neatly in the basket once more. It was beginning to occur to me that Brenda's Mum was not so weird after all. She was perhaps instead crafty. She knew that the best way to protect her daughter was to throw something completely irrational into the situation that had developed with this odd stranger who had lured her away into that secluded corner of the park. Whatever it was, it put paid to all my lustings. We parted not too long after at her back door with an arrangement to meet again at Brian's Café. But this relationship was to founder on another rock, that was just about to rear from the dark waters of the Irish Sea. A party of students from Dublin suddenly landed among us. A few of them were devastatingly handsome, and that, together with their accents, had them stand out – just as we had done not so long before. Brenda was swept away by one of them, as was her small friend with the short dark hair. It happens that I later became friendly with some of the Irish contingent and a marvellously lively and talented lot they turned out to be. Witty conversationalists and one of them was a brilliant trumpet player. Very many years later, I was certain I recognised one of them in a photograph in a newspaper of a group of Irish politicians, but I had not noted their names properly when we parted, and never had any way of checking up. Anyway, there are an awful lot of Brendans and Dermots in Ireland.

Their distinctive approach to life could catch you unawares. One occasion saw a group of us heading back to North Walsham one evening when it was getting dark. The lights of the town were visible ahead, but there was still some distance to go.

"Let's cross this field. That'll get us back quicker," said one of the Irish group.

We all scrambled over a fence and found ourselves, not in a field, but on what was more like an extensive lawn, with high hedges running along it. A large very English-looking house, with mullioned, lighted windows looked frowningly down at us.

"I say", brayed a voice with the unmistakable "accents of the ascendancy".

And striding towards us through the summer evening gloom was the archetypical Colonel Blimp. He was a vision in tweed with white hair and bulging white moustache. His features were puce and his dog by his side looked poised and ready to do its master's bidding.

"What are you hooligans doing on my land? Get off. This instant."

I was already beginning to retrace my steps to the recently clambered-over fence when I saw that the group of Irish were not for moving. It must have been the imperiousness of the barking voice that stirred memories of the oppression that the Irish had suffered over the centuries from people like this that had them boil over. Suffice to say that the sultry evening atmosphere was shattered by the reposts that were directed back at the raging landowner. When the noise died away and we had melted into the night – luckily before Colonel Blimp had had time to telephone the police – I was mightily relieved to get back into the hostel again. The Irish were great company, but were inclined to volatility on occasion.

A few final images from Duncan's Fine Foods factory. First, the name "Norfolk Gold". The provenance of this fine-sounding term was as follows. Duncan's canning factory, along with its own named brands, also canned various lines in fruit and vegetables for other well-known food companies. One of the most lucrative was for Marks and Spencer. All the stops were pulled out for such an order and special care was taken at every part of the process in the factory. Even the labels on the cans had to be one hundred percent accurate in their alignment. Without warning, a team of inspectors from Marks and Spencer would appear on the factory floor, accompanied by a nervous and highly solicitous member of the senior staff. They would go to one of the huge vats where the peas or baked beans were at the final stage of the canning process and lift several cans out with nets. Then these randomly selected ones would be taken to a private laboratory that was installed in the premises and the contents were subjected to a rigorous inspection. Only if the contents were up to the standards of M&S would the consignment be allowed to leave the factory with the M&S label affixed. I well remember the day when the white-coated, silent inspectors had looked at each other after checking the baked beans and had shaken their heads. Within minutes the whole production line was stopped. All the cans in that batch were recalled. If they had been packed into their cardboard boxes, they were removed and all of them were handed on to a squad of workers who set about tearing off all the labels. Then they came tumbling back down towards my, and the other, labelling machines, to have another identity glued on to them. This identity was contained in the neat packets I unwrapped and slotted into the label tray. They were bright orange and red with a garish image of shiny beans swimming contentedly in a wholesome matrix of tomato sauce. And written over this appetising image was the new name: "Norfolk Gold Baked Beans". Only we who worked in the factory were aware of the subterfuge at work here. "Norfolk Gold" were beans that had been rejected by M&S.

Another piece of arcane knowledge brought back from those factory days was that of the contents of large catering tins of strawberry jam that were used then for cafes and restaurants. It could bring back memories of one of the least pleasant jobs we were asked to do. To be told that you were to join a squad for "pulping" was like being condemned to a chain gang. Occasionally, during that summer of 1958 there were spells when the flow of produce to the factory ceased due to bad weather. This was when things like jam could be prepared and canned from huge reserves of pulped fruit that was packed into barrels and stacked in warehouses. So, what was this pulp? A pulping squad would be taken to a conveyer belt where fruit that was not of the best quality was passing before you. Most of the strawberries were partly rotten, so that you had to pick out each of these glutinous berries and throw away the rotten part. The remains were then tossed into barrels. When these barrels were full, some chemical was pumped in and the lids were sealed. This was the last of this ghastly mess that the pulpers were to see – unless they were around when the barrels were unsealed some time in the future. By this time, the contents were deathly white in colour and had a sulphurous odour. You could just make out the shape and consistency of the original strawberries, but that was all. In order to make this dreadful looking mess into something resembling jam, colour had to be added as had flavour and the end product was sealed into the large catering tins I have referred to and no doubt had a bright and wholesome-looking label from the same school of product presentation that had come up with Norfolk Gold for the baked beans. All of this was a life-time ago and more, of course, so I can only wonder if anything like this is done any more.

In spite of these two examples, I did not come away from Duncan's canning factory when my summer job was over with a life-long aversion to canned foodstuffs. My overall impression was of huge efforts to make certain that what the customer eventually emptied into a pan or on to a plate was as safe and wholesome as you would wish.

For some reason that escapes me now, my memories of the rail journey home are of me travelling on my own. My immediate future lay deep in the books I had to study with the frenzy necessary to pass the re-sits that lay about a month ahead. It wasn't till my final year that I learned to pass the required examinations first time around. I was indeed a slow learner.

By sheer co-incidence, I was able to re-visit North Walsham about fifteen years after the end of that working holiday in the canning factory. We had been staying in an exchange house near Norfolk one blistering hot summer in the early seventies. I suggested one day that we point our hired Dormobile in the direction of North Walsham and soon we found ourselves there. My overwhelming memory of this is how astonished I was to find out how much distortion had occurred in my memory over even that fairly short interlude. Few of the places I remembered could I find, except for the dismal "hostel" where we slept. Yes, I found it all right, and it was virtually unchanged since we first stared at it in disbelief. It was totally abandoned by now and not even by peering in through the cobwebbed windows could I discern any relic of the large number of students who had once stayed there. The canning factory was still there close to the railway station, but under a different name. It was almost as if that intense few packed weeks of my life had been some kind of waking dream.

In a spirit of curiosity, I decided to contact North Walsham recently to ask about the canning industry and did it still have an outpost in that community? The reply from the town's tourist organisation was to the effect that they had no record of a

Duncan's Cannery, but that the old HP Smedley's canning factory had been demolished as recently as April 2010. Then they dug a little deeper and found that the original Duncan's Canning factory had been bought up by HP Smedley's not long after my sojourn there in the late fifties. Also enclosed was a series of photographs of the demolition of the old canning factory. They meant absolutely nothing to me and stirred not the tiniest memory. It was just another ragged-looking series of crumbling brick walls being swept away to be replaced by something else. So odd to think that the very name "Duncan's" (that I can still remember seeing on cans of peas in shops when I was young) has been forgotten in that part of East Anglia today.

CHAPTER 28

The High School Folk Group

My first teaching job after leaving Teacher Training College in Aberdeen in 1960, was in Inverness High School. The selection and appointment of the newly-qualified students in the early sixties was quite extraordinary when looked at from this distance in time. In those days, the various of the many Scottish education authorities sent their senior educational figures – the lordly Directors of Education, no less – to select and sign on the young, brand-new teachers. I can remember a corridor in the College with doors with the names of the various authorities pinned up and we walked along its length, selecting the one that we fancied. I had had a brief flirtation with moving somewhere farther afield than the Highlands, to be a bit adventurous, but I just could not pass the door with "Inverness-shire" on it. Inside sat the impressive figure of the then Director, Dr MacLean and an assistant. He looked up and addressed me in the "accents of the ascendency" that he employed and immediately I began to feel a little uneasy. He clearly had some sort of dossier on the desk in front of him that he consulted. Then he would look up at me and return to the dossier. Next a brief *sotto voce* consultation with his assistant and another glance up at me. I had been running through some of the unfortunate episodes during my year in the College: events that had occurred during my classroom teaching experiences that might have thrown doubt on my suitability for the noble profession. Two in particular flashed before my eyes that might possibly have been reported back to the College authorities. The details are too complex to enlarge upon here, but will be returned to on elsewhere in this book – in another chapter, in fact. My uncomfortable interview concluded with me being offered a job as an assistant in the English Department of Inverness High School.

The sheer scale of this school was quite overwhelming to me as were the problems of gigantic classes and the matter of keeping even minimal discipline.

Naturally, I gravitated to fellow youthful members of the staff for moral support out of the classroom and it was this that led directly to the emergence of the High School Folk Singers. These early sixties days saw the explosion of folk music on to the airwaves inspired by, among others, figures such as Hamish Henderson as, mainly Irish, American and home grown Scottish groups became immensely popular. The Irish Clancy Brothers brought a brand of testosterone-driven, fishermen's jersey garbed interpretation of Irish rebel songs on to our television screens and turntables of our record players. The songs were catchy and brilliantly performed by these likeable troubadours. It was now that I bought my first – and only – guitar. A handsome instrument, Hofner by name, and equipped with nylon strings. It proved to be the key to my entry to a mild form of showbiz as well as a constant reminder of my severe limitations musically.

The Folk Group that came together originally consisted of myself, Madeleine MacGillivray, Elsa Stephenson, Irene Brown, Alan Brownlie and John MacDonald. Madeleine, Elsa and Alan were Art teachers; Irene and I taught English and John was head of Geography. All were very talented vocally and some also instrumentally. I was a reasonably workmanlike accompanist on my handsome new guitar and Alan Brownlie was brisk and lively on the tin whistle. The male members of the group mainly threw their energy into Irish songs taken from Clancy Brothers records as well as traditional Scottish material. The female members leaned towards the more Joan Baez melancholy ballads as well as Scottish ballads - sometimes accompanied, sometimes not. All had voices perfectly suited to this medium. Now to my contribution. I did - indeed have – an ordinary sort of voice: I can keep a tune in my head and reproduce it accurately, but there is absolutely nothing in its timbre or resonance to hold an audience rapt. The member of the group who gave me a sense of really contributing something was John MacDonald. He comes from the North East and was steeped in the Bothy Ballad culture. He also had a superb instinctive gift of being able to harmonise to any tune. How I used to revel in the experience when we were giving laldy to "A Man's A Man for a' That". Then and to this day I have been convinced that both in noble sentiment and in sheer musical power, it stands out head and shoulders as the only contender for Scotland's national anthem. Its chances of ever being so are, alas, depressingly slight. Such is the nature of my perverse little native land.

I think I can say that we were pretty good. We practised regularly in each other's homes and it became the pattern of life. No-one was really in charge – all could suggest new songs and we sort of gravitated towards the ones that we liked. Elsa and Irene performed together; Madeleine went solo and the three males did their routines mainly together. I have no idea as to when we first went out into the community to perform in local halls and clubs. It just sort of happened. One of our other attractions for people who were running some concert to get funds was that we didn't charge a fee for our performances. All we looked for was a reasonable supply of drinks and maybe something to eat afterwards.

Then came the day when we were first invited to perform outside the town. We found ourselves giving full concerts in Beauly, in Nairn and in Forres. I think it was in the latter that I found myself introducing an item to a very large crowd and looking up towards a packed gallery and calling out, "Can you all hear us up there?" Heady stuff.

The most memorable of these concerts we gave – as the whole act for the evening's entertainment – were in the already-mentioned Forres Town Hall, the Victoria Hotel – again in Forres – and on the exciting occasion when we piled into cars and headed into the wilds (for us) to entertain the people in Tomintoul. And why Tomintoul? My younger brother, Gregor, was a civil engineer with the Glasgow-based company who had the contract to build a distillery there. He was staying in the main hotel that dominated the square in the centre of the village and would tell me of the lively (very) social life of that remote community. He had told his host and hostess, the hotel proprietors, about the High School group and it was suggested that he invite us up to stay overnight in the quiet close season (before the winter snows closed in). To us, a huge adventure and we agreed immediately. Free board and lodging (and drinks too) and all we had to do was deliver our by-now well rehearsed programme. I have to confess here that memories of that evening are very vague, but it was generally agreed afterwards that it had been a resounding success. My brother's standing in the small, but very energetic, community was done no harm whatsoever.

Things began to change for me and my involvement with the group rather gradually. I simply liked the fun and the thrill of performing to audiences who clearly enjoyed what we were doing. It was entertainment pure and simple. But there was another aspect to the Folk scene in those days that was much more cerebral. The study of the origins of folk songs and their roots assumed greater importance, but I didn't get into that. Additions to our group brought that more serious element into the almost innocent, nicking-tunes-off-records position I had been taking. The more intense approach just didn't work for me. Those were the days immediately before the hugely successful annual Inverness Folk Festival, which was to run for many years, but its early stirrings were discernable and I was being left behind. Others of the group would progress and become highly successful; I eventually dropped out without the slightest rancour. It was just another form of natural selection, I suppose.

Two episodes really drew my involvement to a close. The first was a fairly minor one. It took place in the Victoria Hotel in Forres when we giving a concert there. Two French assistant teachers then training in the school had asked if they could join us. They were young and attractive and brightly talented. They wanted to sing two or three songs from their own land and that was no problem with us. A touch of the sophisticated and exotic in the midst of our normal fare. They had asked me to provide a simple accompaniment and we had had a brief bit of practice. I was already feeling a little uneasy as the tunes were alien to me: very fast with very different emphases and switches of rhythm. The evening arrived and then it was their turn to perform. As was arranged, I stood sort of down from them, just in front, at the edge of the stage – actually a little bit too prominently, I was beginning to think. I had really wanted to blend in with the background as I was in extremely unfamiliar territory. Now I was exposed, with my new, shiny and impressive-looking guitar slung in front of me. Here I have to re-emphasise the mechanical nature of my musical abilities. I had my series of chords and my set number of plucking combinations and routines and that was that. Absolutely no flexibility or shifting of key or adaptations of the sort that real musicians would be able to do without even thinking. It was vital to me that these completely unknowns in our group should behave rationally. They just had to take the lead from me. Life and sanity depended upon it.

I ran my little introductory riff and strummed the chords to lead them in. They were not looking at me. That was the first warning. It was also the last musical contact I was to have with them for the next interminable stretch of agonising time. They scampered away like light-footed gazelles on the Serengeti while I lumbered heavily far behind. I tried to find the key they had randomly selected for themselves. Useless. You have to believe that it is not possible to mime a guitar – especially when the front row of the audience is only a few feet away. I was aware that some of those closest to me had their eyes fixed on my fingers in order to watch what they seemed to imagine would be the technique of a master of the instrument. I made a few tentative plucks, but could not blend in with the musical trail they had chosen to follow. And the bright-animated sounds of French peasant longings for shepherd lovers continued and went on and on as I felt more superfluous and foolish. I have no idea as to whether I remonstrated with them for having abandoned me, after the loud appreciative applause had faded away. It really doesn't matter, as it was not long after that that I was to give my final performance with the High School Folk Singers.

At least I was to go out in a blaze of glory though.

In my last book, I spoke about my Uncle Dave, the proprietor of the general stores at Laggan Bridge, six or so miles west of Newtonmore on the road to Spean Bridge. I had spent two of my most enjoyable working holidays driving his grocery van round the many routes he covered in that part of the world. Uncle Dave was an elder in the kirk and during one visit he mentioned that some church fund or other was getting low. Would I like to organise the High School Folk Singers to come to Laggan one weekend sometime soon and give a concert in the local hall? All proceeds to go to the church fund, and accommodation and all appropriate forms of sustenance would be laid on for us? Absolutely no problem. Our group was by now a pretty polished outfit and completely confident of delivering money's worth to an audience. In addition to our usual members, we had by now attracted a number of highly talented students who were going to make their way to Laggan Bridge from either Edinburgh or Glasgow in time for the concert too. But dark forces were gathering that were to cause disruption to our plans. A tidal wave of influenza was sweeping the land and our northern mountains and glens were being affected by it as well. Some of our group were smitten and on the Friday we were to have been heading off down the A9 after school had closed at 4 o'clock, I was told that John MacDonald had succumbed as well. It was too late to call the date off, as there was a skeleton crew still available. It was made less catastrophic by the promise of the talented students who were to be heading north. From being an extra item in the programme, they now were an absolute necessity. I telephoned to Laggan Bridge and said that we were still coming and would do our best, but asked if there was any chance of having someone to hand who could play the piano or the accordion in case there might need to be a dance to fill in any blank spots. Of that last concert (for me) I have little recollection. I was totally taken up with the fact that I had never sung on my own before. My regular partner's strong harmonising was essential for my self-confidence.

Then there was another spectre rearing up in the background. Our flu-depleted group kept staring at the door of the hall for a sight of the trio of students who were to be helping us out. Especially Donald Davidson with his extensive repertoire and sparkling guitar playing. Meanwhile, the crowds were filing into the small hall and it soon filled. The chink of money at the door clearly pleased Uncle Dave, but I was still agonising over the implications of our depleted numbers and reduced programme. Uncle Dave was now calling the crowd to order and he welcomed the Inverness High School Folk Group. Kind things were said about us and our generosity in coming all that way to perform for the folk of Laggan, especially since some had not been able to make it due to the flu – but in spite of that, give them a big, big hand. Oh, and they are waiting for a contingent from the south who haven't arrived yet. Actually, we had heard by this time that the students had set off to try to get lifts to Laggan Bridge! Ye gods; this was hardly re-assuring. A lift from Glasgow up the A9 as far as Newtonmore would not be all that impossible, but to more remote Laggan. What chance that?

The Singers now took to the stage and we began our programme. Things seemed to be going well enough, but still no sign of our reinforcements. Maybe they hadn't even left Glasgow? Now, it was my turn. I introduced my first song and probably – and stupidly – announced that I was 'flying solo' and would they go easy on me. Bad idea. Now it was my last song: my favourite. The one that usually got some of the audience joining in towards the final chorus of Burns's magnificent hymn to world peace in "A Man's a Man for 'a That". I hurled myself at it and threshed my guitar, to make up for my missing partner's contribution, but nothing could fool me into believing that this was anything other than a third rate performance. The polite applause at the end merely reinforced that.

I decided, there and then, that that was my lot. And that's how it turned out. I told the rest of the group that I was done now and my beautiful guitar has spent the rest of its life either as an ornament in our front room, or latterly just propped up right beside the desk where I am now tapping out this.

But the Laggan Bridge Concert tale is not finished yet. The hitch-hiking students arrived in time to complete our programme and the audience reaction at the end told us that we had done a good job for the local church fund. Now the rest of the evening lay ahead. And what an evening it was to turn out to be. There was an invitation to all of us to head up past Glenshero to Garvamore, near the southern end of the Corriearrick Pass. Great friends of my uncle and aunt lived and worked there. Jock Campbell and his wife Maggie were in charge of the squads of shepherds who tended the vast flocks on the British Aluminium estates and lived in the large, bleak house in the wide strath near Garva Bridge. The house was close to the remains of the General Wade barracks, which had housed the redcoats in the days of Highland revolt and tumult. Jock was huge and booming - a man of loud laughter and hospitality. His drams were downed in the small, traditional Highland glasses – neat. He filled a room and was in all aspects the perfect host for such a gathering. Maggie slaved all evening seeing to the vast platters of sandwiches that were always being refilled. All of us quickly got into the mood and the place soon was awash with music and raucous voices. Party time. Garva style.

The stark, grey house filled with revelry till well into the following morning. One element standing out in my memory was the contribution of my cousin, Jim, son of Uncle Dave. He had been one of the outstanding pupils of the most famous piping instructor of those days, Dr Kenneth A MacKay of Laggan. He took his pipes from their black case and plumped them up and ready for action. I see him yet, pacing back and fore on a landing up above us and having that effect that indoor piping seems to have on people. The pipes are designed for the great outdoors and there can ravish the very soul of most Scots. Indoors, they have a tendency to open the doors to licence and even slight madness. They certainly could have been held partly responsible for some of the excesses of that Dionysian night in the empty places.

The following incident will illustrate. I found myself at one hazy point, in a porch with coats and oilskins draped everywhere. Peering out of all this heavy-duty country gear was the dull sheen of the muzzle of a double-barrelled shotgun. I opened a drawer in the big hallstand and saw a scattering of cartridges. Without a glimmer of thought, I scooped up two of them and stepped out into the moonlight with the gun – intending to knock over some tins. I found one and propped it up on a fence post. I broke open the shotgun and slipped the two cartridges into the breech then snapped it shut. The pale light was adequate and I aimed at the tin, squeezing the first trigger. I was not used to shotguns – in fact, this was actually the very first time I had ever fired one. Rifles, yes, but never a shotgun. The combination of the explosion of the report and the violent recoil on my shoulder snapped me back to my senses. The tin had vanished and I realised that I was no longer alone. A smallish, red-haired figure had joined me. One of the shepherds who stayed at Garva and worked the vast estates. I had been aware of him vaguely on the edges of the mighty party. He just had to have a shot of Jock's gun. As he was as true a man of the country you could imagine, I assumed that a shotgun to him would be as familiar as a knife and fork. I handed over the gun, indicating that there was one cartridge left. Before I could say or do anything, and before my amazed eyes, he held the gun out in front of him with the stock directly in front of his face. The next development was violently predictable. He pulled the trigger. Another explosion of sound rolled over the moonlit hills but this time, there was a yell of pain from the red-haired shepherd. It was the inevitable result of his holding of the gun in that utterly stupid fashion. The gun had recoiled and the butt had struck him full on the face. He fell back and the gun went flying. Blood was pumping from his nose and there was a gap in his front teeth. I remember a rescue party appearing and helping the alcohol-anaesthetised shepherd who was cheerfully chatting to all around him. Our host, Jock, had heard nothing of this foolish episode and no recriminations were to follow. As for the small red-haired shepherd, I have no idea. His injuries were painful but superficial and he was just enfolded back into the shadows of the house.

I have only one record of that wild party in the hills. It is a solitary photograph, taken with my wonderful Voigtlander camera with its two and a quarter inch square colour transparencies on expensive Agfa film. It shows the house at Garva, mottled, shabby grey and white with brooding curtained windows and the rolling hills leading to the Corriearrick in the background. Parked alongside the stark, angular building is a small, grey Mini: YGD 164. It was ours – our first car that we bought second-hand shortly after we got married. It looks tiny and forlorn. But it is the house that is the dominant feature. Only I knew when I took that picture what these mottled walls contained. They enclosed probably the most comprehensively massive hangover that that part of the Highlands had witnessed since the Redcoats were billeted in the nearby 18th century barracks.

For all those years that it had played a major part in my life, between the weekly practices and the frequent dates when we were entertaining at various functions, I find it hard to understand why I don't have a single photograph of us performing. I have always had cameras – and as already mentioned, I had a pretty superior one at Garva with me when I stepped outside to see if anything of the night's madness with the shotgun had left an incriminating trace. But why didn't I ever arrange to capture us in full melodic mode? I really regret that omission even at this late date – 45 years on.

Finally, our success as a group at the various venues where we performed over the brief number of years of our existence was never in question: the reactions of audiences reflected that. Only one occasion stands out as an exception. We had been asked along to the Craigmonie Hotel in Inverness to entertain the Liberal Party who had been holding some major event in their calendar in the town. It was around the time that Russell Johnstone had been elected to represent Inverness-shire in Westminster. All of the Liberal big beasts of that era were there: Jo Grimond, David Steel (then the youngest MP in the House of Commons) and, of course, our own Russell Johnstone. We had decided on one of our most popular selection of songs and when we had called the large gathering to order in the function room and introduced ourselves, off we went. Very quickly we realised that things were going badly wrong. The noise of conversation began to intrude after a few minutes and naively we sort of hoped that it would die away. But it didn't. It just grew louder and more brutish. We adopted that most futile of responses – we sang louder and I threshed my guitar more violently. Quite simply, as far as the Liberals were concerned, we were not really there at all. It was all highly dispiriting as we had been rather proud to have been asked along to such a distinguished gathering. I seem to remember at one point, asking the crowd to quieten down a bit before our next number, but I was completely ignored. I don't think the Liberals did themselves much by the way of favours and garnering votes with that display. Another memory of the occasion was a brief encounter with David Steel. I see him yet as a slender diminutive figure in a sharp, pin-stripe suit and looking quite impossibly youthful. I can't remember if he was a contributor to the racket that all but drowned us out.

CHAPTER 29

COMFORT FARM

In the nineteen eighties I broadcast on BBC Radio Highland a large number of occasional talks about any topic I chose. They came under the heading of "The View From Denoon". The following two chapters are adapted slightly from a couple of them.

It is bizarre, isn't it, that provision for our most basic of comforts is such a vague and ill-organised thing in our society - even today....
Americans call them "comfort stations", and we have our own whole lexicon of names for them.
It's really difficult to imagine earlier ages in which even the most glittering in society made use of facilities that would turn the strongest stomach today? How could they have tolerated it? Since necessity is the parent of invention, it just means that it didn't figure very highly in people's priorities in those days. Mind you in the Edinburgh eighteenth century context, the New Town night soil collectors were a quantum leap in human advancement ahead of the unbelievable "Gardy Loo" mentality of the Old Town. Nevertheless, it can still amaze that the social dynamic that brought forth that same beautiful New Town didn't get around to devising something better than the earth closet or the commode.
Well, today, we can't let ourselves get too smug, as you will sometimes discover to your cost while on that holiday, or just away from home. What about these smallish towns you pass through which apparently don't provide toilets - or meanly

conceal them from the desperate seeker - usually round the back of an abandoned, decaying garage or something?

It was many years ago now, but just such an experience lodges in my memory of the homeward journey from a holiday in Strathnaver.

One such small community on the road south from there is a place of grim recollection.

A little background. We had decided to head off north during the summer holidays. Our small infant was to be left with the doting grandparents and we were to snatch a few brief days on our own in the wilds of our own land. I rented a two-tone Bedford Dormobile with sliding doors, basic amenities for life-support on board and steering-column gear shift. It was soft-springed with good visibility and seemed the perfect vehicle for such an adventure. Like so many Scots, all of our exploration of our own country at that point had been to the south or the west. The urge to go north is a very diminished one in our nation – much to the annoyance of all who live in the north.

We pulled in at a lay-by somewhere in Strathnaver and looked out over a loch with surrounding bleak hills and felt the shiver of the echo of past unhappy events in that place. At that point, we felt just a little depressed - probably as a result of just having been reading about the Clearances. However, I had also recently discovered the guilty delights of making home-made wine and had taken along with us a large bulbous glass flask of raw, dark-red and highly potent, very youthful vintage. This was the place to sample it. No more driving that day and we felt the childish anticipation of bedding down in our small home on wheels after a meal cooked on the small on-board gas cooker. The cork was eased out and the glasses primed. Toasts to the coming holiday and soon the bleak-looking hills began to seem more soft and enticing. The evening sky was a perfect symphony of summer colours and all was indeed well with our world.

But a large black car was approaching, and it was soon clear that it was about to join us in our own private lay-by. Irritating, but not a disaster. Perhaps they would only pause. The white-haired driver stepped out and in a flash of panic, I recognized the then Deputy Director of Education for the County of Inverness. In these days, a Director of Education was almost god-like to humble teachers and because my father was headmaster of Fort Augustus Junior Secondary School, I had been in the presence of Mr Lawson, the Deputy, on more than one occasion in the past. He had now recognized me and was coming, with his wife, to chat to us. We both realized that this was about the most inopportune moment for such a meeting as the dark-red wine-type liquid we had been drinking for the past hour or so had had a pretty devastating effect. Conversation was lumbering and crippled by the rising fumes and by the time we watched the departing car, we knew that we had not made a very good impression on the exalted ones. In later years, our response to such an encounter would have just been to get a couple of glasses and offer hospitality. Somehow, in the late sixties, a different set of values prevailed.

The next day, we both arose late and suffering. When we did get under way, it soon became clear that the Dormobile was in distress. In fact, it would only move at a painfully slow pace with ugly noises rising from its darker recesses. We headed back the way we had come, till we drew up at a small village. I saw a telephone box and decided to phone to the garage in Inverness from which the vehicle had been hired. The wretched phone was out of order. What more by way of misery could be laid across our slumped shoulders as we contemplated our wrecked holiday. I saw what looked like the local small school, and sensing that a kindred spirit must live there, I rang the doorbell of the schoolhouse and put on my most appropriate face for asking a favour off a stranger. A more felicitous choice I could not have made, as the young head teacher of the school could not have been more helpful. Her husband worked for a local estate and soon arrived on the scene. Phone calls were made and assurances came up the line that the Dormobile would be fixed the following day. We had an evening of merriment and perhaps, excess, with memories of bucketing along a narrow winding road in the back of a small, khaki-coloured mini-van, as we headed to a stark, white-washed inn in the centre of a vast moor with a rudimentary bar where drams were consumed. Drinking and driving was not considered such a shocking thing in those days, of course.

After a late breakfast, we said goodbye to our new friends and headed south in our repaired vehicle. After some miles, I began to feel the effects of two consecutive nights of over indulgence and the dreadful internal pressures began to make themselves felt.

The ill-timed urge became even more pressing round about Lairg, but we drove on in our Dormobile that was becoming a bit troublesome again. So, here we are at the next small town - a reasonably sized place; no problem as far as toilets are concerned. Look for the sign. None. Blast. At least, none visible. Now it's terminal desperation. Aha. Small cafe by the roadside. So here's the strategy: my wife goes in to the counter to buy something, while I head rapidly for the Armitage Shanks.

When I emerged back into the cafe, it was to find the proprietrix - an elderly lady of dragonish aspect - getting torn into my wife for being part of a conspiracy to make illicit use of her toilet. I turned my full withering contempt on this person, but to no avail. There isn't the tiniest shred of dignity you can wrap around you when you try to defend yourself from an accusation like that. And remember that this was a cafe, and all the customers were staring at us and listening.

As we went out the door, I tried one Parthian shot about what such behaviour would do to the place's hopes as a tourist resort, but she was armour plated, and I didn't dent her. God, it was really appalling. The embarrassment in front of that array of smirking strangers in the cafe, and our absolute annihilation by the fearsome owner is something that will live with me forever.

Revenge. We found the local tourist office just a little way down the road where I was to make my fury plain. It was shut. Immediately I got home, I wrote to their local newspaper the most skilfully phrased and wounding letter about unacceptable behaviour towards distressed travellers in small northern towns but, surprise, surprise, it wasn't printed.

I would like to stress that all this happened a long, long time ago. Today, I have no doubt, that small community has wall-to-wall toilet facilities - one for every tourist.

And while on this topic, what does the inside of a public or institutional toilet tell you about its clientele - apart from obvious things like scabs of graffiti (in our inner-city sites) or the gleam of tiles and antiseptic atmosphere of the up-market and well-ordered?

I will tell you. The biggest give-away is whether it has a mirror or not.

If there isn't one, it's because successive waves of yobs have smashed it so systematically that the management have decided not to bother any more. You are in a place, which even gives the term down-market a bad name.

I have come across only one exception to this.

A while ago, when I was an energetic activist in teacher politics, I was at a conference in the Assembly Hall on the Mound in Edinburgh. This was long before that building had been lent to the Scottish Parliament until its own building at the foot of the Royal Mile had been completed. I'd never been there in my life before, and was much impressed. From the statue of John Knox near the entrance to the green padded benches in the auditorium, and the magnificent wooden beams and panelling. The Fathers and Brethren have sure done themselves proud.

Anyway, at a suitable point in the proceedings, I thought it time for the wee stroll. The door with the appropriate sign was just opposite a rear exit, and in I went. It was elderly and tiled and exactly reflected the dark-suited propriety of the whole place.

Except for one thing. NO MIRROR.

There could be one of two explanations. Either the Fathers and Brethren have over the years been vandalising the gents and regularly smashing up the mirror in their eruptions of wrath and frustration at being defeated in theological dispute in the debating chamber, or, perhaps the more likely explanation: among such a body of men, the deadly sins would not find such fertile ground for seeding and sprouting into rank growth. Vanity, in other words, would be almost totally absent, so a mirror would be quite unnecessary - in fact the mere presence of one would be bordering upon insult.

By their facilities (toilet), indeed, shall ye know them...

CHAPTER 30
The Perfect Round

How often have you observed that people who appear on the airwaves, on TV or in print, who are involved in the theatre or in the creative arts – oh, all right, arty types – such people are always swift to get around to telling us how useless they are at doing all practical things. It is paraded as some badge of honour. Such is the high level of their sensibilities that the grubby mundane things of daily life are just completely beyond them.

In programmes like "Desert Island Discs", the question placed before the great philosopher or composer of "would you be able to build a shelter?" would inevitably elicit the response, "Oh dear! I should be absolutely HELPLESS! I can scarcely tie my own shoelaces ..."

If you are very intellectual, then you must also be very other-worldly and impractical.

All a bit of a pose, is it not?

Now I am preparing the ground for myself here. I have prefaced what I am going to say with this opening about apparently helpless types who fancy themselves, flapping their hands feebly when confronted with say, setting the TV to record a programme. You will not be able to accuse me of adopting this lordly pose.

I am going to talk about golf. Particularly that bizarre phenomenon – the perfect, or almost-perfect, beginning-of-season round.

This used to be a regular punctuation mark in the unfolding story of my life in my golf-playing days. Its regularity and its predictability never took away the sense of wonder it afforded.

So, first of all, a confession. And this is not a high-domed, intellectual-poseur confession. I am NOT good at ball games. I never was and in my present retired state from all such activities, never will be. All versions I have attempted, from the ridiculous of marbles to the sublime of shinty, have had the same dull accompaniment: just able to keep a place in the team but always destined to be the spectator to the curving arabesques and flashing brilliance of more talented colleagues. I used to pretend to myself that my real problem in shinty was my shortsightedness. Without my specs, things more than a few yards away were hazed in vague and misty outlines. I couldn't wear my specs on the shinty field, of course, so I had to develop a highly sensitive 'instinct' for sensing the ebb and counterflow of play. I am referring to the days when they only used the jet-black ball, which was well-nigh invisible against autumn-darkened skies and trees. I remember yet, the curdling embarrassment in my university days when we were playing Newtonmore at the Eilan. Under a leaden sky, I had hopelessly misread the movement of play and had set off with concentrated, frenzied energy to where I reckoned the ball was about to land – only to discover that I was all alone, hurtling towards a totally empty part of the field, while the real game was being contested at the other end. A spectator called out that there were lavvies at the garage if I was desperate. How could I explain that I couldn't see the ball? Oh, and one final word on shinty. I was at a game in Strathpeffer some time ago when there was still a lot of snow lying around and on the boughs of surrounding trees. Guess what was the colour of the ball being used? Yes, white! Who says that it is only the Irish who have a complex way of looking at life?

But to get back to Golf, and that perfect round.

Rabbits at the game, such as I, will know precisely what I am talking about. It's the first round of the short summer season. You haven't played since the clock changed last October. No play over the winter: leave that to the lions and sabre-toothed tigers of the game – the kind who battle into a force ten gale with horizontal-driven sleet. As you take that first practice swing and look down the fairway, you know with an absolute certainty that you can almost pick the precise blades of grass on to which you will waft the ball. And you do. The second shot will roll on to the apron of the green while the putt will wriggle over its knap - drawn inexorably into the cup. My patient partner will look on quietly. He knows the score. He will have had his own quota of "*divinus afflatus*" – this heavenly inspiration – already this new season and can only stand back resignedly and watch. Drives rifle up the middle. Wood strikes off the fairway rise with that sort of elastic, bending, slow-hissing climb that denotes the perfectly struck shot. And the approach shots and putts convince me that if I were just to strike the ball with the golf bag, it would continue to obey its pre-programmed instructions of perfection. It all comes to an end of course. From the usual blue sky, speeds the lightning-bolt. Off one of the last tees, I curved my, as yet unmarked, ball over some tall trees into a distant hopelessly irretrievable garden to my far left. Calmly I unwrapped from its crisp wrappings a brand-new ball and sent it bending in exactly the same numbly pitiless trajectory. It probably rolled up to the base of the same garden gnome as the first. My third brand-new ball was sent swooping to its watery grave in the fast-rushing burn - this time to the far right. The door to my magic world had now closed. A brief glimpse of what being a scratch golfer was like had been given to me. Now, like Orpheus seeing his Eurydice fading back into the shades of the Underworld of Hades, I now had to face the pain of loss and the dull reality of my natural skill levels once more.

But, you know, on another level, I wouldn't have cared if I had lost a score of cadmium-coated, titanium-cored, carbon-indented, Vulcan, super-macho brand-new balls. I was actually supremely happy with my once-a-year spell of perfection. It would ensure that through the following summer, I would trample the rough of the golf course with that desperate, gnawing hunger of the rabbit golfer's yearning to re-live, even just a few, of these golden moments.

If it wasn't for this phenomenon, I do not think that golf could survive.

Now, I wonder if the following footnote to my golfing days might have you doubt my sanity, but I assure you that the following is the unalloyed truth. Please do not think the less of me when you have read it and made your assessments of my character.

It happened like this.

I had succumbed at one point in my playing days to my insecurity as a player, and for lengthy spells, would get up really early in the mornings of summer – and I mean really early – so that I could be out on the course long before the main waves of players were unloading their equipment from the boots of their cars. Only then, could I - and I alone - witness the strange bendings of natural laws that accompanied so much of my play. I was pulling my golf trolley behind me at one point on the final three holes, heading back towards the clubhouse. It had been an unspectacular round and not too many balls had been lost.

As I recollect, I was feeling quite benign and looking forward to breakfast and lots of coffee when I got back home. I noticed that the first of the main groups of players for the day had driven off from the first tee and would soon be passing me as I moved up the last fairway. These were the big beasts of the club and were settling down to what would be their drive, medium to short iron pitch, and then putt that would constitute their golf round – the kind that was natural to them. I barely recorded their presence.

Then I saw that one of them had detached himself from the foursome, and was heading in my direction. My direction? Why on earth? These types who would normally not have even recognised my existence in golf terms just did not do that sort of thing. I stopped and waited. The question was fired at me.

"Didn't you read the notice in the clubhouse? No more narrow-wheeled trolleys allowed."

No, I had not read the notice in the clubhouse. A glance told me that the passing foursome all had trolleys with wheels like Formula One racing cars, whereas mine were of the now-obsolete, thin, turf-lacerating variety.

As in similar situations in life when vast humiliation is visited upon me, my sky turned deep crimson. The rest of the foursome were looking vaguely at me, while my informant was turning away to resume his round.

Now it's what happened next that will bring down the gales of cruel laughter – I really don't care at this stage in my life – but my first thought then was that the large windows of the clubhouse were looking accusingly out at me on the final stages of the playing area of the course. Any senior official of the club could be standing behind the blank glass and preparing to confront this dim and thoughtless member who was prepared to defy the rules of the club, and he would be waiting for me by the final green. One public rebuke was enough for me that morning. I could not face another – this time in front of an audience.

I folded in the wheels of my golf trolley and hoisted it, with the dead weight of the full set of clubs, on to my shoulders. It was akin to heaving the equivalent of the Eiffel Tower on to my back, but I was prepared to do that rather than face the opprobrium of the majesty of a senior golf club official.

Yes, I know. Pretty pathetic.

CHAPTER 31
No-body's Fault

This is a short story that was published in the Shinty Year Book.

The arguments raged in the pub smoke-haze.
The local team had been beaten again - this time by their near-neighbours. Always the hardest to swallow.
The game was shinty.
Danny MacLean was standing at the edge of the group listening.
In his late forties, he was slight and had reddish thinning hair. A good shinty player himself when younger, but he'd given up about ten years ago.
The drift of the conversation was really getting him down. Badly down. This time it was all the ref's fault.
Finally.
"Look. If he'd given us every foul, it wouldn't have made the slightest difference. We didn't bloody deserve to win..."
They turned to look at him. He didn't often intrude.
"God, Dan, you know he's got it in for us. It's thirteen lined up against us when he's there."
Someone else. "Trouble with you, Danny, you can't see what's going on under your nose."
Danny looked at the group. They sensed his anger.
"It's far worse than that. Shinty's had it in the village here. It's on the way out. It's dying. Ten years, that's all. Ten years from now - maybe sooner - there won't be a team left. And what are you lot doing about it. Just standing around, blaming a referee. It's pathetic. Bloody pathetic."
The argument dragged on, but he was finished. He'd had his say. Why couldn't they see what was happening? It was so depressing. The village was steadily losing something that was so important to it.
Smoke was beginning to get at him now. He'd given up the fags long ago, and found the pub was getting difficult - especially in winter, with all the windows tight shut.
A long-delayed closing time, then the frosty air biting into his lungs.

"God, it's sharp. Time to get the pipes lagged." A voice from the crowd.
"Too late - like the shinty," said Danny. "When it's too late, then you might do something."
"For God's sake, Dan, gie's another tune. You're getting bloody obsessive, you are,"
The voices died. Cars crunched and lurched over the hotel's gravel car-park, glittering in the frost, then nosed carefully into the darkness of what they hoped would be police-free roads.
Danny had a few offers of lifts, but he preferred to walk the half-mile or so back to his own place - one of a row of forestry houses. The frost was sharp enough, but not too bad. The pub argument was still pounding in his head.
Why couldn't they see what was happening? All the signs were there, stark and clear. Shinty was on the way out. It was getting more and more difficult to raise a decent team. The older players were not too bad, but some of the younger ones had a daft cockiness about them; they hardly ever turned out for training sessions either.
Then there was the boozing. There had been some in his playing days - fair enough - but nothing like today. Saturdays were now nearly always the same - swimming eyes and parchment faces of the heavily hung-over. How could they put in a decent performance like that?
He continued turning over the main obstacles to the game yet again and examining them individually as he walked down the moonlit road. There was the big secondary school in the nearby town that waited for the boys when they left the village primary school. Playing fields bristled with football, rugby and hockey goals, but of shinty goals no sign - nor ever likely to be.
But the biggest loss as far as shinty was concerned was the retiral of the headmaster, Angus Fraser, last year. He had been the game's best friend, and the primary school had lifted trophy after trophy in competitions. But he was gone now, and a successor had been appointed.
His place had been taken by a much younger man. Lean and black-bearded and a keep-fit enthusiast. The track-suit and head-band had become familiar early-morning sightings on the roads and paths.

Peter MacLaren was his name. He was an incomer. To his incomer's eye, shinty was more than a slight cultural shock. When he saw the wide swing of the club, the ball being struck well above shoulder level - and on either side - indeed the hardness of the actual ball: all this, together with the hard body contact of the sport brought the inevitable day when a new school rule was introduced. From then on, shinty could continue at the school, but just like any other game, taking its place with football and anything else. The boys would only be allowed to take their clubs to school on the visiting PE teacher's days, and on occasional days when he himself could supervise at the interval.

There was also a painful and embarrassing incident too. Not long after he had taken up the post, he had joined in with some of the older boys one lunch break. The game rapidly exasperated him. He was used to adapting to most ball games quite easily, but the way the boys played this one with such casual ease, scooping the ball away from him, bouncing it lightly on the club and sending it flitting to the other end of the field - all this got him rattled.

He made a clumsy tackle from the wrong side.

Pain flashed and exploded.

Boys came running. "Are you all right, Sir?"

Voices in the dark, red distance.

The boy who had hit him was trying to help him to his feet. Peter MacLaren just treated it all as an accident - however, the episode did play a part in that decision.

That evening, his wife said, "Don't you think you've gone a bit far? You know, actually banning the game ..?"

"Just a minute; haud on - it's not a ban. It's not you that's got to watch them swinging these bloody great lumps of wood about. One of them gets hit, and it's me that's responsible. That I can do without. They'll still get it at PE anyway, so what's the problem?"

"I think you're going to be hearing more about this. They take that game pretty seriously around these parts."

When the reaction did come, it was all a bit low key. It happened at a meeting of the parent-teacher association. One of the mothers there asked if there was the chance that the boys

might be allowed to take their sticks to school again every day, like they used to be able to do.
His answer had been well rehearsed.
"Mrs Grant, rest assured that shinty will still have its place in the school. I've entered all the competitions, and we'll work to winning like in the past. But try to see it from my point of view. It is a dangerous game. I just can't let it be played unsupervised. And I can't always supervise myself; I've other things to do - including having my own lunch ..."
("Reasonable answer," he thought, "And a timely wee reminder at the end.")
However, no response. The row of parents looked back at him impassively.
Nobody else said anything on the subject, and the meeting just moved on to other business.
That was Peter MacLaren's cue.
To his wife that evening: "If they really wanted shinty all that badly, they'd have put up a bit more of a fight..."
What he didn't say to her was that if there had been any threat of a serious falling-out, he would probably have given in to them.
Danny MacLean was getting close to his house now.
All right, he was obsessive - but why shouldn't he be? Shinty was central to the village's life - and to his own too.
The outside light had been left on, and it was when he was sliding his key into the lock it struck him what he had to do.
He would call on MacLaren after practice tomorrow. There was no scheduled game, and he had a training session lined up. He would go up to the schoolhouse afterwards and have a word.
As he lay just before sleep, he turned over the points he would make when he met the headmaster.
There was a knot in his stomach when he got up. "God almighty," he thought. "It's just a chat with the man; he's no more than a lad himself anyway."
The practice session was only hindered by the lack of numbers. Several of those who had promised to be there just didn't appear. That's the way things were now.
Eventually he blew the whistle and they all trooped back to the local hall where they changed and cleaned up.
That was it. Nothing now between him and the meeting. The knot had returned. So stupid. It would be no more than a talk

between neighbours. The last of the players had left, and Danny locked up.

He sat in his car for a few minutes, holding the steering wheel out at arm's length, breathing deeply.

This was getting ridiculous but just to be certain, he rehearsed his arguments once more before heading for the schoolhouse.

In the playground, unchanged since he had been a pupil there himself, he slammed the car door - sort of to announce his arrival. He didn't like to ring the doorbell.

No-one came.

Reluctantly he tugged the old-fashioned bell-pull and heard a distant jangling. A brief pause, and then footsteps, young and energetic, came leaping down a staircase and headed towards him.

"I'll get it." Peter MacLaren's voice, and the heavy door was hauled open. He was wearing tracksuit bottoms and a very damp tee shirt.

"Hullo. Mr ... ah.... MacLean, isn't it?" He was talking in gasps, as if he had been exerting himself

("God, he's young; not much older than my own" thought Danny.)

"Hello, Mr MacLaren. It's, well ...I'd like to talk to you about the shinty; that's if you've got the time just now ..."

"Sorry about the appearance," Peter MacLaren said, not addressing the subject. (The first faint stirrings of unease.) "I've been doing a bit of a work-out upstairs. I've got a wee gym I made. I must be mad. Shinty, is it? Look, don't stand there. Come on in. It'll have to be the kitchen, I'm afraid. The wife's slapping paint on almost everything else." He winked: man-to-man complicity.

Danny caught a brief glimpse through a door he was passing. She was on a stepladder. He saw a multi-coloured sort of blouse thing, and the slim lower body in the inevitable jeans.

In the kitchen, the headmaster pulled out a couple of chairs.

"Drink? Cup of tea ..... Coke or something?"

Danny shook his head. He just wanted to get this over and done with. He was in strange territory now. Alone with, to his generation, a powerful figure of authority - albeit one the same age as his own son. And none of these figures seemed to speak with local accents. Was it Edinburgh the MacLarens came from?

"It's something that's been bothering me for quite a bit now, Mr MacLaren. Not just me. A few others I've been mentioning it to as well."

Peter MacLaren sat quietly and listened to the carefully-delivered story of a perceived decline of the community's traditional game; how it was beginning to lose ground in the school even over the past year or so. How it might disappear completely if something wasn't done.

He didn't interrupt or comment; he just let his visitor have his say. Yet, as he was listening, something inside began to react. It surprised him - even shocked. It was a quite naked and angry resentment. When Danny MacLean had finished and looked for his response, there were to be no concessions.

"Mr MacLean. You weren't at that last parent/teacher meeting. If you were, you'd have heard me say that shinty was to stay at this school. I do not intent to change anything in that department..."

"It's not that," Danny interrupted. He was getting reckless now. "I know all about what you said then. The problem is what you are actually doing now."

He sensed a sort of digging-in on the part of the headmaster. Things were slipping away. He lowered his voice, trying to take the edge out of it.

"Look. They got their best early training at school. It was always like that. It made them good team players - you've only got to look at the record book. Do you think that by organising football teams you are going to do anything but harm shinty. It will do for it - completely. You must see that."

MacLaren's resentment now surged. Who was this middle-aged, mock deferential man, sitting in his kitchen, who was reading him lectures from the basis of his narrow, small community outlook? (When he was appointed to this post, he was excited at the prospect of bringing his liberal, urban experience to a Highland village. To his last breath he would have denied the accusation of cultural imperialism.)

"Mr MacLean. I don't think there's any more point in this conversation. I'd like to clear up one point though. Before I came here, I knew damn-all about shinty. All right, it's a good game, and all the rest of it. But one thing I do know: you're not going to get me to disadvantage these boys the way they were disadvantaged in the past. They leave this school, and head off into the town. Damn it; shinty isn't even played there. They have to be taught the basic rules of football - at that age! I even heard that some of them used to think there were twelve players in a football team. How do you think that made them look in front of their new pals...?"

Danny was ready for that one. The fault lay with the town schools for not providing for the traditional Highland game. They would have to change their ways ......

" .... and before you try to tell me that it's the town schools that are all wrong, what difference would it make if they all changed over to shinty tomorrow. None at all. Football's the reality, man. That's where we have to start from. I'll say it once again. There is no plan to do away with your shinty in this school. I just don't see that it ought to be the only organised game they play. Yes, and one other thing, in case you've forgotten it. My job here is to teach them to spell and to count. All this sport's by way of a bonus. Too many of you seem to be forgetting that."

Danny knew he'd blown it. Yes, MacLaren was right. He hadn't been appointed as an unpaid sports organiser. To him, the survival of a game that existed in such a small corner of the world as the Scottish Highlands wouldn't seem all that important. No world stage - nothing like that.

The confident young man, now unsmiling, with his damp towel still pulled tight round the back of his neck with the ends drawn down, was looking directly at him.

"Look, Mr MacLaren. I'm not here to teach you our job. All I wanted was a bit of help. We're all grateful for what you're doing for the school and the village. It's just that you're missing out on something. It means a lot to the locals here. And especially when you think of what Angus Fraser used to do in his time ...."

Now he'd really blown it.

Peter MacLaren stood up and his chair rasped back.

"I've got a lot to do, Mr MacLean. Thanks for dropping by."

And the door, moments later, thudded with finality behind him.

Danny drove back home down the avenue of black forestry trees.

God, but he'd made a right muck of that! But what else could he have said? It was always so hard to get through to incomers. They always know what's best for us, and we sit back and let them. We'll girn, but do nothing about it.

He sat in his car outside his house, till the cold made him move. He paused again in his small patch of front garden. He was feeling tired and depressed. But about one thing he was absolutely determined - not a word about his botched-up visit to the schoolhouse to anybody. He had failed and that was that.

He opened his front door, and heard himself saying, half-aloud: "One thing's sure: no football or new schoolmaster or anything else is going to do for shinty here. Not as long as I'm around. By God, no-one's going to be able to blame me."

Back in the schoolhouse, Peter MacLaren was talking it over with his wife.

"You weren't rude, or anything?" she asked.

"Hell, no. Mind you, it was touch and go. He had the impertinence to suggest that I wasn't doing my best for the place. What more do they expect? Anyway, I'm only the teacher here. They're damn lucky I do more than I'm paid for as it is..."

Then, as an afterthought.

"Them and their bloody shinty. It's just an accident of history it's survived this long anyway. They'll find that out for themselves soon enough. It'll just vanish and no-one'll give a damn. One thing, though, by God, they won't be able to blame me. It certainly isn't going to be my fault."

CHAPTER 32

That's Him, Your Honour
This appeared originally in the Glenurquhart Bulletin

My daughter's call to do jury duty in Glasgow recently brought a rush of memory of just such a call to me, many years ago, when I was teaching in a large Inverness secondary school.

Actually, I have been called to court duty twice in the past 5 – 6 years. I was summoned as a witness after my pride and joy, my new car, had been savaged by a night prowler in the South Side of Glasgow. He had smashed in a rear window with something blunt and heavy and then torn out the CD/ radio system from the dashboard. It had been a night of driving rain and sleet so that what awaited me in the grey morning was only a sad memory of what I had proudly parked there the evening before. Smashed glass; soaking, torn upholstery and a gaping, ragged hole in the dash with strands of wire and sad components protruding like broken teeth. To my amazement, I was called, not all that long afterwards, as a witness at the trial of the likely villain in Glasgow Sheriff Court. I duly appeared there on two occasions, within a month of each other, and each time was told that the case would not be going forward. On the second occasion, the whole thing had been abandoned on some technicality. I received my expenses, and that was that. Material for reflection on the workings of the Scottish legal system and its apparent wastefulness. My expenses for the journey to and from Glasgow together with board and lodgings on each occasion were not cheap.

But it is back to the late nineteen seventies I have to take you for the real tale to unfold. My earliest memories of this incident in my life are the reactions of my staffroom colleagues. Strange to think of it now, but in those days, it was an all-male staffroom where the civilising influence of female colleagues was not present to lay a restraining hand on some of our more brutish excesses.

"No problem," seemed to be the consensus. "They have to select you for the jury first. One thing they do not want is a smart-*rse."

Someone else then said, "Be sure to carry a newspaper that suggests you're a leftie as well. They don't like that either."

And the final advice. "Try to LOOK like a teacher. That's the absolute turn-off for the defence lawyers."

I'm pretty sure I didn't pay too much attention to all of this. The staffroom I worked from in those days was a boisterous and raucously mickey-taking environment where the Scottish art of flyting was perfected and raised to dizzy heights. You had to be sharp and on your guard at all times. Yet, just maybe ……

I turned up at the Sheriff Court on the appointed day and found myself in a fairly large gathering of potential jury members – to be narrowed down to that uniquely Scottish assemblage of fifteen citizens. And yes, I was prepared. I was wearing my corduroy jacket with leather patches on the sleeves. My trousers were suitably baggy. I had my leftie magazine – a "New Statesman", as I recollect – under my arm. I sat, ostentatiously looking as if I was doing the crossword. That latter detail was all a fake. I never could do crosswords. My wife is the expert in that arcane skill.

If the truth be told at this stage, I was beginning to think that it mightn't be all that bad an idea to get involved in the solemn ritual that was about to unfold. It was starting to get a bit interesting. And it was a day away from the rigours of the classroom. Not to be sneezed at. At this point I don't think I had the faintest idea about what facet of the dark side of our species was to be held up to public scrutiny and ultimate judgement, but with a bit of luck it might just be something intriguing or macabre or even titillating. But this was only the Sheriff Court. That sort of stuff was surely only for the higher courts. Well, you never know. It was all completely new and mysterious to me. These and many other thoughts were crowding in as I suddenly heard my name being called out and I found myself moving forward to join the others who had also been selected. So much for the "New Statesman" and the shabby teacher get-up then.

The case, when the main details were revealed to us, was about an assault in a boarding house somewhere in the town. A lodger had been pressing his unwelcome attentions upon another member of the household and it had all become rather messy. And that's about all that you require to know for the purposes of this tale. The fifteen of us eventually were seated in the jury box looking directly across the floor of the court towards the witness stand. The sheriff, in gown and wig, sat in his elevated throne to our right, while the accused (or "Panel" as he is termed in Scots Law) sat between two policemen, facing the bench. All members of the jury had been provided with notebooks and pencils as well as sketches and plans of the interior of the house where the alleged incident(s) had taken place. By now, it was actually getting to be a bit exciting.

It chanced that I was seated in the front row, on the far left looking into the well of the court. I vaguely knew only one of the jurors – another educationalist: a member of the inspectorate in fact. We nodded to each other. He was sitting directly behind me. Note these tiny details: they are important later. It was then that the unfolding of a dingy little tale of clumsy, drink-fuelled violence in the small boarding-house was spelled out by one of the legal presences – presumably the prosecution – and I made up my mind, there and then, to listen with heightened concentration to every nuance of the evidence. My official pencil was already scribbling. You never know – I might be selected by my fellow jurors to be the foreman so that I would need all the forensic skills I possessed to hold the rest of them in order and see to a clear and unambiguous verdict emerging.

But none of this was to happen. For several reasons.

A witness was called by the prosecution. Let's call her something ordinary like Mrs Mackenzie: the first name to come into my head as I relive these long-ago events. Mrs Mackenzie was very elderly and was helped into the court by an official. She was a small wispy figure in a navy coat and with a vague expression on her bemused features. Instead of going into the witness box, she was helped into a chair just in front of it and sat impassively there. She was very deaf and the opening questions about her identity and so on had to be enunciated loudly and very slowly. Then this question was put to her. "Mrs Mackenzie. Would you please look round the court. If you see the panel (this term was explained to her), would you please point to him."?

A long and agonised pause.

Mrs Mackenzie remained silent and motionless, just staring in front of her.

Again the ponderous question and again the same response.

It was at this point that the Sheriff, Scott Robinson (for it was he), decided to take over. In strong, resonant tones, he commanded instant attention. He leaned forward and said to the mute witness: "Would you please look carefully round the court room, Mrs Mackenzie. If you can see the panel, I want you clearly to point him out."

This time, she reacted. So very slowly. She looked first of all at Sheriff Scott Robinson, then her gaze carried on along the front row of the jury with me at the (to her) right hand corner – over the dock with the figure of the panel sitting impassively between two of the Highland's finest in their smartest uniforms and with their white gloves. No reaction whatsoever from Mrs Mackenzie. Back swept the slow, elderly questing gaze till she was once more looking up at the Sheriff. Then she made up her mind. She turned her head smartly, looked directly at me, and raised her arm dramatically and pointed straight at me.

A lacuna in the flow of the time froze reality.

The implications of the absurd error were all too obvious and then the first slight beginnings of reactions among those present began to stir. I turned to my fellow jurors who were trying not to break into that dreadful laughter that can strike at the most inappropriate moments in life – like in a church: or a courtroom!

The magisterial tones of Sheriff Scott Robinson restored solemnity and decorum to the proceedings.

"Mrs Mackenzie. I would like you to have another careful look round the court. Take your time. After you have studied the faces of all present, I would like you to point directly at the panel. Would you do that now? Please."

By now, I was becoming distinctly alarmed. Surely not this time? Not again? What if I was to have a net of suspicion thrown around me? I was now one very nervous juror.

Again, the slow ritual. The solemn scanning by the rheumy eyes, in the same order as before. The same slow drifting of the gaze along the front row of the jury – over the panel and his uniformed escorts - then the same evidence of a mind being made up. The only difference this time was when the arm was raised and the finger was aimed directly at me, Mrs Mackenzie pronounced to the world, clearly and unambiguously, "That's him, your Honour!"

I was appalled. I remember leaning to one side so that the invisible laser beam she was projecting fixed on the one in the row behind me: Her Majesty's Inspector of Schools.

A ripple of suppressed mirth agitated the courtroom solemnity. I could have sworn that the shoulders of the two constables on either side of the panel were heaving gently. It was all hugely and totally embarrassing.

And that was really it. The rest of the courtroom drama was total anticlimax. A very superior young-looking lawyer in gown and wig stepped up to the bench. He was immaculately suited and affected a foppish gold watch chain and fob across his waistcoat. His accent had the metropolitan drawl of the most exclusive Edinburgh clubs. Whatever he conveyed to the Sheriff, it resulted in the jury being told that the case could proceed no further. Some legal technicality had been detected somewhere in the thickets of the law and that was it. All the panoply of Scottish justice collapsed around us. The jury were thanked by the bench for giving up our time and told that lunch had been prepared for us in a nearby hotel (the Haughdale, as I recollect) and to it we were taken in a bus – also paid for by the state.

And that is all that I know about that long-ago incident in that boarding house. All I could have told you anyway. Jury members are barred from disclosing their deliberations.

I phoned home to my wife for a lift after lunch. As we were driving along Academy Street and I was gabbling my extraordinary story to her, I suddenly yelled out, "That's him! That's the bloke the witness thought was me!!"

Standing at the edge of the pavement was the unmistakable figure I had so recently been studying in the court. He was tall, thin and with a pale cadaverous face. Clean-shaven, no glasses and he had a head of thick jet-black hair. And he was wearing a grey jacket.

I am not very tall – very medium, in fact. In those days I wore a pair of what were called "Umbramatic" specs: the lenses reacted to the light and were dark for most of the time – even indoors. I had a black beard wrapped round my features and was getting thin on top. Oh yes, and there was my shabby brown corduroy jacket too.

To this day, I cannot for the life of me imagine how I could have been mistaken for a man who in every important point of appearance was the exact opposite of me.

But I have realised the dangers if I was ever called in off the street as they used to do in TV police dramas, to take part in an identity parade. A hand would have been raised, a finger would have pointed and a voice would have intoned:

"That's him, Your Honour."

CHAPTER 33
Abriachan

As I described in my first book, I spent the first eight years of my life in the tiny community of Abriachan, high in the hills on the northern side of Loch Ness, about nine miles along the lochside from Inverness. Memories are, therefore, scattered and sharply episodic.

The following lines were written in the mid-eighties, and were my attempt to collect as many of these fleeting moments of recollection as I could and link them together in verse.

Was it a crown of thorns:
The hawthorn bush
I used to look through
At the old, dull, mottled
Rust-patched shed
Beside the road, that was
The village hall?

Not 'village', just a
Random vague deposit,
Grey-stone, lumped together:
The crofts and little farms
That answered to the name
'Abriachan'.

The hill fell sharp and green,
And houses' roots were deep
Along the edge and down
The face.
God knows how cows and sheep
Could ever have the time
To pluck the grass
Before they slid down to
The loch, black-deep,
That waited for them
Far below ……..

The school, the tiny hall,
The only focuses;
No church,
A wooden bridge across a burn
And woods:
Woods of pine and fir
That hissed and sighed, or
Lounged in summer, up against
The garden's wall.

My father made the garden;
Shaped the stones and made the
Pond I shoved my brother in,
One day of reckless folly.
From the corner at the top, beyond
The raspberry canes, I'd look
Where moor began and heather
Spoke the end of cultivation,
Stretching up towards the other arm of woods
That flung away towards the south,
Pointing to the hills beyond
The loch's deep cleft,
Invisible from here.
Close to hand,
The yellow rasps,
Velvet-heavy, hanging
On their soft white cones:
Maybe now an extinct breed,
I liked them better than the red.

Down the path now, past the dull
Green cabbages, across the lawn
And back to my captain's bridge:
The corner of the wall below the
Tangled bushes and the spiky hawthorn.
From here I have command,
The road is mine.
This is my turnpike gate, my castle tower,
My pilot's cockpit.
Close by, the muscled, edge-of-forest trees

Drop cones for us to throw,
And dip their gnarled, flaked branches:
Their Scottish metaphor of pine:
Flayed beaten bark like prehistoric skin,
Yet wood, so soft and vulnerable.

I'd guard that road
And see the hall as
Crouching enemy – tank or ship –
To be repelled.

Inside that hall,
I see a crowd of children.
A film is promised,
Outing from the school perhaps.
A film to take us by our infant hands,
And show us,
Sanitised, hygienic,
A pageant: flat-topped helmets
Straight from Agincourt;
Simple, jaunty, kindly even:
Ours,
Seeing safely off, the square, black
Brutish downward-sweeping, shadowed,
Embossed-with-swastika,
Evil helmets of the foe.

A scene still sits in memory:
A wall of bricks, it seems,
And, rising slowly, like a nightmare
Comes the helmet.
Its jutting brim makes eyes
Seem lit within
With all the evil in the world
I know up till that point in time.
Slowly then the rest:
Black uniform and gun,
Face now visible,
Metallic sheen of grey
Gun-metal face.

All the monsters of my darkest dreams
Are pressed into that one
Lean German shape.

A shot rings out.
The reptile features lock.
Teeth gleam sharp.
He topples slowly
And slowly slides from sight,
But not before the
Hands that grip the wall
Are seen to spasm, firm
Perhaps to haul him back again,
Restored, healed
Unkillable.

But no. The cold grey fingers slip
And slip in jerks, and then
Are gone from sight.

The credits roll.
"Salute the Soldier"
And we did! We did!
By heaven, how we cheered …..!

Still inside
The dark, pitch-pine lined walls
Another sound:
A voice, a song and
Faint piano, drifting down to me.
Who were these "Kerry Dancers"?
Or their Dance; or choice of time
To dance? I still don't know.
But every time I hear these words
I'm tugged back to that wooden bench
And child's ambivalence to parent
Standing up before the gaze
Of neighbours and of
Friends.

I was young enough to be proud
I think ………

The peaty loch to me
Was vast. My father's boat
Would nudge the rushes at
The edge and peer
Into the black for trout.
The magic rasping of the reel;
The amber gut that curled
From crumbs of vivid greens
And yellows, ruby-reds
Of flies, set in their crinkled
Waxy paper – coiled and ready,
The underhang of hook
And barb that thrust from each
Bright beauty didn't give me slightest pause.
My father used them
And they must be right.

The sound of hook being torn
From upper jaw's ribbed cartilage –
A crunching sound – and
Smell of fish, still quick,
With firm, elastic life, tail threshing
Empty air, before the
Swing against the wooden seat
Brought final gasping silence.
Not death, of course.
My father – no – he
Never would do that.

In any case, the word
Meant nothing to me.

A howling dog,
A moon as white as sheets.
A small, cramped room.
My bedroom for a night or two,

With fingerprints of light
Thumbed on the facing wall.

Eyes snap open.
Disbelief.
      Silence.
The cry again, quite close.
It shivered in the moon-white air and
Laid its weight upon
My bed and me.

I still can see,
A shape come hunching
Over the gleaming, shadowed lawn
To meld through doors and walls
And stoop across my counterpane.

But Kerry Dancers move,
And point their toes and circle;
Meet and part and weave their patterns
Endlessly.
My mother's voice still leads them
Through their strange pavane
That never has resolved itself
In any manner I can understand.
This pointlessness of time,
Just clicking up the years, remote
Abstract, absurd,
And sounds of notes, just
Three or four enough.
They'll steal up close behind
And reach inside, and take a hold
And twist and twist, and have me stare
Behind,
In pointless silly yearning.

So many other things
That happened to me
In that distant place;
So many people, friendly, huge.

The simpleton who visited the house,
The kitchen door.
Tobacco was his craving, and
I think he got his fix.

His mistress, Mrs Findlay,
Her huge soft aproned bosom
Held a heart whose vastness
Would engulf our house
And all of us.
Even the flayed sheep's carcass
I once saw, hung from her ceiling
Over grey stone flags, did nothing
More than have me wonder
At the colours of its
Marbled, layered, opened, spread
Insides.

Imagination sees a crook-winged
Shape come hurtling, black, tree-high
Past our house.
A German raider, lost, and
Swooping down our indentation
In the hills.
Incongruous to think that
Such a shape that sent its shadow
Flitting over upturned staring face
Of far-off tortured Europe,
Could look along its gun sights
At our small Highland
Aimless huddle.

All that and so much more.

I now go by that way and see the house,
The hall, the little battered bridge at Leault.
The new woods, almost now
As high as those
That were hacked down
Right at end of war.

Like heroes on the day of Armistice
Being struck by wandering shrapnel
As bells ring peace.

One day I stood before
The crumpled little school,
And saw the soft remains:
A tree stump.
Once it had a jagged edge with
Pointed peaks of wood where
Trunk had hinged
Its slow, resigned toppling
When it fell.

I was just tall enough, once,
To peer into the tiny pools
That formed,
And made my mountain-scape
With deep-set fjords and
Monster-teeming seas.

And, so,
A "crown of thorns"?

The now arthritic
Twisted, almost dead remains
Of that old hedge
Of over forty years ago ....
That's far too simple.

Out of scale,
Inept.

No image I can muster up
To place on page (or centre stage)
Of memory,
Can hold it all:
My complex universe, expanding still,
Till all its several elements
Have reached that point

Where none is visible
From any other.

And when that happens
That's
My lot ………..